THE
ROMAN YEARS
OF
MARGARET FULLER

The portrait of Margaret Fuller by Chappel.

THE
ROMAN YEARS
OF
MARGARET FULLER

A Biography by

Joseph Jay Deiss

THOMAS Y. CROWELL COMPANY

ESTABLISHED 1834 · NEW YORK

OTHER BOOKS BY JOSEPH JAY DEISS

A Washington Story

The Blue Chips

The Great Infidel

Captains of Fortune

Herculaneum

*(Various titles above have appeared in nineteen for-
eign editions.)*

Designed by Barbara Kohn Isaac

Manufactured in the United States of America

L. C. Card 70-81941

1 2 3 4 5 6 7 8 9 10

Foreword

Who was this Margaret Fuller?

I have been asked that question many times in the course of writing this book. The book itself is intended to provide an answer. As much as possible I have tried to let Margaret tell her own story and answer the question in her own way. It was a question she asked herself.

So rapidly turns the newsreel of American history that Presidents, titans of finance, heroes, and film stars rate no more than oblivion after the passage of a generation. Yet, after her death, the name of Margaret Fuller remained well known in America for the last half of the nineteenth century; and for the fifteen years preceding the Civil War her name was almost a household word in the East. Nor was it unknown in Europe, especially in Britain, where her reputation was impressive.

As both unhushable exposé-columnist and overcandid literary critic for Horace Greeley's New York *Tribune*, Margaret Fuller created sociological and literary sensations one after another. Her book, *Woman in the Nineteenth Century*, was the first American plea for women's rights. It raised a tempest. As the first American woman journalist abroad she covered a vastly important Italian revolution, which mirrored much of European history to come. And in her personal life abroad she exploded so great a scandal that even the fighting reformer Greeley found it advisable to drop her from his pages. With all this, she was easily the outstanding American woman intellectual of her time; and European countries, with few exceptions, would have been hard put to find her peers.

It seems strange that such nineteenth-century middling names as Julia Ward Howe, Louisa May Alcott, Susan B. Anthony, are commonly remembered in the United States, while Margaret Fuller is not. Today she is known only to an intellectual elite—an elite so restricted that it includes few but students of American literature and occasional scholars in the general humanities. Vernon L. Parrington, in his *Main Currents in American Thought,* evaluated the Margaret Fuller matter precisely: "Misunderstood in her own time, caricatured by unfriendly critics, and with significant facts of her life suppressed by her friends by a chivalrous sense of loyalty, the real woman has been lost in a Margaret Fuller myth and later generations have come to under-estimate her powers and undervalue her work. Yet no other woman of her generation in America is so well worth recalling."

In the light of events in the second half of the twentieth century, it must be added that no other American woman of any generation is so well worth recalling—not for her sake, but for ours. Observed Charles A. Madison in *Critics and Crusaders,* "Her great intellectual vigor, her extraordinary generosity of spirit, and above all her passionate criticism of the parochialism and materialism about her, made her the effective leader of those who resented the restraints of their calvinistic environment and sought to enthrone the precious freedoms of civilized man. It is this championing of human rights, this abhorrence of oppression and inequality of any kind, that still endears her name to all lovers of liberty and democracy."

In Rome, in one of the municipal parks (the gardens of a villa where Goethe used to stay), a tree-shaded walkway just inside the Janiculum walls is called the "Viale Margaret Ossoli Fuller." How amazed and delighted Margaret would be if she could know that in the Rome of the millennia she is thus remembered. In America she had never lived as she wished to live, never loved as she wished to love. In Rome she heard the subtle echoes of antiquity, and answered them. It was a dialog of deep emotion.

"History is not a compilation of facts, but an insight into, a moving process of life," wrote the late Sigfried Giedion, with whom in Rome I discussed Margaret Fuller. "Such insight is obtained not by the exclusive use of the panoramic survey, the bird's eye view, but by isolating and examining certain specific events intensively . . . ."

This was the method intuitively adopted by Margaret when it fell to her to report the story of the stirring defense of Rome against its multiple enemies in 1849. But the public history of the Roman Republic was so intricately interwoven with the private history of Margaret Fuller that neither is complete without the other. In her letters and dispatches the personal and historical, the historical and personal, are inseparably intermingled. Her love for Giuseppe Mazzini, the revolutionary Triumvir, differed in kind but not in intensity from her love for the citizen-sergeant Giovanni Angelo Ossoli, fighting on the walls. Together all three shared an intense belief in the importance of unity and nationhood for dismembered Italy—a concept of the nation-state underlying the chain reaction of revolts by oppressed peoples throughout Europe in 1848–1849. (It is a concept now paradoxically outmoded by the economic requirements of the new technology, capitalist or communist.)

Margaret's earlier rejections of Puritanism and Transcendentalism were of course significant forward steps philosophically; but perhaps the progression from nineteenth-century liberal to nineteenth-century radical was not so great as it might seem. Both, measured by today's brutal realities, were essentially romantic. The liberal was a gradualist; the radical wanted immediate action. Both believed, naively, in absolute goodness as an ethical norm, in progress as inevitable, and in "the People" as an abstraction. Yet toward the end of Margaret's European sojourn, she had parted company with romantic radicalism and was beginning to probe for both social and economic understanding. She never ceased to grow.

The image of Margaret Fuller, as handed down by her friends and enemies for posterity, included relatively little about her Roman years—certainly the most important and dynamic period of her life. Her imprint was established largely by the efforts of one cold and overly fastidious man: Ralph Waldo Emerson. Though Margaret's so-called *Memoirs,* published soon after her death, were also edited by William Henry Channing and James Freeman Clarke, Emerson without doubt was the chief of these New England triumvirs.

The copy of the *Memoirs* that came into my hands through the American Academy in Rome chanced to be the original two-volume edition owned by George T. Davis, Margaret's kinsman and first adolescent "crush." (How oddly symbolic that these volumes should somehow find their way to Rome, scene of Margaret's final and mature love.) Davis had gone through all of Volume I, filling in the names that had been left as blanks; and beside one of Emerson's rather waspish remarks about the vastness of Margaret's ego, had written in the margin, "sublime bosh!"

Unfortunately Emerson's editing cannot be dismissed so lightly—however well-meaning his intentions. It is maddening to compare texts in the *Memoirs* with such texts as chance to remain in manuscript. Emerson modified words from simple to complex, revised sentence structure from spontaneous to ponderous, ignored dates and time sequences, shifted paragraphs from one document to another, and sometimes changed names or misstated the recipients of letters. It was a cut-and-paste job, with the scissors acting as censor's shears. Suspect material was deleted—whole sections snipped from letters, masses of pages ripped from the notebooks. A part of Margaret which Emerson did not approve was destroyed. Yet, in spite of Emerson's literary libertinage, more than sufficient material exists for the not infrequent reconstruction of Margaret's innermost thoughts and feelings—and even monologues. It has been my task to restore wherever possible both the authentic version of Margaret's works and the authentic version of Margaret's life. I totally agree with her statement that "writing is worthless except as the record of life."

When in 1883 Thomas Wentworth Higginson (who as a child had known Margaret) undertook the first really serious biography, he chided Emerson gently for an incomplete portrait. But it was more than incomplete: It was distorted, as if Emerson had used tricky mirrors, and Higginson was well aware of the fact. The kindlier Clarke also seemed aware, for he wrote to Higginson, "Margaret had so many aspects to her soul that she might furnish material for a hundred biographers; not all could be said even then."

Since then biographies have appeared at more or less regular intervals—all overstressing Margaret's American years as compared with the dramatic Roman climax of her life. The reasons are obvious: the authors' lack of familiarity with the Roman scene, or the Italian historical events of 1847–1850, or the Italian language—all of which are essential to a new portrait of Margaret Fuller full-fleshed. It has been my good fortune to be able to correct some of the errors made in the earlier biographies. For example, I have been able to establish the radicalism of Margaret's Italian lover *before* she met him, and the probable time and place of their belated marriage. Also, her relations with Emerson were much more intimate than previously believed. But no doubt I have made errors of my own.

Something needs to be said about the love letters of Margaret Fuller. The first set, addressed to James Nathan, was published in 1903, under the editorship of Julia Ward Howe. The letters had been sold by the son of the man to whom they were addressed. They are the essence of the romantic, high-flown, fantasy Margaret. The second set, addressed in Italian to Giovanni Angelo Ossoli (a nobleman, a marchese—not a waiter, as some of Margaret's enemies whispered), is herein largely published for the first time. These letters are the essence of the radical, warmly human, real Margaret. To this correspondence have been added other critically important letters from Adam

Mickiewicz, the Marchesa Constanza Arconati Visconti, and Lewis Cass, Jr. These have been mentioned by other American biographers, if at all, only in passing. New letters from Mazzini to Margaret are also included.

Margaret once referred to her life as a Greek tragedy. Truly the fates played interesting games not only with her but with other lives tangential to hers. Had not the Papal Ossoli family driven Angelo away for his republicanism and association with Margaret, the family line might not today be approaching extinction. (It was long a family opinion that Margaret had ruined Angelo's life because she was "older, not beautiful, Protestant, and poor.") Today, of the Ossoli only one aged, childless woman remains; and she finds herself living not in the family palazzo but in an apartment just off the Viale Mazzini —hated name! Ironically, the family palazzo was pulled down in 1886, to make way for the enormous white marble monument to King Victor Emanuel II, representing the *Risorgimento* and the unity of Italy. It was not, however, until the Vatican Concordat of 1929 that the Ossoli family condescended to recognize the actual sovereignty of the King instead of the vanished temporal sovereignty of the Pope. They consistently refused to set foot in the King's Palazzo Quirinale, once the Papal palace.

Such were the Ossoli. Yet, as late as 1963, Prof. Perry Miller of Harvard could write that Angelo "on somewhat vague premises claimed to be a Marquis."

As for Margaret's dear old friend Waldo Emerson, a final touch after her death is worth recording. While Emerson was plaintively writing in his journal, *"I have lost in her my audience,"* it was Henry Thoreau who rushed to the scene of disaster. Thus it was Thoreau, not Emerson, who searched for any trace of her manuscript on the Roman Revolution—a manuscript that almost surely would have added Margaret Fuller's name to the front rank of historians.

Already she occupied the front rank of human beings.

Joseph Jay Deiss
ROME

Author's Note of Thanks

Research on this book was significantly aided by the following institutions and organizations: The Houghton Library of Harvard University, Cambridge, Massachusetts; the manuscript division of the Boston Public Library; the Fruitlands Museums, Harvard, Massachusetts; the Istituto per la Storia del Risorgimento, Rome; the Museo del Risorgimento, Rome; the Centro di Studi Americani, Rome; the United States Information Service Library, Rome; and the library of the American Academy in Rome.

I am grateful for the assistance given by Elizabeth del Amo Ruspoli in the translation of the Ossoli-Fuller letters, and by Nina Contini in the translation of general letters and documents. As both are bilingual, they acted as a constant control over my own translations. (Many of the Ossoli-Fuller letters were translated by Margaret's friend Elizabeth Hoar, but her Italian was literary and not colloquial; nor did she understand all the political references.)

I was particularly fortunate in being given access to the Ossoli family archives by the Marchesa Maria Ossoli-della

Torre Genuardi. From them I was able to establish many facts about the Marchese Giovanni Angelo Ossoli not previously reported.

And finally, to my wife Catherene for her general assistance goes more than a note of thanks.

J. J. D.

Illustrations

Yet me also, the wonderful bird, singing in the wild forest, has tempted on, and not in vain.

—Margaret Fuller

I

The little Italian steamer chugged into a dream. With its sidewheels grinding rhythmically, it drew close to the rocky slopes of the island of Ischia in the Bay of Naples—and so into the lee of a cutting March wind. The wind ruffled the azure sea with whitecaps, and the troughs flecked golden from the bright sun. Yet the sun's warmth remained illusory; the buffer of the land was more than welcome.

As the ship steadied in the calmer water, one passenger—an American woman, not young not old, not beautiful not plain, shawled and bundled but obdurate against the wind—sighed with relief. She disliked the rumbling machinery and the smells and smoke of the steamer; she suffered too, in spite of the exercise of supreme will, the sickness of the sea. But these were as nothing compared with the exaltation she felt, after years of longing, at seeing for the first time the legendary beauty of the Bay of Naples.

With her three companions—a man, a woman, and a boy—she gazed at the hazy blue hump of the island of Capri in the far distance, at the wave-bitten cliffs of the remote Sorrento peninsula, at the cone of Vesuvius with its plume of smoke blown horizontal by the wind, at the mauve shadows and mirrored light reflections from the mass of the ancient Greek city of Neapolis. The amphitheater form of the bay was perfectly familiar from the engravings which since childhood had fascinated her back home in Boston. But the bay's color was unimaginable—a color opalescent and changing like some gigantic jewel. As a young girl she had believed in the mystical significance of jewels, choosing the blood-red ruby—the carbuncle—as her magic stone. Then she had longed for demoniacal power; and at length had found it within herself.

So the old dream of the Bay of Naples had become present, living, and real. She breathed a profound excitement. The palpitation of her heart was like that of a woman in love.

Ischia's rocks seemed perilously close, but the steamer remained serene. A medieval storybook castle clung to a peak amid tall cypress trees. Pink and blue and white stone houses of a fishing village clustered about a tiny harbor full of varicolored sailboats. On the hillsides terraced vineyards led down to the sea. In the chill wind it was difficult to imagine naked satyrs playing among the grape leaves, but certainly Pan himself frolicked among the goats under the umbrella pines. And long ago, Roman villas with palms and fountains and statuary had adorned these coves. Ulysses had sailed this way, and the god Hercules. Here was history; here was antiquity.

And here also was Sarah Margaret Fuller, child of the New World, daughter of New England, heiress of Puritanism. For all the brilliance of her mind, she was unaware—consciously—that she was about to renounce her heritage, about to embrace the ancient cult of Eros. It was the Christian year of 1847, but in Italy the ancient gods lived on.

A week after landing, in a *dolce* mood, she wrote her first impressions of the new-old, unfamiliar-familiar land. The letter was addressed to a long-time friend, who was more than friend but less than lover: Ralph Waldo Emerson—austere, tightly self-contained, remote and frostbound in Concord, Massachusetts. "Dear Waldo—At Naples I have at last found *my* Italy," she exulted, though regretfully she was aware that Emerson would have no inkling of what she meant. She might have added, but she did not yet know, that at last she had found her true life. And she had come so close to losing it . . .

Her relief at reaching Naples was not only relief from the discomforts of a small ship, but for the joy of being on solid earth. In chatting with Emerson, she described how, between Livorno and Naples, she had "only just escaped being drowned." It was an omen, serving to reinforce her instinctive fear of the sea.

In an article for Horace Greeley's prickly and already famous New York *Tribune* she described the incident in some detail: "We started . . . in an English boat, highly recommended, and as little deserving of praise as many another bepuffed article. In the middle of a fine, clear night, she was run into by the mail steamer, which all on deck clearly saw coming upon her, for no reason that could be ascertained, except that the man at the wheel said *he* had turned the right way, and it never seemed to occur to him that he could change when he found the other steamer had taken the same direction. To be sure, the other steamer was equally careless, but as a change on our part would have prevented an accident that narrowly missed sending us all to the bottom, it hardly seemed worthwhile to persist, for the sake of convincing them of error. It ended at last in the Neapolitan steamer taking us in tow for an inglorious return . . . . She made a long detour, with her black hull, her smoke and lights, which looked so pretty at night, then came round to us like the bend of an arm embracing. We changed the boat, and . . . came at last to Naples."

Soon the cold March wind slackened, became a zephyr. Flowers burst everywhere; the scent of lemon and orange blossoms perfumed the air. The shivering Neapolitans came out of their slums, and with ironic laughter and love songs tried to compensate for their poverty.

Scorning the "raptures of sentimental tourists," Margaret hired a carriage and flung her party into an orgy of tourism. Her zest was such that she very nearly exhausted her three companions—the benign Quaker, Marcus Spring of New York; his

3

wife, Rebecca; and their twelve-year-old son, Eddie. For them the trip was merely the Grand Tour, while for Margaret Fuller it was the Ecstasy. Even Eddie was hard put to keep up with her; but, as he adored her, he followed blissfully everywhere. In New York, Eddie—like a grown-up lover—almost every day had left reverentially on her desk at the *Tribune* a single pink rose. With children she had a special rapport. She explained everything, made history come alive, and told fascinating tales of Greek and Roman gods and goddesses. Though her health was frail, she never seemed to tire, and it was she who spurred Eddie up steep mountain slopes, through archaeological ruins, into spray-drenched rowboats.

To the *Tribune* she wrote: "I have passed through the Grotto of Pausilippo, visited Cuma, Baiae, and Capri, ascended Vesuvius, and found all familiar, except the sense of enchantment, of sweet exhilaration, this scene conveys . . . . Baiae had still a divinity for me, Vesuvius a fresh baptism of fire, and Sorrento—O Sorrento was beyond picture, beyond poesy, for the greatest Artist had been at work there in a temper beyond the reach of human art."

Lovingly she noted everything in her journal, jotting with scratchy pen fragmentary sentences in telegraphic style, as if a transatlantic cable existed to rush her turbulent thoughts to the dullard stay-at-homes. The expedition up Vesuvius was at night, and while her feet sank deep in the ashes near the cone of that treacherous mountain, she marveled at the vast roseate fires and sulphuric fumes, as if she stood at a vent of hell.

At the base of Vesuvius, on one slope, lay the ruins of Pompeii, buried by ashes, and on another, the ruins of Herculaneum, suffocated by a deep, hardened crust of mud-lava. Twelve years ago she had reviewed Bulwer Lytton's *Last Days of Pompeii*. Now she was less moved by its false and sentimental Christian portrayal than by a fresco of the Greek hero Achilles and his dead lover-friend, the youth Patroklos, killed by Hector before the walls of Troy. At Herculaneum the unexcavated city could be explored only by means of dank and dangerous tunnels, which had been bored through the volcanic alluvium. But neither the frescoes nor the tunnels impressed her so much as the pile of carbonized books that had been salvaged from a single Herculaneum library.

Her literary bent was evident, too, at Sorrento. She paid a respectful visit to the house of the famed sixteenth-century poet Torquato Tasso, whose epic *Jerusalem Delivered* she so often had discussed. At the age of twenty-five she had translated Goethe's *Tasso* from the German, marveling over the pathos of the poet's life. Humbly she read one of his autographed letters, and asked her diary: "Why was he always so unhappy?" How could he have been, in a place "so . . . beautiful"?

No detail escaped her. She entered her "first acquaintance" with: the lizards emerging to bask in the sun's springtime warmth; the orange trees heavy with the last lingering fruit of the winter season; the pink and white camelias in bloom; the olive trees silver-gray with their delicate bouquets of white blossoms; the figs sprouting their new leaves in all the fecund suggestiveness of an ancient plant sacred to fertility. She was struck, as are all visitors to Italy, by the abundance of bronze and marble statuary, particularly the nudes. Aside from Christian saints and madonnas, everywhere were ancient gods and goddesses, young and beautiful, perfect in form and naked—a heritage from antiquity and the Renaissance. Everywhere were naked *putti,* plump little winged angels, and naked adolescent boys with bows and arrows playing the role of the youthful Eros, their genitals uncovered and all unashamed. Everywhere, it seemed, were fountains ornamented with lovely nymphs with water spurting in tiny streams from bare breasts. Everywhere the human body was adored, in spite of almost two millennia of Christianity, as something divine. And in Margaret Fuller the response was strong and elemental.

"It is to the pagans we must turn to learn the secret of a happy and virtuous life," she had once written. "To the Saxon, the body is a convenience, to the Italian a thing alive with beauty." Boldly, in Puritan-bound New England, she had found occasion to deplore the smug American horror at nude statuary, saying, "If the body is the temple of the spirit, why should it be regarded as something evil?" And how could she fail to recall that secretly and impetuously she had confided to her closest friend, the much-envied beauty Anna Barker, some of her early fantasies: "An altar stands at the end of a grove . . . . A group of dancing-girls comes through the grove, carrying baskets of fruits and garlands of flowers; their white bodies glisten like alabaster, for they wear no clothes. They dance around the altar and they chant an old pagan melody . . . ."

Naples, an ancient pagan city, she noted in her diary, was "divine," and full of "delightful bands of music" playing operatic airs and Neapolitan love songs. But, as she wrote in her dispatch to the *Tribune*, "Beyond this, reader . . . I shall tell you nothing of Naples, for it is a thing apart in the journey of life, and, if represented at all, should be so in a fairer form than offers itself at present."

Then suddenly, without any warning, the new, expanding, political Margaret Fuller rises to the surface, sweeping aside both fantasy and the self-conscious platitudes of a journalist-tourist: "Naples—priest-ridden, misgoverned, full of dirty, degraded men and women, yet still most lovely Naples—of which the most I can say is that the divine aspect of nature *can* make you forget the situation of man in this region, which was surely intended for him as a princely child, angelic in virtue, genius, and beauty, and not as a begging, vermin-haunted, image-kissing Lazzarone [Lazybones]."

Already she had taken a forceful stand opposing Ferdinand II, ruler of the Kingdom of Naples and Sicily. His was the degenerate House of Bourbon, a dynasty imposed by the Spanish occupation early in the eighteenth century, and against whose brutal rule the hapless subjects had revolted again and again. Soon Ferdinand would endear himself to his people by his profligate use of cannon against them, and ironically they would dub him "King Bomba." In crusading against this perfidious man, the Boston "Transcendentalist" Miss Margaret Fuller had found a worthy cause. Soon the King's censors would wince from the lancelike thrusts of her freshly sharpened pen; then, with reckless courage, she would tilt at the pope, potentially a far more dangerous enemy.

But while the new political Margaret Fuller was finding release, the new psychically liberated, passionate Margaret Fuller yet remained hidden under the cool porcelain glaze of a New England spinster, resisting primly the casual Neapolitan banter about *amore,* frowning sternly on *lazzaroni,* who sought to escape all sorrow in festas, fireworks, and the careless interplay of love. To the Neapolitans, love was tactile, not spiritual—a pleasure of the body, not of the mind. Nor did they make any effort to conceal their feelings. As is customary in Italy, the male stared openly at the female. In every masculine eye was a candid appraisal of the physical Margaret Fuller—her elegant clothes, her regal walk, her womanly bosom, her fine blond hair, her clear complexion, her vivid, remarkable eyes. Her age meant little or nothing. Lustful men were gazing at the sexual Margaret Fuller, and their expressions showed that they desired her.

Her only recourse was to lower her lashes and turn aside. It was all too blatant. A true Puritan could not be other than shocked. But the Puritan, years before, had confessed to her secret diary, for her eyes alone, that she strongly felt the urge "to live, love, and perish!"

Now indeed she was shocked . . . but not repelled. Else how could she have written with such exuberance, *"My* Italy!"

Perhaps she sensed that so little time remained. She confided to her travel journal that, although she was fascinated with Naples, she was "so anxious to arrive in Rome." Perhaps she knew intuitively that *amore,* like Rome itself, was eternal . . . and awaited there.

2

The prismatic Margaret Fuller was born May 23, 1810, in Cambridgeport, Massachusetts. From the very first awareness she "detested" Cambridgeport, and considered the big square two-and-one-half-story house on Cherry Street at the corner of Eaton "ugly." She was touched by the fact that her father had planted two elms in front, inside the picket fence, in honor of her birth. But she liked only the garden and the gate that framed the sunset; the pump and the toolshed she ignored. Besides, the "port" was blighted by a rotting wharf, salt marshes, and a soap works. So Margaret longed to live in Cambridge—a village of Georgian mansions, stately trees, and the seat of Harvard College, only a mile away.

Boston, to which the 2,500 people of Cambridge and its port were satellite, had less than 40,000 inhabitants. The fledgling United States of America had less than ten million. James Madison was President—the fourth incumbent. The "Indian problem" and freedom of the seas were the main topics of the day; slavery was yet to become a major issue which would rend the nation into two parts.

In Europe the battle of Waterloo was five years in the future.

The Old Order strove mightily with the New. And Italy, Margaret's eventual magnet, was a peninsula inhabited by twenty-four million Italians unhappily divided into eight separate states. In America's one-time mother country, the Victorian era was yet to dawn.

Timothy Fuller, Margaret's father, had done his best to increase the United States population. She was the eldest of eight children, of whom two were to die in childhood, and one, the youngest boy, was to develop mental illness. Timothy had married, at thirty, Miss Margarett Crane, a slender, blond, sweetly timid young woman ten years his junior. At fifty-five he was to die suddenly of Asian cholera, in retreat on a barren farm, leaving little money and Margaret as head of the household, for his wife was incapable of assuming that responsibility. It was Margaret, anguished, who closed Timothy's eyes.

The Fullers were among the earliest immigrants to the Massachusetts Bay Colony. The pious, poetry-writing Thomas, entitled "Lieutenant" in his will, arrived in 1638, almost hard on the wake of the *Mayflower*. He settled in Salem, principal haunt of New England witches. His descendants industriously sought to better themselves. Timothy's father was a divine, driven from his pastorate for his Tory sympathies during the American Revolution, and consistently opposed to the Constitution because it recognized human slavery. Timothy opposed the Missouri Compromise for the same reason.

Timothy was one of five brothers who became lawyers. He worked his way through Harvard College. In due time he was elected to Congress as a Jeffersonian—to the House of Representatives. He tried to play king-maker during John Quincy Adam's first campaign for the office of President, and had ambitions of becoming an ambassador—ambitions, unfortunately for Margaret, never fulfilled.

When Margaret was fifteen, the family moved from Cambridgeport into the long-desired and elegant Dana mansion in Cambridge. A year later, Timothy gave a party in honor of President Adams, followed by a ball marking Margaret's debut in society. The President, who was in mourning, left shortly

9

after dinner, and those who came to the reception to shake his hand found only embarrassed explanations. With the new paneled drawing rooms, wax candles, lavish food and wines, Timothy had overextended himself financially, and the affair passed down in local legend as "Fuller's folly." Margaret's vision of the occasion was otherwise. Though her stays were too tight, she was happy with her new pink satin dress (a bright pink which clashed, people said, with the high color of her complexion). She danced vigorously until her carefully set locks became frazzled and uncurled, and laughed the night away.

Timothy was a strong-minded man with all the rigid determination of his Puritan forebears. He resolved to overlook the unfortunate fact that his firstborn was not male, and to educate her precisely as if she were a boy. At the end of the War of 1812 with Britain, he took the five-year-old Margaret to Boston to hear the bells and see the illuminations celebrating the peace. He devoted himself to her education, instructing her himself. He assigned her lessons and heard her recitations, accepting no "if's," "but's," or "maybe's." As an adolescent, she was sent away to boarding school; she found it a painful experience because she was so far in advance of her fellows.

At the age of four and one half years, Sarah Margaret could read. At six she was reading Latin with the fluency of English; at seven she was running through Vergil's *Aeneid,* with expurgated selections from Horace and Ovid for amusement. Later she learned other languages: a little Greek plus a fluent reading knowledge of German, French, and Italian. The German led her to Goethe, Schiller, Heine; the French, to Molière, Racine, Rousseau, Fourier; and the Italian, to Dante, Petrarca, Boccaccio, Poliziano, Cellini, Tasso, Alfieri, Manzoni.

Though called to Washington, Timothy kept up with his young daughter's education from afar. In one letter, the Congressman informed his wife, "I have written Sarah Margaret a short Latin epistle," and admonished, "She must rise early and shake off sloth . . . . I hope the good girl is pleased when we exert ourselves to give her those qualities which will make her useful to others as well as respectable and happy in herself." He also insisted that she take piano lessons. It is hardly surprising that her schoolgirl companions believed she could rock the cradle, eat an apple, knit a stocking, and read a book, all at the same time.

For her precocious advancement Margaret, not Timothy, paid the price. "The peculiarity of my education had separated me entirely from the girls around, except that when they were playing active games, I would sometimes go out and join them," she wrote in a fragment of her unfinished autobiography. "I liked violent bodily exercise, which always relieved my nerves." But the relief of her nerves was not sufficient. She was plagued by dreadful nightmares and by sleepwalking.

"No one knew why this child, already kept up so late, was still unwilling to retire. My aunts cried out upon the 'spoiled child, the most unreasonable child that ever was—if brother [Timothy] could but open his eyes to see it—who was never willing to go to bed.' They did not know that, so soon as the light was taken away, she seemed to see colossal faces advancing slowly towards her, the eyes dilating, and each feature swelling loathsomely as they came, till at last, when they were about to close upon her, she started up with a shriek which drove them away, but only to return when she lay down again. They did not know that, when at last she went to sleep, it was to dream of horses trampling over her . . . or, as she had just read in her Vergil, of being among trees that dripped with blood, where she walked and walked and could not get out, while the blood became a pool and plashed over her feet, and rose higher and higher, till soon she dreamed it would reach her lips. . . . Often she dreamed of following to the grave the body of her mother, as she had done that of her sister, and woke to find the pillow drenched in tears. No wonder the child arose and walked in her sleep, moaning all over the house, till once, when they heard her, and came and waked her, and she told them what she had dreamed, her father sharply bid her 'leave off thinking of such nonsense, or she would be crazy,' never knowing that he was himself the cause of all these horrors of the night."

Margaret could not have been aware how common are the rampant stallions and dead mothers in the dreams of neurotic little girls with father fixations, or have analyzed fully her own emotions of jealousy and guilt. But she did not lack insight. She refers candidly to her relationship with her father, "all whose feelings were now concentrated on me." Further, "He had no conception of the subtle and indirect motions of imagination and feeling. His influence on me was great, and opposed to the natural unfolding of my character, which was fervent, of strong grasp, and disposed to infatuation, and self-forgetfulness. He made the common prose world so present to me, that my natural bias was controlled. I did not go mad . . . I had too much strength to be crushed . . . ."

Only once did she overtly display toward her father any trace of hostility. At Groton, on the rocky isolated farm she so loathed, and where he had dragged the family, he had constructed for her a little woodland bower, a "retreat," a private place to read and think. For all his urging, she declined so much as a single look, and thanked him in terms so coldly polite as to be curt. After his death she was overwhelmed with remorse—but all her tears could not make the bower less lonely and repelling.

Finally, she was able to be almost dispassionate when she spoke of her childhood: ". . . The child fed with meat instead of milk becomes too soon mature . . . . Certainly I do not wish that instead of masters I had read baby books, written down to children, and with such ignorant dullness that they blunt the senses and corrupt the tastes of the still plastic human being. But I do wish that I had read no books at all till later—that I had lived with toys and played in the open air. Children should not cull the fruits of reflection and observation early, but expand in the sun, and let thoughts come to them. They should not through books antedate their actual experiences, but should take them gradually as sympathy and interpretation are needed."

True is the note of pathos when she adds: "With me, much of life was devoured in the bud."

But for all that, she never ceased to cling to the dream that in Europe her life would flower. There, surely, the canker worm could be thrust aside.

3

Sarah Margaret Fuller was not yet thirty-seven, but in the eyes of her New England contemporaries she was irrevocably a spinster. They had so viewed her even from girlhood. When she blossomed into puberty, she begged that "Sarah" be dropped. Though "Sarah" is "princess" in Hebrew, its meaning did not occur to her; she complained, instead, that there was no Latin equivalent. " 'Tis a proper old-maidish name," she told a cousin; "I will not take it until I am sixty. Then I will sit and knit, look cross and be Miss Sarah Fuller for the rest of my life." Her father had frowned and told her that to eliminate "Sarah" would require an act of the General Court. Sarah was his mother's name.

Margaret did not behave like a repellent spinster, however; from girlhood on, she magnetized large numbers of persons, female and male—and with them explored the whole range of intellect and emotions . . . except sex.

Nor did she look like a spinster. At thirteen her breasts were so developed that she seemed eighteen or twenty. And in her fantasies she enacted becoming a wife. At the age of eight she had read *Romeo and Juliet.* Her father was much dismayed that she should choose such a tale on the Sabbath. Even for "emancipated" Unitarians, Sunday was a day of family prayer; novels and plays were forbidden in the Old New England tradition. When the book was seized, and Margaret put to bed for disobeying, she soared away to Italy and the Verona of her star-crossed lovers. Later, she wrote: "At eight or nine years old the passions are not infrequently felt in their full shock." She knew, because she had felt them.

She was a striking young woman. The proper Harvard College boys with whom she was so "passionately fond of dancing" found her lacking in femininity because she neither chattered nor fluttered her fan in the accepted manner. When she talked, she went, instead, straight to the point—and duller wits than hers could not but feel inferior.

"She had no pretensions to beauty," said her New England contemporaries. Then readily they admitted: "she was not plain." Her hair was blond, fine and softspun, reflecting light like buckwheat honey when poured from a pottery jar. Her mouth was soft and curving, her teeth exceptionally white, her nose a trifle prominent. Her large blue-gray eyes, set wide apart, ranged from intense vivacity to withdrawn melancholy. She was nearsighted, and had a mannerism of half closing the lids to see more sharply. Her hands and arms were beautifully shaped, her figure notable. She was sufficiently athletic to be able to ride twenty-two miles on horseback without fatigue. She carried herself gracefully, with a certain dignified, almost queenly set to her head. Her voice was clear, cultivated, and her words were articulated with the rather high-pitched, precise Yankee accent—in contrast to Southern slurring or a Western drawl. Emerson found her tones too nasal (no doubt as counterpoint to his own celebrated mellow organ notes, developed in the pulpit); but those who attended her famous public "Conversations" in Boston, and listened to her in private conversation, were enchanted and adoring.

Why, then, did her fellows consider that she lacked beauty, when she attracted-repelled them more strongly than any other woman of their time? All—Ralph Waldo Emerson, Bronson Alcott, William Henry Channing, James Freeman Clarke, Henry David Thoreau, George Ripley, Nathaniel Hawthorne, Edgar Allan Poe, James Russell Lowell, Oliver Wendell Holmes, Theodore Parker, Edward Everett, William Cullen Bryant, Henry Wadsworth Longfellow, Horace Greeley, Julia Ward Howe, Elizabeth Peabody—all these and many lesser persons felt the tingling shock of her electricity.

She had, they all said, a man's mind—and they were fascinated, drawn, and repelled by it. When they were afraid of it, they loathed her, and heaped scorn on its possessor. They said, when they disliked her, that she was sarcastic, critical, self-centered. To her admirers she was brilliant, exciting, often wildly gay, often satiric, always witty and stimulating. And this, too, they said publicly. Her gift for mimicry had the power to wound, unless restrained, as well as amuse. Horace Greeley wrote that Margaret, ". . . . had she condescended to appear before the footlights, would soon have been recognized as the first actress of the nineteenth century."

Of them all, it was Emerson who most loved and most hated her, guardedly admitting his "strange, cold-warm, attractive-repelling conversations with Margaret." Often she had taunted him with phrases like, "You are intellect, I am life!" Or, implying a perilously close relationship, she wrote, "Your prudence, my wise friend, allows too little room for the mysterious whisperings of life." In revenge he said she was like the "crackling of thorns under a pot"—yet "her talk was a comedy, she made me laugh more than I like." He confessed, ruefully, "I found she lived at a rate so much faster than mine, and violent compared with mine." Then his great ego took umbrage at another ego: She had, he said, "a rather mountainous ME."

Edgar Allan Poe affected scorn. His prose work had been well reviewed by her, and he had returned the compliment. Nevertheless he was greatly piqued because she had said that his poems, with one exception, The Raven, were "all fragments." "Miss Fuller is an ill-tempered old maid," he declaimed. "Her acts are bookish, and her books are less thoughts than acts

. . . . Avoid her!" But unconsciously he had paid a compliment, for it was ever her aim to combine thought and action into a single harmonious whole.

Bronson Alcott, the harassed father of Louisa May and a covey of squealing little girls, was not unfamiliar with feminine temperament. Alcott wrote in his diary that the temperamental Miss Fuller was "clearly a person given to the boldest speculations, and of liberal and varied acquirements . . . . With the gift of intellect [she has] that of prudence." Thereupon he hired her to teach in his celebrated "progressive" school, where all the children sat in individual chairs instead of upon long benches.

Elizabeth Hoar, a dry New England intellect who met Margaret at Emerson's house in Concord, wrote a friend a detailed list of all her graces, and wound up, at a loss for more words, saying simply, "Only her presence can give you the meaning of the name Margaret Fuller."

Negative and positive, it all added up to what everyone believed: An exceptional woman was exceptional because she had a man's mind. And Margaret was fully aware of what was said about ". . . a chameleon like me." Candidly she appraised herself: "I am 'too fiery' . . . yet I wish to be seen as I am, and would lose all rather than soften away anything." She pretended disdain of other people's remarks. Nevertheless she was made prostrate by blinding headaches, a hysterical reaction. "My character is, after all, still more feminine than masculine," she wailed—and waited impatiently for the opportunity to prove how profoundly she understood herself. As a young girl she had decided that if she must be "ugly" she would be bright. "I am determined on distinction." And distinction came partially as a result of her defense of the feminine, which was a defense of herself.

"I love best to be a woman," she told William Henry Channing, "but womanhood at present is too straitly bound to give me scope. At hours I live truly as a woman, at others I stifle . . . . Desperate as a gamester I feel at moments, yet I cling to the faith that God cannot lose His great throw of Man. Men disappoint me so. I weary in this playground of boys! . . . I wish I were a man and then there would be *one.*" In her pioneering and history-making book, *Woman in the Nineteenth Century,* she stated her case to the public: "Let it not be said, wherever there is energy or creative genius, 'She has a masculine mind'. . . . There is no wholly masculine man, no purely feminine woman."

But she was far from immune to despair. To her journal she confided: "With the intellect I always have, always shall, overcome; but that is not half of the work. The life, the life! O, my God! shall the life never be sweet?"

Then, in a single phrase, she summed it up: " 'Tis an evil lot to have a man's ambition and a woman's heart."

4

On the first of August 1846 she steamed-sailed aboard the *Cambria*. It was a record crossing of the Atlantic: only ten days sixteen hours from Boston to Liverpool. The ship's speed was maintained by both sail and steam—and the *Cambria* was hailed as a symbol of the new industrial age.

The crossing was notable, too, for its smoothness. Yet for all the ease of the voyage, Margaret paid "too dear"—she was seasick, and stated that she preferred to view the sea "from a firm green shore." The stewardess in reply observed that "anyone tempted God Almighty who complained on a voyage where they did not even have to put guards on dishes!" But Margaret had not complained—merely recorded an opinion.

Already she was known in Europe, especially in England. Her editorship of the transcendentalist magazine the *Dial*—a chore she had assumed first alone and then jointly with Emerson—had given her a start toward fame. The Brook Farm experiment in collectivist living had been widely publicized; and though Margaret never resided at the farm and held many reservations concerning it, her name was associated with this idealistic venture which simultaneously aroused wild enthusiasm and violent ridicule. Later she characterized it as a "pastoral masquerade, or a masquerade pastorale." (The Brook farmers named a cow after her.)

Her little travel book, called *Summer on the Lakes,* published in Boston in June 1844, had helped establish her fame. She had traveled by steamboat, stagecoach, and wagon to the frontier region of the Great Lakes, and had reported colorfully on Indian problems, rattlesnakes, settlers in log cabins, shooting rapids in an Indian canoe, and what it was like for a lady to spend the night in a barroom. (While editing her western journal, she became the first woman ever admitted to the Harvard College library.) But it was the book titled *Woman in the Nineteenth Century,* published in New York in February 1845, that truly made her famous. When it was finished, she felt that "the measure of my footprint would be left on earth." It was a controversial and passionate outpouring which sparked the feminist movement in America. To a modern critic it is "poignant, frequently bold, even breathtaking." To her contemporaries it was all this and much more—scandalous, hysterical, revolutionary. To many Americans the idea of equal rights for women was simply preposterous. Yet the first edition was sold out within a week.

The frenetic suspender-snapping Horace Greeley, coiner of the never-to-be-forgotten phrase "Go West, young man," saw Margaret Fuller as a Donna Quixote for his new and crusading newspaper, the New York *Tribune.* It was his firm that had published her *Woman.* Nor, to impress the intellectuals, was he averse to having a former editor of the *Dial* as one of his journalists. So Greeley called Margaret to New York from Boston. He tugged at the chin whiskers that were like a ruff around his face, and surveyed her sharply through his oval steel-framed spectacles. He admitted afterward that his first impression was "not favorable." But, under his wife's urging, he took her home as a boarder, and opened his columns to her as both critic and roving reporter—he gave her such disparate tasks as reviewing the poetry of Longfellow, or describing the condition of women in Sing Sing prison. She dissected Longfellow with scalpel precision, revealing his plagiarism and lack of style. Her visit to Sing Sing led to an indignant attack on prostitution, one of the most unmentionable shock words of the time. While many people were horrified by both articles, immediately she was invited to all the most important literary salons. Almost overnight she became a kind of literary lioness . . . who always wore a white japonica in her hair.

When at last an opportunity opened for Margaret to go to Europe, Mr. Greeley saw his chance. He engaged her to write a series of travel letters at eight dollars per dispatch—perhaps shrewdly aware that he was contracting for a set of remarkable historical documents, which long will continue to be read for their vivid picture of Europe and Europeans in the throes of industrial and political revolution.

Europe was a goal she had set for herself in girlhood, when at the age of thirteen she had seen a fascinating English lady at church. She became infatuated with both the young lady and the idea of Europe. The fulfillment of this glamorous dream had to be deferred year after year, because of her father's declining financial circumstances, and eventually because of his death. When she became head of the family at twenty-five, she resolved to banish thoughts of foreign travel until she had put her brothers through college, had seen her sister safely married, and could leave her mother secure. This she did by teaching and by her public "Conversations for Women" on such subjects as Greek Mythology and Faith. Not until she was thirty-six, however, did the cherished moment arrive. Brother Eugene, the eldest and her favorite, had become a partner in a New Orleans law firm; William Henry had broken with his father long ago on the farm at Groton, entered trade, and made a new life for himself in Cincinnati; pretty Ellen was married to the charming but irresponsible young poet William Ellery Channing; Arthur Buckminster was embarked on a career as a clergyman; Richard had worked his way successfully through Harvard Law School; and poor addled Lloyd was for the moment tranquilized by the continual singing of hymns. So at last she was free to travel—but she lacked the funds.

Among the people she met in New York were Marcus and Rebecca Spring, wealthy, kind-hearted Quakers, who enjoyed philanthropy. They had gone so far as to buy shares in the Brook Farm Community. Once they had noted Margaret's dilemma, they proposed that she join them on the Grand Tour in exchange for helping with their twelve-year-old boy, Eddie. The money was to be considered an advance against some future day when she might be rich in royalties. As this arrangement avoided any hint of charity, she could not refuse. Greeley's offer did the rest. Elated, she launched her new career with emotions surcharged because of the long years of delay.

Emotionally, as well as intellectually, the voyage was overdue. Not long before, she had involved herself with a blue-eyed German one year her junior. To her surprise he revealed himself as a Jew. He had been born in Hamburg, but had immigrated to New York some fifteen years before, and had made something of a success in the commission business. He protested that he did not like his work on the grounds that he had a poetic nature. Also he had a soulful way of playing the guitar. He met Margaret at a particularly difficult moment in her life, when it seemed that she had no alternative but to succumb to spinsterhood. On James Nathan she projected all her pent-up hunger for a man's love, and visualized him as a finer person than he was in fact.

At first the affair had to be conducted with clandestine meetings, as she was staying at Greeley Farm overlooking the East River, and Horace Greeley did not much "take to" Nathan. The couple met on the street, in bookstores, in tearooms, and innumerable letters passed between them. Though Nathan definitely was not interested in marriage (what would his orthodox Mama back in Hamburg have said of his marriage to a goy?), he was led by the passion of Margaret's letters to attempt a physical intimacy closer than she was yet prepared to experience. She professed herself repelled by his "lower nature."

Yet without reserve she had written him: "I hear you with awe assert power over me and I feel it to be true. It causes awe, but not dread . . . for I feel deep confidence in my friend and know that he will lead me on in a spirit of holy love . . . . Psyche was but a mortal woman, yet as the bride of Love, she became a daugher of the gods, too."

She was spinning rapidly toward some sort of physical denouement, when Nathan felt compelled to escape possibly serious complications. He sailed for Europe on the first of June 1845, and the affair was over—though Margaret was not willing to admit this truth to herself. Certainly she sensed the end, or she would not have requested the return of her letters, to be burned. He did not comply.

Once he had returned to Europe, Nathan's communications were sporadic and brief, concerned only with favors for himself, such as a note of introduction to a Washington Cabinet member who happened to be Margaret's friend. After four months of silence Margaret ventured a letter. Its theme she made no effort to conceal: "I have felt . . . a desire for you that amounted almost to anguish." In one of her replies to Nathan, Margaret expressed both the pathos of an old maid spurned and the first taste of bitter reality: "We said farewell the first day of summer and now it is the last. It is again Sunday, the same hour in the evening. I am by the window in the little study recess with the tree looking in, and the stars looking through it, 'but where art thou!' It is gone forever, the beautiful summer, when we might have been so happy together, and happy in a way that neither of us will ever be with any other person. Oh, it is very sad! My friend, shed some tears with me. Why, why must you leave me? . . . Yet, all through it, have I been growing in knowledge of you. You would be surprised to find how much better I know you than when we parted . . . ."

She continued to fret and grieve, nevertheless, and against her better judgment, hoped to see Nathan again in Europe. Through intermediaries she arranged for him to communicate with her in Britain, and part of her eagerness to be off to England lay in this tremulous wish fulfillment.

To America and her friends she bade a peremptory good-bye. Not long before, she had written about her own country: "Since the Revolution . . . the tendency of circumstances has been to make our people superficial, irreverent, and more anxious to get a living than to live mentally and morally. The superficial diffusion of knowledge . . . is likely to vulgarize rather than raise the thought of a nation." Now she wanted to evaluate for herself Europe's long cultural traditions and compare them with American institutions. In the *Tribune* she said, "America is as yet but a European babe; some new ways and motions she has, consequent on a new position; but that soul that may shape her mature life scarce begins to know itself yet."

In her farewell to New York, which appeared in the pages of the *Tribune* on the day of her sailing, she wrote: "I go to behold the wonders of art, and the temples of old religion. But I shall see no forms of beauty and majesty beyond what my country is capable of producing in myriad variety, if she has but the soul to will it . . . ."

Neither she nor anyone in America could have foreseen what in fact she would behold in addition to the wonders of art and the temples of the old religion . . . or the true import of the message she would so vividly and passionately convey to her native land.

Margaret Fuller approached European shores as not only the first American female foreign correspondent, but one of the first American correspondents anywhere. She was astonishingly well informed about European conditions, and foresaw that much of Europe was on the verge of revolution. In an early dispatch to the *Tribune* she made an open declaration of her sympathies. She trumpeted herself as one of those Americans "who take an interest in the cause of human freedom, who, not content with the peace and ease bought for themselves by the devotion and sacrifices of their fathers, look with anxious interest on the suffering nations who are preparing for similar struggle."

Before Margaret's eyes, submerged classes and submerged nations, from Paris to Warsaw, from Palermo to Vienna, soon were to rise like waterspouts from an angry sea and swirl against their tormentors. Nationalists, republicans, socialists, openly and secretly joined together in their several causes against the old regimes, which held them in such tight bondage. In England, in 1848, a pair of unknown Germans with names like a music hall team, Marx and Engels, would publish a document which has not yet ceased to challenge: *The Communist Manifesto.* The French would strike down their fraudulent "Citizen King." North Italian patriots would attack their Austrian oppressors, while Neapolitans and Sicilians would fling themselves in fury against their Bourbon overlord. In Rome a slack and pleasure-loving people would suddenly stiffen, declare the Papal States no longer a theocracy but a democracy, and the Pope would flee. And far away to the east, revolutionary turmoil would increase tenfold.

The Napoleonic upheaval was only a generation past—Napoleon himself had died when Margaret was eleven years old. The democratic freshets loosed in the early Napoleonic era had been dammed and repressed by the aristocratic governing classes against which the French Revolution had struck. The old order had been restored by tyrannies more ruthless than before, and the restlessness of incipient revolutionaries rose in direct proportion to the degree of oppression. Now, with the increasing pace of the Industrial Revolution, a new situation was forming, giving rise to new tensions demanding new solutions.

Britain led the way in the construction of railroads and mass-production factories, while the Russian, Prussian, Austrian, Turkish autocracies of the east, like the Papal theocracy and the Bourbon monarchy in Italy and Spain, lagged far behind. In Britain, France, and parts of Germany and the Low Countries, two new classes were developing and were given new names: the industrial "bourgeoisie" and the industrial "proletariat." These new classes found themselves trapped between the old land-owning aristocracy and the illiterate peasant hordes. A dual economic crisis—in finance and in factory overproduction—created a depression, with extensive unemployment.

To add to the general woe of the working people of western Europe, two bad harvests in succession had been capped by the "potato famine." A potato disease had spread to the continent from Ireland, where thousands literally faced starvation. (Hence the mass Irish immigration to the United States, totally changing the character of Margaret Fuller's Boston.) Thus poverty and famine were coupled with enormous new industrial riches, while the old land-owning aristocracy clung to the feudal past with a nostalgia at once both romantic and pathetic. The need for change for the better was urgent. And such was the temper of the times that almost any change was welcome.

During this revolutionary turbulence, Margaret was to chance across two men who would have a profound effect on her life: Giuseppe Mazzini, Italian patriot and exile, who was to inspire her to new political heights during the liberation of Rome; and Adam Mickiewicz, Polish patriot, poet, and exile, who was to counsel her to liberate her suffering inner self along with the suffering people.

In London she would meet Mazzini. In Paris she would meet Mickiewicz. Then the road led on to Rome . . . and its dual liberation.

5

Liverpool in 1846, except for the vastness of the cement docks, did not look particularly strange to American visitors. The three- and four-story row houses, built of red brick, were not unlike those of Boston, New York, or Philadelphia. The white stone steps were nearly identical with those of Baltimore. And all the bleak, ugly factories looked the same.

On the other hand, the small town of Chester, with its mossy walls, ivy-covered towers, arcaded streets, half-timbered houses, crumbling Gothic cathedral, Roman ruins, was a new experience. The placid river Dee, with mullion-windowed tearooms along its banks and swans floating on its mirrored surface, was truly England. And not far away was Eton Hall, magnificent estate of the Marquis of Westminster, set amid a grassy park so tamed and trimmed that comparison with the raw New World inevitably was invited. It was "a country of that soft, that refined and cultivated loveliness, which, however much we have heard of it, finds the American eye—accustomed to so much wildness, so much rudeness, such a corrosive action of man upon nature—wholly unprepared. I feel all the time as if in a sweet dream. . . ."

So Margaret reported to her faithful readers. But there were other aspects to Queen Victoria's realm she did not wish her audience to overlook. Once having mentioned dutifully the conventional sights and sounds, she drew a deep breath like a diver and plunged into troubled waters. She discussed the evening classes for workers in the mill town of Manchester; the "squalid and shameless beggars" of Liverpool; the lack of bathing facilities in English hotels; the "coarse, rude" girls from the cotton mills; and, like Zola a generation later, "seeing through the windows of the gin palaces the women seated drinking, too dull to carouse."

During her four-month tour of Britain with the Spring family she was indefatigable. They traveled by coach, canal boat, and railroad. The first two modes of transportation, she approved; the third, she detested. Once she continued to ride atop a diligence throughout a rainstorm, though the horses splattered mud and the wind disordered her hair, that she might not miss anything of the landscape. The canal boat was enchanting, because she met "a beautiful youth, about eighteen" whose "profile was like one I used to have of Love asleep, while Psyche leans over him with the lamp." He was an East Indian, dressed in his native costume, the first she had ever seen. But the iron horse, with its rattle and sway and soot, she scorned. It was "that convenient but most unprofitable and stupid way of travelling," and she never became reconciled to it—though later she wrote that it was useless to protest against the new inventions and machines.

For her *Tribune* readers perhaps the most exciting of all her adventures was the entire mid-September night she was lost on the slopes of Ben Lomond, like a Scottish Bacchante who had missed the trail of some MacDionysus. They had "done" Loch Lomond, complete with Gaelic songs from the boatmen, and she and Marcus decided to climb Ben Lomond, leaving Rebecca and Eddie at the inn. It was a four-mile ascent, boggy at the base and rocky at the top. On the way down they overshot the path, and Marcus, in seeking it, became separated from Margaret. They called to one another, but echoes led them farther astray. All night she wandered, several times narrowly missing injury or death in ravines and bogs. At last she succumbed and, exhausted, waited in one spot, chilled and frightened but nevertheless calm, for rescue. At dawn she was found by shepherds sent by Marcus Spring. For many hours they had searched with dogs and lanterns, and shouted her name without results.

The following day Marcus gave a dinner to the shepherds as part of their reward, but she could not attend, as she was sick from fatigue and excitement. This incident she described in full in the columns of the *Tribune,* but in her travel diary she dismissed the whole affair with two cryptic sentences: "Ascent of Ben Lomond. Lost, and pass the night on a heathery mountain." Then she added: "Love Marcus and Rebecca for ever"— and so betrayed her true emotions.

Other emotions she made no attempt to conceal, most especially her indignation at the misery of the poor contrasted with the luxury of the rich. It was "a most lovely day on which we entered Perth," and "visited . . . the stately home of Lord Grey. The drive to it is most beautiful, on the one side the Park, with noble heights that skirt it, on the other through a belt of trees was seen the river and the sweep of that fair and cultivated country. Returning, we were saddened by seeing such swarms of dirty women and dirtier children at the doors of the cottages almost close by the gate of the avenue. To the horrors and sorrows of the streets in such places as Liverpool, Glasgow, and, above all, London, one has to grow insensible or die daily; but here in the sweet, fresh, green country, where there seems to be room for everybody, it is impossible to forget the frightful inequalities between the lot of man and man, or believe that God can smile upon a state of things such as we find exist here."

Though she called Edinburgh "a beautiful city," she added tartly, "if cleanliness be akin to godliness, Edinburgh stands at a great disadvantage in her devotions." At Sheffield, "I saw the sooty servitors tending their furnaces. I saw them also on Saturday night, after their work was done, going to receive its poor wages, looking pallid and dull, as if they had spent on tempering the steel that vital force that should have tempered themselves to manhood." At Newcastle she descended into a coal mine in a bucket and picked her way along a mile of underground galleries with a flickering tallow candle. Here she was moved by the plight of the horses, which "see the light of day no more after they have once been let down into these gloomy recesses, but spend their days in dragging cars along the rails of the narrow passages."

London she found most disturbing of all. She was horrified by "that pomp and parade of wealth and luxury in contrast with the misery—squalid, agonizing, ruffianly—which stares one in the face in every street of London, and hoots at the gates of her palaces more ominous a note than ever was that of owl or raven . . . when empires and races have crumbled and fallen from inward decay." Then she sums up: "Poverty in England has terrors of which I never dreamed at home," and she prays, therefore, "that the needful changes in the condition of this people may be effected by peaceful revolution, which shall destroy nothing except the shocking inhumanity of exclusiveness, which now prevents . . . the treasures created by English genius [from] being used for the benefit of all."

With relief she turned from "these clouds of the present," to more "pleasant" thoughts—to the literary figures who fascinated her. She had come armed with a whole arsenal of introductory letters to the heavy artillerymen of English literature, and such was her fame that she was received without hesitation —evoking not a little envy on the part of some New England colleagues she had left behind.

With the florid, white-maned, seventy-six-year-old Wordsworth she was distinctly disappointed, though she qualified carefully her disappointment. To have done otherwise with the Jehovah of English poetry would have seemed so blasphemous that all her friends would have been roused against her. Apparently she expected some sort of wildly romantic setting, and found his respectable suburban house not quite the proper haunt for a poet who wrote about trailing clouds of glory. She clucked regretfully over his neat rows of hollyhocks, though she herself was a lover of flowers. Nor was she content to confine her comments to poetry and flowers: "Mr. Wordsworth spoke with more liberality than we expected . . ." but "his habits of seclusion keep him much ignorant of the real wants of England and the world." It was clear that she believed an artist belongs in the world and should not attempt to escape from reality.

Her visit to the famous novelist Harriet Martineau was characterized by severe restraint—but not on the part of Miss Martineau. By a curious irony it had been Miss Martineau who introduced Miss Fuller to Mr. Emerson. Margaret had become very friendly with Miss Martineau in America, but subsequently had not permitted friendship to interfere with some negative judgments about Miss Martineau's book *Society in America*. The nervous Miss Martineau, smarting from Margaret's criticism, filled her journal with feline remarks on Margaret's atrocious behavior while visiting in her house. Miss Martineau, deaf from childhood, had an interesting clinical history; she had been freed of another debilitating illness by mesmerism. At thirty-eight she had become bedridden in hysterical protest against a blind and overwhelmingly dominant mother. She dreamed constantly of her mother's falling to her death from high places. Given up by the medical doctors, Miss Martineau's dramatic cure by hypnosis had for Victorians all the elements of an occult scandal. But for Margaret Fuller it was fascinating. Miss Martineau's recovery, she wrote, was of "magical quickness," and "we found her looking far better than she did when in the United States."

Also, Mr. Atkinson, Miss Martineau's mesmerizer, was fascinating. Had Miss Martineau been willing to share with Margaret his platonic attentions, it seems probable that the adventurous Miss Fuller would have leaped into a series of experiments with hypnotism . . . and Mr. Atkinson. He had "a head for Leonardo to paint," she wrote, with "*beaux yeux* and extreme sensibility." Through her ear trumpet Miss Martineau had heard enough of such remarks from Margaret, and became intensely jealous. What remained of her literary friendship with Miss Fuller came brusquely to an end.

Another famous invalid, Elizabeth Barrett, Margaret failed to meet, for in defiance of a morbid, tyrannical father she had risen from her couch at the age of forty and eloped with Robert Browning. Margaret reported the news to New York at once, but factually and not as gossip. The meeting, however, was only deferred, as the lovers had chosen Italy for their idyll.

Though De Quincey, famed as an opium eater, was difficult of access, Margaret managed to see him for several hours. She felt no sense of shock at taking opium, as it was commonly prescribed for babies to keep them quiet, and she herself had been given a drop or two when her headaches seemed to split her personality. Fortunately De Quincey was in a conversational mood, and though at seventy-six he tended to ramble, she found him "an admirable narrator," eloquent and subtle. "I admired, too, his urbanity, so opposite to the rapid, slang, Vivian-Greyish style current in the literary conversation of the day."

There were others, dead and alive, whom she mingled together in her dispatches to the *Tribune:* Robert Burns and Walter Scott and Mary Queen of Scots and Shakespeare and contemporary playwright Joanna Baillie and the skeleton of Jeremy Bentham, still propped up in his clothes. Tennyson and Landor were away. Somehow Dickens was overlooked, though she was well aware of what she called his "cockneyism . . . his graphic power and love of the odd corners of human nature." In place of the missing ones she was able to report that she had gone mad over the Greek and Egyptian rooms at the British Museum, and equally mad over a public bath and public laundry. This last was impressive because it provided, "for almost nothing, good tubs, water ready heated, the use of an apparatus for rinsing, drying, and ironing, all so admirably arranged that a poor woman can in three hours get through an amount of washing and ironing that would, under ordinary circumstances, occupy three or four days." Marcus Spring was impressed, too —so much that when he returned to New York he installed similar plants as a philanthropy.

"In London, for six weeks, we never saw the sun for coal-smoke and fog." Yet it hardly seemed to matter, for she flung herself into the life of the city in a deliberate effort to find new sensations. She was still fluttering from the pain caused by a note from James Nathan, received at Edinburgh. Callously he smashed the eggshell hope that remained to her, by indicating his intention to marry someone else. He added insult to injury by declining to return her letters, as she had begged, unless she agreed to a consideration. In bitterness and fury she sent word to Nathan, through a mutual contact, that she had received his communication but was "too much involved in the routine of visiting and receiving visits to allow her mind a moment's repose to reply to it." Such was the collapse of her relationship with her "dear companion." She did not hesitate to stigmatize his apostasy in her diary, but the pathos of her curt "I care not" certainly did not escape her.

It was in London that Emerson's seminal letters to Thomas Carlyle bore for Margaret the ripest literary fruit—not surprising in view of Emerson's description of her as "an exotic from New England, a foreigner from some more sultry and expansive clime." But for all that, Carlyle listened to barely a word from Margaret, and himself drowned that great talker in a flood of talk. Carlyle was fifty and famous, craggy and crotchety, and had no intention of being lectured by "a strange, lilting, lean old maid," as he afterward described her. Margaret's antennae, as ever, were sensitively attuned; if not to Carlyle's words, then to his wife's eyes. She had been invited to dinner at the Carlyle's house overlooking the foggy Thames, and was received in the red, black, and gold drawing room by Jane Carlyle, wearing black velvet. Anticipating some such elegance, Margaret had put on her lilac silk dress, with trim of black lace. Dinner, she reported to Emerson, was one long harangue by her host, but "I had, afterward, some talk with Mrs. C., whom hitherto I had only *seen,* for who can speak when her husband is there? I like her very much—she is full of grace, sweetness, and talent. Her eyes are sad and charming." Yet Margaret, for all her acuteness, could hardly have guessed the well-kept family secret: Thomas Carlyle's impotence.

Jane Carlyle, in her sorrow, turned to men more delicate and subtle than her husband, though she remained loyally his wife.

One of her dearest friends was an Italian political exile who twelve years earlier had been condemned to death *in absentia:* Giuseppe Mazzini of Genoa. This name, too, was on Margaret's list, and once she had met him, she commented that he was "by far the most beauteous person I have seen." For his part, he was already acquainted with her work, through the Carlyles, and was eager to make personal contact with her. Nor was it very long before he was writing her: "You do not know how much I esteem and love you . . . ."

One evening the Carlyles came to call when Mazzini was visiting Margaret. "All Carlyle's talk," Margaret wrote to Emerson, "was a defense of mere force—success the test of right; if people would not behave well—put collars around their necks; find a hero—and let them be his slaves, etc. It was very Titanic, and anti-celestial . . . . Unluckily, Mazzini was with us, whose society, when he was there alone, I enjoyed more than any . . . . But his being there gave the conversation a turn to 'progress' and ideal subjects, and C. was fluent in invectives on all our 'rose-water imbecilities.' We all felt distant from him, and Mazzini, after some vain efforts to remonstrate, became very sad. Mrs. C. said to me, 'These are but opinions to Carlyle; but to Mazzini, who has given his all, and helped bring his friends to the scaffold, in pursuit of such subjects, it is a matter of life and death.' "

This slender man, with his thin face, his domelike forehead and scanty graying hair, his short-cropped beard and moustache, his long and cleanly chiseled nose, his enormous dark and intense eyes, was to Margaret "pure music." He was no more than five years her senior, and they held many things in common—"many important things," as Mazzini was to admit in a letter to his mother. His imprisonment and banishment for political activities appealed strongly to the ecstatic elements in Margaret's nature, and his scholarly accomplishments appealed strongly to her intellect. In exile he had mastered the speaking and writing of English so that he might present not only his program for "Young Italy," the revolutionary organization he had founded, but also his long-term goal of a united Italy, a republican Italy. Invariably he dressed in black, "in mourning for my country." Because of recent revelations that the British Government had opened his letters, a public scandal had been created which aroused much sympathy for him. He was known to be trailed constantly by spies, but he showed no fear. He behaved always like a man who knew that he had been touched by a special destiny.

"The name of Joseph Mazzini is well known to those among us who take an interest in the cause of human freedom," wrote Margaret to her *Tribune* readers. "It was no superficial enthusiasm, no impatient energies, that impelled him, but an understanding of what *must* be the designs of Heaven with regard to man, since God is Love, is Justice." The choice of these words could not have been accidental on Margaret's part, for Mazzini's outlook—in contrast to that other famous revolutionary whom he physically resembled, Lenin—was actively spiritual. Long since, he had dropped all the dogmas of the Roman Catholic Church, in which he was brought up, but retained a kind of theism related to the growth and development of Man. One of the slogans he unfurled on his banners was "God and the People." His other great emphasis was on the idealistic role of youth in social reform.

Not content with theory, Mazzini from early manhood had been a practicing revolutionary. Hunted down by the police, hounded from his native land, Mazzini nevertheless continued his political agitation. In addition to speaking and writing for a united Italy, he organized from afar clandestine groups for actual revolt. As he believed that only the young had both adequate strength of body and firmness of purpose to carry through his grand design, he limited membership in "Young Italy" to persons under the age of forty (except himself, when he passed that age). And in London, tireless in his drive, he turned his attention to the poor Italian boys who roamed the city's streets. He established a free night school for the education of these largely illiterate immigrants, and with education they became his devoted followers.

On the evening of November 10—the school's fifth anniversary—Margaret Fuller addressed the students. She had been packing all day, preparing to leave for Paris. Mazzini saw that she was willing to carry on in his cause even when exhausted. He nodded approval throughout her talk, and afterward wrote to his mother that she "made a touching speech." The celebration lasted until one-thirty in the morning. Margaret described the evening in the *Tribune's* columns, and to remind her readers of the importance of Mazzini's work, added that Americans should have "an especial interest in Italy, the mother of our language and our laws, our greatest benefactress in the gift of genius." She said not a word, however, of having joined Giuseppe Mazzini in a plot.

In fact, not only Margaret but the Springs had joined with titillation in a plan to smuggle Mazzini into Italy. It was decided that he would follow them to Paris in disguise, and become a member of their party. With a false American passport —to be provided by Margaret and the Springs—they would set out together for Rome. The only difficulties were the Mazzini death sentence waiting to be enforced, and the potential dangers to Mazzini's new American conspirators.

As the new American conspirators had never breathed the sulphuric fumes of a European torture chamber, they could not have been more casual. They felt no misgivings at the prospect of so romantic an adventure and, bearing letters to one of Mazzini's agents, cheerfully departed for Paris and The Revolution.

6

Perversely, Margaret chose to describe Paris, not as the legendary city of elegant boulevards and glittering crystal chandeliers, but as a city of "mud and mist." She assured her *Tribune* readers that their winter climate of gales, snow, and ice was delightful in comparison with that of Paris.

Nevertheless, she admitted rather grudgingly that one could find in Paris "wax-lights, mirrors, bright wood fires, vivacious ejaculations, wreathed smiles, and adroit courtesies." In passing, she took a couple of nicely honed razor swipes at both the English and the French. John Bull, she wrote, "is prone to the most solemn humbug, generally of philanthropic or otherwise moral kind . . . . Not so with your Frenchman; who can cheat you pleasantly, and move with grace in the devious and slippery path."

In France she repeated, with the Springs, the pattern that had been established in Britain. She looked into the night schools for adults—a necessity of the rising new capitalism—and was impressed by "how much can be done for the working classes" with education. She herself, she said, would attempt to establish similar classes, "should I ever return." (It is curious that she did not say *"when* I return.") Then she launched into praise of the *crèches,* where children of the poor could be left while the mothers were at work. This too, she said, would be a good arrangement in America, "even when we cease to have any very poor people, and, please heaven, also to have any very rich."

Passing through Lyon, she visited the garrets of the weavers, and was horrified at the inhuman working conditions. Entire families, including children from the age of nine, slaved at the looms night and day for the barest subsistence. Near Paris she toured the wards of a school for idiots, and "wept the whole time I was in this place." And everywhere she went, she inquired about prostitution, intending to write a comprehensive study of its many aspects.

In contrast, she attended a presentation at court and the royal ball given afterward at the Tuileries. It was an ideal opportunity to use the gold lorgnette that compensated for her nearsightedness. She was pleased by the beauty of the women, their chic clothes, "their graceful vivacity." She approved of the "great variety of costume, color, and decoration" among the men, as compared with "the sombre masses of men that overcloud our public assemblies." She described the queen, and noted that the king was rumored to have his eye on a certain beauty from Philadelphia. But for all the dazzle she was not fooled. Already she had seen too much of the slate gray poverty that lay behind the bright gilt facade. "The poorer classes have suffered from hunger this winter," though "all signs of this are kept out of Paris." A pamphlet, called *The Voice of Famine,* had appeared, but had been suppressed immediately in the name of the king.

The "bourgeois King," as Louis Philippe was known, was the fattest in person and in purse of all the monarchs of Europe. It was not surprising that François Fourier's utopian socialist doctrine was making headway, said Margaret, though she herself had serious reservations concerning it. The followers of Fourier, she wrote to a friend, "are full of hope, and their propaganda has a real and increasing influence." In the columns of the

Tribune she stated flatly: "The need of some radical measures of reform is not less strongly felt in France than elsewhere, and the time will come before long when such will be imperatively demanded." She was, as events would prove, prophetic.

Yet for a moment her optimism deserted her, and on Christmas Eve she set down her gloomy thoughts in a letter: "I have been today in one of the great Roman [Catholic] cathedrals (St. Roch), and have heard there beautiful music to celebrate the birth of Jesus. As I looked on the countenances of the crowd and saw inscribed there the woes and degradation of which I see such glaring evidences on every side, when I saw the gilt coaches of royalty leaving the door, I marvelled at the faith of men, that they would still be celebrating a fact which at the end of 1800 years has produced so little of the result desired by Jesus."

Perhaps part of her depression was derived from the failure of Mazzini to arrive in Paris on schedule, and she had so greatly desired his coming. On that very Christmas Eve Mazzini was writing her: "The scheme has unavoidably been protracted to some indefinite period. You guess it by my sending the introductory notes [to friends in Italy]. I am bound here, not without a faint hope of revisiting my country in a different manner." He was alluding to the Italian revolution, which he felt was soon to come. Nonetheless, Margaret's disappointment was profound.

Another part of her depression certainly derived from the last letter to arrive from Hamburg. Just before she left London, she had written her congratulations, stiffly and properly, to Nathan. With his reply he proved himself, if possible, even more the poseur and prig. Again he refused to return her letters, assuring her that "I shall do nothing with them but what is right, manly, and honorable." But: "Your sudden change of heart will not permit me to ask a favor even though I needed to. To that interesting portion of your letter where you say, 'Mr. Nathan, you have deceived me,' I reply, Keep cool! I shall in time disprove all charges and establish that (whatever I may or may not have been to others) I have been true to you. A few charges, it is true, I have against *you!* . . . Yes, Miss Fuller, *you have judged me without a hearing, you have condemned and insulted me . . . !"* Yet for all his floods of rhetoric, the essential fact was that he held her all-too-passionate letters for ransom or blackmail.

Characteristically, she bounded into action, to forget or not to think. She went to the theater to see the famed actress Rachel in *Phèdre.* She attempted to attend a Sorbonne lecture by the astronomer Urbain Leverrier, discoverer of the planet Neptune, and was indignant when she was denied entrance because she was a woman. She turned to the musical offerings of Paris, going first to the Opéra Comique. She found it tolerable and no more, unconsciously agreeing with Stendhal's verdict on French music when she wrote: "I find the tolerable intolerable in music." The Italian Opera was more agreeable, and she saw, among other offerings, *Norma* and *Don Giovanni.*

The romantic *Don* offered an unexpected psychosomatic dividend—though both the idea and the term were then unknown to the medical profession. She had been suffering with a severe toothache for several days, and resolved on an extraction with the aid of the newly discovered anesthetic, ether. She was "not sorry to try its efficacy, after all the marvellous stories I had heard." Her faith in the wonder drug was sorely tried, however, when at first she failed to feel its effect. She was just thinking, "Alas! this has not the power to soothe nerves so irritable as mine," when suddenly she wandered off—"many impressions, but all pleasant and serene." Then the dentist gave her a stronger dose, and when she awoke, the tooth was gone—but not the effect of the ether. For three days she seemed to taste the anesthetic constantly, and suffered neuralgic pains.

She had bought her ticket to *Don Giovanni* before the trip to the dentist's office, and so could not bear to give up the opera, despite her aches and pains. To her astonishment "the music soothed the nerves at once." The pain disappeared and did not return after she left the opera. And of course, being Margaret Fuller, she drew a conclusion: "Ah! if physicians only understood the influence of the mind over the body, instead of treating, as they so often do, their patients like machines, and according to precedent!"

Her stalking of French literary lions proved unsatisfactory. In a letter to Emerson she was forced to admit: "My steps have not been fortunate in Paris, as they were in England." Part of the difficulty lay in the unfamiliar sound of the French language —she read fluently, but she could not speak. Almost at once she began lessons, yet to Emerson she confessed: "French people I find slippery, as they do not know exactly what to make of me, the rather as I have not the command of their language. *I* see *them,* their brilliancy, grace, and variety, the thousand slight refinements of their speech and manner, but cannot meet them in their way. My French teacher says I speak and act like an Italian, and I hope, in Italy, I shall find myself more at home." For all the difficulties with French, it was at least a pleasure to seem Italian—the implied rebuke was really a compliment.

But for all her lack of success in finding entrée into the French literary world, she did not cease to try. Her *Essay on American Literature* had just been published in translation in a leading Parisian journal (to her disgust, her name was misstated as "Elizabeth"), and she hoped that doors hitherto closed would open to her. At first little changed. She was not even fortunate enough to hear Alexandre Dumas speaking musketeerlike in his own defense in a law suit—the courtroom was jammed with spectators long before she arrived. She was compelled to content herself with the manuscripts of that dangerous radical (in American judgment) Jean Jacques Rousseau: "Yellow and faded age has made them, yet at their touch I seemed to feel the fire of youth." Then her luck changed, and while visiting Robert Lamennais, the elderly once-imprisoned "apostle of democracy" who had campaigned for separation of Church and State, she met the anticlerical Pierre Jean Béranger, whom she hailed as "the great national lyricist of France." Béranger was all the greater in many eyes because he had refused every formal honor, including nomination to the Academy of France.

Her real coup, however, was even more totally unexpected: a

long, warm meeting with Mazzini's friend the notorious novelist George Sand (Madame Dudevant)—a meeting that Margaret chose not to describe in the *Tribune,* as Madame Sand was alleged to be the most licentious woman in Europe. In *Woman in the Nineteenth Century* Margaret had coupled the names of George Sand and Mary Wollstonecraft in defense of women's rights, and thus had suffered at first hand the outraged shock of American Puritans. In an essay on French novelists in the *Tribune* (February 1, 1845) she had gone much further, and publicly mentioned George Sand's irregular sexual arrangements, "independent of the civil and ecclesiastical sanction," without a word of condemnation. In self-righteous American eyes any woman who condoned the behavior of a George Sand could herself be no better than a hussy. So Margaret confined her report to dear old Elizabeth Hoar in Concord—a rather strange choice for such a confidence, as Elizabeth yet remained faithful to the memory of her fiancé, Waldo Emerson's dead brother, Charles.

George Sand, said Margaret, "had every reason to leave her husband—a stupid, brutal man, who insulted and neglected her. He afterwards gave up their child to her for a sum of money. But the love for which she left him lasted not well, and she has had a series of lovers, and I am told has one now, with whom she lives on the footing of combined means, independent friendship! But she takes rank in society like a man, for the weight of her thoughts . . . . Even an American here, and with the feelings of our country on such subjects, Mrs. ———, thinks of her with high esteem . . . . She needs no defense, but only to be understood, for she has bravely acted out her nature, and always with good intentions . . . . Also, there may have been something of the Bacchante in her life, and of the love of night and storm, and the free raptures amid which roamed on the mountain-tops the followers of Cybele, the great goddess, the great mother."

Of the personal interview Margaret wrote: "Madame S. opened the door, and stood looking at me an instant. Our eyes met. I shall never forget her look at that moment. The doorway made a frame for her figure; she is large, but well-formed. She was dressed in a robe of dark violet silk, with a black mantle on her shoulders, her beautiful hair dressed with the greatest taste, her whole appearance and attitude, in its simple and lady-like dignity, presenting an almost ludicrous contrast to the vulgar caricature idea of George Sand . . . . It made me very happy to see such a woman, so large and developed a character, and everything that *is* good in it so *really* good. I loved, shall always love her."

"Afterwards," she concluded, "I saw Chopin, not with her, although he lives with her, and has for the last twelve years." Chopin, "always ill, and as frail as a snow-drop, but an exquisite genius," played the pianoforte for her in his pearl-gray suite above Madame Sand's apartment. So, quite logically, Margaret discussed Chopin, and Franz Liszt, Madame Sand's former lover, with Chopin's countryman Adam Mickiewicz. It was a discussion that might have been concerned only with music or revolution, but that instead led on to personal subjects—with an impact even more lasting than the memorable interview with Madame Sand . . . for Margaret, too, longed to act out her nature.

This "real and important relation," as Margaret described her feelings for Mickiewicz, began with a note attached to a gift volume of Emerson's most recent poems. "As I had heard a great deal of him which charmed me . . . I asked him to come and see me. He came, and I found in him the man I had long wished to see, with the intellect and passions in due proportion for a full and healthy human being, with a soul constantly in-spiring."

Adam Mickiewicz was indeed an extraordinary figure. His vitality denied his almost fifty years, and he remained strik-ingly handsome. Blue-eyed and blond, vigorous and athletic in body, this national poet of Poland totally negated popular con-ceptions of poets as feeble intellectuals. He was not only the epic poet of Poland, with his *Pan Tadeusz,* but also the revolution-ary leader of his country, for he had been driven into exile by the Russian czar. His wife, unable to bear the life of homeless refugees, had lost her reason; and lately he had been deprived by Louis Philippe of his professorial post at the Collège de France. Like his friend Mazzini, he called not only for the freedom of his country from external oppression, but for political rights, freedom of speech, land reform, rights for women . . . in short, democracy.

Margaret Fuller was not the first American Mickiewicz had known, for James Fenimore Cooper (*The Last of the Mohicans*) had been his friend in Rome. But it was Margaret who made the most profound impression on him. Their encounter, he said, was one of those which "consoles and fortifies." She was "a *true* person." More—she was "the only woman to whom it has been given to touch what is decisive in the present world and to have a presentiment of the world of the future."

He spoke to Margaret with a directness which must have been wonderfully refreshing to her after the miserable convolutions of James Nathan. Mickiewicz detested Puritanism, and was even suspicious of Margaret's Quaker companions, the Springs, because of the proper bourgeois aspects of their life. He assured Margaret: "For you the first step of your deliverance . . . is to know whether you are to be permitted to remain a virgin."

His words no doubt were like a lightning bolt striking perilously nearby, and afterward she remained quivering in the electricity of his intimacy. Yet in her last Paris dispatch to the *Tribune* she could not have been more bland. She mentioned nothing of having made the acquaintance of Mickiewicz, and wrote instead a critique of Turner's paintings. And while "brother Adam" was urging her on to the sensuous land of Italy, Mazzini's parting admonition was singing in her ears: "I would like you to learn to love not only Italy, but the Italians."

On February 25, 1847, Margaret and the Springs "bade adieu to Paris, just as we had one fine day"—the first wholly fine day of the winter, and the boulevards were jammed with gay crowds, "full of quick turns and drolleries." She professed herself sorry to leave; in fact she was ever more eager to reach Rome, and almost regretted that their itinerary called for Marseilles, Genoa, Livorno, and Naples. At Arles, however, with its ancient amphitheater, she found some compensation: "Here for the first time I saw the great handwriting of the Romans in its proper medium of stone, and I was content . . . ."

7

For all Margaret's sense of urgency, they took the diligence from Naples to Rome, because there was no other way overland. So indolent were the Bourbons, and so irreconcilably opposed to industrial progress were the clerical rulers of the Papal States, that no railroad or telegraph had been constructed between these two of the three greatest cities in Italy. The bulky coach, drawn by six horses, rumbled and bumped and swayed, but Margaret was not sorry to be aboard. The route from Naples lay along the ancient road built by the Emperor Domitian in the first century A.D.; and at Formia it joined the Via Appia Antica, built by the censor Appius Claudius Caecus in 312 B.C.

The continuing existence of these two roads, with their ancient pavement, culverts, and bridges, was to Margaret proof positive of all she had learned of Roman character as a child. It was easy now to hear the creak of Roman wagon wheels bringing commerce from the ends of the known world, and the tramp of the legions returning victorious from such savage lands as Germany and Britain. Her father had instilled in her "Roman virtue," and in the beginnings of her autobiography she had written about "the influence of the great Romans whose thoughts and lives were my daily food during those plastic years . . . . ROME! it stands by itself, a clear Word. The power of will, the dignity of a fixed purpose is what it utters."

Formia had been the site of many Roman villas, and ruined remnants of their boat landings and interior painted walls could be seen all along the coast. But at Gaeta, later hands had constructed a vast and imposing medieval castle on the point of the peninsula. It was a castle that soon would have a role to play in the events Margaret Fuller was fated to record. Always curious, she took the trouble to note Gaeta in her travel diary.

She found the journey to Rome "exquisite." She saw "picturesque villages in the hills," "gnarled old olive trees on the slopes," and "graceful bell towers in the valleys." It was the end of March, and spring was everywhere. Toward the Pontine marshes she seemed to feel no fear of malaria, but noted the marshes' "ecstatic character . . . dear frogs . . . fellow citizens all croaking and singing." They were characters from Aristophanes' play, and the chorus chanted "Brekekekex, ko-ax, ko-ax"—just as in antiquity. But from Albano on, though the travelers passed ruined aqueducts, temples, and tombs set among umbrella pines and tall dark cypresses, she ceased to make notes. She was too impatient, too eager to be at the center of her world. The coach she calumniated as a "slow, jogging *vettura*"—she was already beginning to garble English and Italian. Winding down from the Alban hills into the hazy Roman plain, she saw a city of stone glowing like golden terra cotta in the morning sun. *"Ecco Roma!"* was the coachman's cry. It was, she said, "all light and calmness."

At first it was a bewildering world, for Rome was not the Roman city of her dreams but the shadow of a shadow. Of the city of the Caesars, with its two million inhabitants, there remained but a few crumbling ruins and the Pantheon intact. A medieval and then baroque city had been built above and among the ruins—a city containing hardly two hundred thousand people, and not one seemed to care about the immensity of the past. Of the Latin language, in which she was so fluent, there

46

remained only the Italian tongue, which despite her reading knowledge she could hardly speak at all. And of the rocklike Roman character she could see no trace. Yet, somehow, a mysterious metamorphosis took place. It was not long before she was writing to her dear and trusted friend, Caroline Sturgis: "Rome was much poisoned to me. But, after a time, its genius triumphed, and I became absorbed in its proper life . . . the whole heart must be yielded up to it. It is something really transcendent, both spirit and body." But she did not yet report to Caroline the special reason for this change.

A letter from Adam Mickiewicz was waiting for Margaret, a letter calculated to help her yield "both spirit and body." In his ebullient French he advised her to seek "the society of Italians, conversations with Italians, the music of Italians . . . . Now enjoy what surrounds you. Breathe life through all your pores. . . . Learn to appreciate yourself as a beauty, and, after having admired the women of Rome, say, 'And as for me, why, I am beautiful!' "

She began by opening her eyes, if not her heart, to the life around her. With the Springs, she had found lodgings on the Via del Corso. The Corso had become the promenade, the fashionable parade ground for the Roman aristocracy. From her windows Margaret could see the elegantly dressed ladies and gentlemen in their carriages, bowling down the Corso as if it were a racetrack, the coachmen never giving way, and constantly crying out "*Guarda! Guarda!*" at unwary pedestrians. To Emerson she wrote, "All night long, after the weather became fine, there was conversation or music before my window: I never really seemed to sleep while there." The Corso was also the locale of spontaneous demonstrations against the clerical regime, and not long ago had been the scene of an international incident when papal cavalry had mistakenly sabred two American onlookers.

The young men of the nobility rode their horses—stallions —as if they were all centaurs at heart, and no more beautiful mounts were to be found anywhere in Europe. But even on foot the young noblemen carried themselves with a special air of intense but graceful bodily freedom, which was reflected from the unself-consciousness of the people in general.

It was Margaret's friend the sculptor William Wetmore Story who took the time to put on paper the pagan lissomeness of the people: "All the windows are wide open and there is at least one head and one pair of shoulders leaning out at every house. The poorer families are all out on their doorsteps, working and chatting together, while their children run about them in the streets, sprawling, playing and fighting. Many a beautiful theme for the artist is now to be found in these careless and characteristic groups; and curly-headed St. Johns may be seen in every street, half-naked, with great black eyes and rounded arms and legs . . . . All things are easy and careless in the out-of-doors life of the common people—all poses unsought, all groupings accidental, all actions unaffected and unconscious. One meets Nature at every turn—not braced up in prim forms, not conscious in manners, not made up into the fashionable or the proper, but impulsive, free and simple. With the whole street looking on, they are as unconscious and natural as if they were where no eye could see them . . ."

And, most shocking to Anglo-Saxon Puritans, among such a people the basic bodily functions were accepted as quite natural. Babies were suckled openly at uncovered breasts, and were constantly hugged and petted. Children urinated at will in the streets, and men made little effort to conceal themselves in the public urinals. Boys and men strolled arm in arm, and lovers caressed and kissed on public benches. Thus antiquity had survived in spite of all the strictures of the priests, and Margaret was immediately aware of what she saw. Here was an expansion of human warmth and feeling in accord with her most secret dreams.

But she had work to do for Greeley's *Tribune,* and wrenched herself from subjective things. Like a good topical reporter she visited all the American sculptors and painters at the moment in Rome: Thomas Crawford, Luther Terry, Thomas Hicks, and Christopher Cranch. William Story was to arrive a few months later, and others had established their studios in Florence.

Then, for contrast, she toured Michelangelo, Raffaello, Leonardo, Guercino, Carracci, Titian, and Il Domenichino. Nevertheless her comments were desultory, and she confessed in a letter to William Henry Channing, "Art is not important to me now . . . I take interest in the state of the people . . . I see the future dawning."

Immediately she frequented the Caffè delle Belle Arti on the Corso, a sort of underground clearing house for persons seriously working for the freedom and unity of Italy. All the latest posters were on the walls, and amid the barrels of wine, speakers carried on a seemingly perpetual harangue. At the Caffè Greco, founded in the middle of the eighteenth century, an atmosphere of thick cigar smoke and theoretical revolution prevailed among the artists and writers who inhabited the place. It was small, dark, untidy, but the owners shrewdly provided excellent coffee and freedom of speech—managing somehow to avoid the strictures of the secret police, whose spying activities were notorious. Here the latest news from all countries was discussed and dissected by citizens of all countries, and so diverse were the languages that sometimes the shouting sounded like the Tower of Babel. The Caffè Greco was a long way from Beacon Hill in Boston, and provided the kind of excitement on which Margaret thrived.

For all her growing interest in politics, events did not yet justify her giving precedence to political reporting in her Italian dispatches. The travelog was still surefire with her readers; but to this, like art, she was resistant. "There is very little that I can write about Italy. Italy is beautiful, worthy to be loved and embraced, not talked about." Thus she began her first column from Rome, and continued, "I find it is quite out of the question to know Italy, to say anything of her that is full and sweet, so as to convey any idea of her spirit, without long residence . . . "

Italy—a geographical expression, not a nation. In the south, whence she had come, was the kingdom of Naples, which included Sicily. In the north was the kingdom of Piedmont; the duchies of Parma and Modena; the grand duchy of Tuscany; and the Austrian overlordship of Lombardy and Venetia. Splitting the peninsula in two, from sea to sea, were the Papal States. And finally, like the head of a pin on the map, was the fortress-fastness of the republic of San Marino.

Everywhere, however, "the great features of the past pursue and fill the eye," and most especially in Rome. Brushing aside the swarms of wheedling beggars, she galloped off to: The Pantheon, built by the Emperor Hadrian; the Castel Sant'Angelo, originally Hadrian's tomb; the Arch of Constantine and the Colosseum by moonlight, where she heard owls hoot; and the vine- and weed-encumbered Roman Forum, where goats grazed and pigs grunted amid the imposing ruins. She climbed the Janiculum Hill, and like Goethe and Stendhal and many another notable person before her, stood on the Roman wall of small San Pietro in Montorio Church and gazed at the rose-colored domes and towers of the city at sunset. She attended Mass in the Sistine Chapel. She ascended the Michelangelo dome of vast St. Peter's and surveyed Bernini's colonnades and fountains. By torchlight she saw the stone popes where they lay on their tombs. "St. Peter's must be to each one a separate poem," she said. "It is all rich, and full—very impressive in its way."

In her dispatch from London describing Mazzini's school for poor Italian boys she had mentioned the new pope, Pius IX, for the first time. These youths, she had said, were encouraged by "some traits of apparent promise in the new Pope." Her incipient political acumen was clearly demonstrated by the lucid and dispassionate position she took from the very beginning: "apparent promise"—while others were offering lavish and uncritical acclaim. And from Rome she struck another dubious note: "We may see that the liberty of Rome does not yet advance with seven-leagued boots; and the new Romulus will need to be prepared for deeds at least as bold as his predecessor, if he is to open a new order of things."

Pius IX was large, handsome, aristocratic, and distinguished —he looked like a portrait of God, clean-shaven. Moreover, he was a "liberal." As Cardinal Mastai Ferretti, bishop of Imola, he had read the controversial book by the exiled Abbot Vincenzo

Gioberti, *The Moral and Civil Primacy of the Italians* (1843), which asserted that by moderate reforms, under the moral leadership of the papacy, a national Italian federation could be achieved. The army of Piedmont would drive out the Austrians; the Bourbons would bow to the pope. A revolution on the Mazzinian model therefore was not necessary. Less than a year before Margaret's arrival in Rome, the dark-horse cardinal had been elected to the apostolic throne left vacant by the death of the aged and suspicious Gregory XVI. Gregory was a pope so unpopular that his subjects first whispered and then said aloud: "Better the Turk than the pope!"

At once Pius granted amnesty to the 394 political prisoners in Gregory's jails and pardons to the 605 political exiles from the Papal States. These acts were greeted with undamped enthusiasm, and cries of *"Viva Pio Nono!"* ("Long live Pius the Ninth!") were heard everywhere in Italy. Then, to the pope's embarrassment, "Death to the Austrian overlords!" was added. Undaunted, however, the pope took a further step and liberalized the censorship of the press. For the first time the subjects of the Papal States could read something of the facts of world events. Overnight Pio Nono became the worshipful object of a hero cult.

Using Holy Week as a point of departure, Margaret described the pope's popularity with the masses:

"The ceremonies of the Church have been numerous and splendid during our stay here; and they borrow unusual interest from the love and expectation inspired by the present Pontiff. He is a man of noble and good aspect, who, it is easy to see, has set his heart upon doing something solid for the benefit of man. But pensively, too, must one feel how hampered and inadequate are the means at his command to accomplish these ends. The Italians do not feel it, but deliver themselves, with all the vivacity of their temperament, to perpetual hurras, vivas, rockets, and torchlight processions. I often think how grave and sad must the Pope feel, as he sits alone and hears all this noise of expectation.

"A week or two ago the Cardinal Secretary published a circular inviting the departments to measures which would give the people a sort of representative council. Nothing could seem more limited than this improvement, but it was a great measure for Rome. At night the Corso in which we live was illuminated, and many thousands passed through it in a torch-bearing procession. I saw them first assembled in the Piazza del Popolo, forming around its fountain a great circle of fire. Then, as a river of fire, they streamed slowly through the Corso, on their way to the Quirinal [Palace] to thank the Pope, upbearing a banner on which the edict was printed. The stream of fire advanced slowly, with a perpetual surge-like sound of voices; the torches flashed on the animated Italian faces. I have never seen anything finer. Ascending the Quirinal they made it a mount of light. Bengal fires were thrown up, which cast their red and white light on the noble Greek figures of men and horses that reign over it. The Pope appeared on his balcony; the crowd shouted three vivas; he extended his arms; the crowd fell on their knees and received his benediction."

The Italian people believed that it was Pius IX, and Pius alone, who would lead them out of the wilderness of oppression. Alas that Margaret was only an American journalist—a woman whose doubts could be of little interest to her hosts.

8

Easter that year fell on April 4. After vesper services in St. Peter's, Margaret proposed to her companions, the Springs, that they wander independently among the various chapels, that they might view with leisure the objects that most interested each individual. So it was agreed, and a meeting place and time selected. But at the appointed time Margaret did not find the Springs at the appointed place. Some confusion had arisen in the mutual understanding.

Margaret then began to search among the chapels for her friends, viewing each group with the ever-handy lorgnette which was strung about her neck. But the Springs seemed to have been swallowed up in the vastness of the largest church in the world. The hour grew later, the shadows longer, the people fewer. As the church emptied, each footfall echoed from the marble pavement into the soaring vaults. It was during these moments of a kind of haunting loneliness that Margaret was approached by a young man who reminded her vaguely of her favorite brother, Eugene. He walked with unconscious grace and serenity.

Dressed in the most fashionable mode, he wore a flowing cravat, a long form-fitting jacket with wide lapels, light tight trousers, and sported a bamboo cane. He had rather long dark-brown hair, parted on the right and combed naturally across his forehead and back around his ears. His moustache was soft and broad, following the whole curve of his upper lip. All of his features were strongly marked. His eyes were a very dark brown, deep set, and so calm as to be almost melancholy. When he spoke, his Italian was enunciated with a beautiful clarity and rhythm.

Then as now, Italian males were always eager to be of service to unattached females. Then as now, the introduction was always some variant of the phrase which has become classic with time: "Signorina (or Signora), is there anything I can do for you?" No doubt Margaret was astonished, and at first she hesitated to answer. But the young man was so polite, so diffident, so obviously well-bred, and so handsome, that she could not resist. She said, in her halting Italian, "I am separated from my friends —either they or I am lost."

"May I be your guide?" he answered.

And in that statement she was not lost—but found.

At once it was apparent to Margaret that he was at least ten years younger than she, though to the casual observer he appeared older and she younger than their ages. Intuitively she felt a fleeting sense of regret; but she also felt a certain protection in her superior age. Though she wore no wedding ring, only the old familiar ruby, surely this young man regarded her as an elderly woman—and his offer of help equally surely was made in good faith. She need have no fear of any impropriety in permitting him to accompany her for a few minutes through the mazes of St. Peter's, which evidently he knew well. Yet it was oddly illogical that she should feel pleased at having worn one of her most becoming dresses and, from her center-parted, severely swept-back hair, having permitted two soft curls to escape along the sides of her neck. Nor, happily, were the few strands of gray visible in the honey-colored mass. Given

Margaret's meticulous care for her personal appearance (she always took at least an hour to dress), she could not have felt otherwise.

She accepted his offer straightforwardly, with gratitude. And, as was her habit with everyone, narrowed her eyelids and looked directly into his eyes. She was unaware of what an Italian man reads into the look of a woman.

They wandered together about the church, but it was clear that the massive pile was empty. "I fear your friends have gone," he said. "It will be necessary for you to take a carriage." But when they sought a carriage, all the carriages had gone. There was no way left but to walk, so he offered to escort her.

Together they descended the broad flight of steps from the main portal into the piazza, flanked on either side by an elliptical colonnade for giants. In the center was the towering Egyptian obelisk surmounted by a cross, and to right and left a great fountain gushed like living sculptural forms. Behind the dome the sun permeated the whole atmosphere with the famous rose-gold light of Rome near sunset. The myriad colossal statues of the apostles and the saints, standing free above the facade and along the colonnades, cast lengthened shadows indistinguishable from the shadows of the marble gods of ancient Rome. Here indeed was ancient Rome, but Rome subdued by Christianity. The name of the power had changed, but the power remained.

Together they cut through tangled medieval streets to the river Tiber. They followed its green and sloping bank to the Castel Sant'Angelo, the oldest castle in Europe, secretly connected with the Vatican and for so many centuries the treasure house and fortress of the popes. They crossed the ancient Roman bridge, now Christianized with its double file of stone angels, and sought the Corso.

As they walked together, they began to talk of personal things. Margaret spoke Italian with difficulty, and sometimes it was necessary for her to rely on French, for the young man knew no English. Yet no matter how she garbled her sentences, he seemed invariably to understand. And he must have been amazed at the rapidity with which she—always the mother-confessor to her friends—drew information out of him.

His name was Giovanni Angelo Ossoli. He had three older brothers and two older sisters. As in Margaret's family, two other children had died. He was circumspect in his references to his brothers, but he spoke of his sisters with warmth. All were married except him, and one sister—amazingly—had married an Irishman and gone to Ireland to live. At last he spoke of his mother, sadly. She had died when he was six. Now his aged father was very ill. He was silent for awhile.

But how did it happen that he was so familiar with St. Peter's Basilica? The reason was very simple: His father was the Marchese Filippo Ossoli, high functionary at the papal court, his older brother was the papal functionary for one of the regions of Rome and secretary to the pope's privy council, and the other sons except him were colonels in the *Guardia Nobile* of the pope. The Ossoli were an old and noble family, and for generations had been associated with the apparatus of the papacy.

But would he someday enter the *Guardia Nobile*? No, not he. Though in his opinion no Catholic could be more devout than he, he did not approve the temporal power of the pope. He believed in a united, not divided, Italy, a republic. He admired Mazzini. When she told him she was Mazzini's friend, he was markedly impressed.

It was then that Margaret knew something extraordinary was happening to her old maid's heart.

The walk was all too short. At her door he kissed her hand—a conventional gesture among the nobility—bade her a polite good evening, and went away. Yet his reluctance to leave was apparent. She told the Springs her adventure; but the telling only emphasized its poignancy. She hastened to write Mickiewicz in Paris; he would be certain to understand.

It must have been a difficult night for Margaret. In a few weeks she would face her thirty-seventh birthday, and with every passing year the full realization of her womanly self became more remote. She had suffered so many rejections from men. It was not for nothing that she once had made this sad and solemn entry in her journal: "No one loves me. But I love many a good deal, and see some way into their eventual beauty. I am myself growing better, and shall by and by be a worthy object of love."

She could not but wonder: Was she yet a worthy object of love?

9

Two decades since her earliest, adolescent, love had passed, but she still could not think of George Davis without regret. How painful is first love!—as she had learned. And how candidly and unsubtly one reveals oneself, implicitly opening oneself to rebuff—forever assuming that the other's emotions are identical with one's own.

Dear old George, who in afteryears had tried to make amends by offering her brother Richard a job in his law firm in Cincinnati. It was one proof that he had not forgotten her. Almost since childhood they had played together, for George Davis was her father's kinsman, and they called each other "cousin." She had been so shocked when, at thirteen, she had discovered he was reading *Gil Blas,* and had taxed him with its "devious intrigues and the impure atmosphere of actresses and picaroons." George was a very bright boy, and with his classmate Oliver Wendell Holmes made a reputation for wit at Harvard. "His mirth," Margaret wrote, "unsettled all things from their foundations." He was, she said, "the first and only person who so excited her." When suddenly he moved to another town, and rumors flew that he was courting another girl, she became so desperately ill that she had to take to her bed—and no one seemed to understand the source of Margaret's fever. All her friends were getting married and "expecting." On the day of George's wedding she busied herself with copying her translation of Goethe's lines on Queen Elizabeth's lament for her lover Essex:

> *Alone! This day the cup of woe is full.*
> *. . . This deadly blow! I feel it here*
> *But the low prying world shall not perceive it.*

The name Samuel Gray Ward also produced a hollow ache. In the end the affair had been almost incestuous, because in addition to Margaret he had loved Anna Barker, and Margaret had loved them both. The infatuation with Anna had been much more than an adolescent "crush." The rich and beautiful Anna Barker, kin of the Astors, had come to Cambridge at the age of fifteen to acquire the culture that was not to be had in New York. She visited in the house of her cousin, the wealthy, elderly Harvard professor John Farrar. His young wife, Eliza, cultivated and widely traveled, earlier had seized on the ungainly Margaret like a fairy godmother, and smoothed out the roughness in her manner and appearance. So Margaret at eighteen was invited by Mrs. Farrar to help add intellectual polish to an already lustrous jewel called Anna. At once the girls, so unlike, were intensely attracted to one another, and gave talismans of their affection. Anna's gift to Margaret was a ruby; and Margaret's to Anna an amethyst and a poem which concluded with the hope that the stone "Keeps thee steadfast, chaste and wise."

A decade later Margaret mused in her journal: "It is so true that a woman may be in love with a woman and a man with a man . . . . It is a love all intellect and spirit. Its law is that of love between the sexes, the desire of the spirit to realize a whole. What one finds not in oneself one seeks in another. The strong seeks the beautiful, the beautiful the strong . . . . Why did I love Anna? I loved her for a time with as much passion as I was then strong enough to feel. Her face was always gleaming before me and her voice echoing in my ear . . . . Anna loved me too, though not so much. Her nature was 'less high, less grave, less deep.' She loved more tenderly, less passionately. She loved me, for I well remember when she first felt my faults how she wished to weep all day. I remember too the night she leaned on me and her eyes were such a deep violet-blue; we felt a mystic thrill and knew what we had never known before. . . . She wished to be with me always."

By the time of the journal entry Sam Ward for several years had been in Margaret's orbit—and while she was the sun, he nevertheless could not resist spinning in a secondary plane about so lovely a planet as Anna. Sam was Margaret's junior by seven years, but in the intellectual young the age gap is easily bridged by common interests and exciting creative projects. Sam Ward was full of creative projects—one moment he was a painter, the next a writer, and the next a combination of both. And to Margaret he was so special that she called him "Raffaello," he who was "so sensuous, so loving, and so lovely."

She urged him constantly to develop his not inconsiderable talents, and when at length he followed the demands of his wealthy banking family and became a banker (eventually a lobbyist in Washington), she mourned him as if "her votary" had committed suicide. It was he who had brought her from Italy a bursting portfolio of engravings of great Italian art and architecture; it was he who returned from the German universities, with his friend Henry Wadsworth Longfellow, speaking fluent German and French and brimful of literary projects. He was more than a little stimulating even to his sister Julia (who as Julia Ward Howe was to become so famous in the Civil War). And he was more than a little exciting to his most intimate friend, Ellery Channing—the erratic Ellery who married Margaret's sister Ellen, but who idealized Sam and used to write him "the wildest letters of devotion and gratitude."

Sam Ward was London-tailored, handsome, amusing, intelligent, and for a long while wholly devoted to Margaret—until he met the glamorous Anna Barker. And the ultimate irony lay in the fact that it was Mrs. John Farrar who had done the matchmaking—that very Mrs. Farrar, too, with her tales of Europe, who had instilled in Margaret such passion to see Europe at first hand. Not Margaret, but Sam and Anna had summered in Switzerland with Mrs. Farrar, and the results were a foregone conclusion. The year Margaret was thirty, Sam married Anna at Mrs. Farrar's house. Not Margaret, but Waldo Emerson went to the wedding. For Emerson, Anna, the all-captivating Anna, was a new experience with Beauty. Tactlessly he had written to Margaret about Anna, calling her "that very human piece of divinity." And knowing that Caroline Sturgis was Margaret's confidant, he nevertheless wrote Caroline that Anna's "unique gentleness unbars all doors and with such easy & frolic sway she advances & advances & advances on you with that look." Accepting the inevitable, Margaret wrote to her "dear Raffaello" somberly in the spirit of renunciation. "We were truly friends—yet not as men are friends or as brother and sister. There was that pleasure—possibly conjugal—of finding oneself in an alien nature. Was there a tinge of love between us? Perhaps!"

A year earlier, at the breaking point, she had written: "You love me no more. How did you pray me to draw near to you! What words were spoken in impatience of separation! How did you promise to me, ay, and doubtless to yourself, too, of all we might be to one another. . . . At an earlier period I would fain have broke the tie that bound us, for I knew myself incapable of feeling or being content to inspire an ordinary attachment. As soon as I saw a flaw I would have broke the tie. You would not —you resented, yet with what pathetic grace, any distrust on my part. *Forever, ever* are words of which you have never been, are not now afraid. . . . All I loved in you is at present dead and buried, only a light from the tomb shines now and then in your eyes."

Who could have guessed—including Mrs. Emerson—that Margaret might finally fall in love with Waldo? Henry Thoreau, maybe, for whom Emerson bore more affection than is usually allotted a "hired man." Thoreau invited Margaret to row with him on Walden Pond in his homemade boat, and they talked of many things, including Emerson. "Last night I went out quite late, and stayed till the moon was almost gone," she wrote her brother Richard. Though she liked Henry, a hint of jealousy existed between them, not as authors but as competitors for Waldo's attention.

Other than Thoreau, only friend Caroline Sturgis might have guessed the secret, for she too was greatly admired by the defensively Platonic Mr. Emerson. Caroline Sturgis was considered by many to resemble a lively, dark-haired gypsy, who made no pretensions to the vastness of Margaret's intellect, yet nevertheless loved and admired Margaret. "With her," said Margaret, though Caroline was nine years younger, "I can talk of anything. She is like me. She is able to look facts in the face."

Margaret first met Emerson when she was twenty-five, and he, thirty-two. Not surprisingly, they met at the home of Mrs. Farrar. "He is a ray of white light, and she is a prism," said Elizabeth Hoar. From the very first Emerson was repelled and fascinated by Margaret, while she adored the lean and craggy clergyman in his splendid long blue coat. When she visited him at his home in Concord, they carried on an intense correspondence from room to room, using Emerson's small son as their messenger boy—unable to bear the distraction of each other's physical presence.

When it became evident that Sam Ward was to be denied to Margaret, her preoccupation with Waldo Emerson increased. The Ward-Barker wedding took place during the first week of October 1840, and the preceding month of September witnessed the full crisis of Margaret's private communications with the "Dear Wise One." As everybody knew, Mr. Emerson had a habit of carefully indexing and filing all his correspondence; but during the climactic period of his relationship with Margaret all of her calorous letters to him disappeared, with a single exception in transcription, which he himself copied for the file.

Toward the end of September (the twenty-fifth), he wrote Margaret that "certain crises must impend," and "perhaps it [is] better to part now. In your last letter you . . . do say . . . that I am yours and yours shall be, let me dally how longsoever in this or that other temporary relation." In his journal next day he entered without specifically using Margaret's name, "You would have me love you. What shall I love? Your body? The supposition disgusts you. What you have thought and said? Well, whilst you were thinking and saying them, but not now. I see no possibility of loving anything but what now is, and is becoming; your courage, your enterprise, your budding affection, your opening thought, your prayer, I can love —but what else?" On the date of Emerson's letter, Margaret was writing to Caroline, "Of the mighty changes in my spiritual life I do not wish to speak, yet surely you cannot be ignorant of them."

Four days later she wrote to Waldo (or at least he copied it thus for his file, probably leaving out phrases that did not suit him), ". . . I have felt the impossibility of meeting far more than you; so much that, if you ever know me well, you will feel that the fact of my abiding by you thus far, affords a strong proof that we are to be much to one another. How often have I left you despairing and forlorn. How often have I said, This light will never understand my fire; this clear eye will never discern the law by which I am filling my circle; this simple force will never interpret my need of manifold being . . . . Could I lead the highest angel captive by a look, that look I would not give, unless prompted by true love: I am no usurper. I ask only mine own inheritance. If it be found that I have mistaken its boundaries, I will give up the choicest vineyard, the fairest flowergarden, to its lawful owner . . . . But did you not ask for a 'foe' in your friend? Did you not ask for a 'large formidable nature'? But a beautiful foe, I am not yet, to you. Shall I ever be? . . . To L.[Lidian, Mrs. Emerson] my love. In her I have always recognized the saintly element. *That,* better than a Bible in my hand, shows that it cannot be wholly alien. Yet I am no saint, no anything, but a great soul born to know all, before it can return to the creative fount . . . ."

A month later she confided to Caroline: "I have just written a letter to our dear Waldo which gives me pain. It was all into the past. His call bids me return, I know not how, yet full of tender renunciation, know not how to refuse." His reply was blunt: "I have your frank & noble & affecting letter, and yet I think I could wish it unwritten."

Suddenly, with Margaret's assumption of the editorship of the *Dial,* the temperature of the Fuller-Emerson surcharged atmosphere rapidly cooled. But occasionally flashes of heat lightning reflected the electric storms of the past. A year later (October 1841) Emerson in his journal remarked of Margaret, "I always admire, most revere when I nearest see, and sometimes love— yet whom I freeze, and who freezes me to silence, when we seem to promise to come nearest." In March of 1842 occurred a further exchange, which was a measure of Margaret's already rapid flight from Emerson. "I have thought of you many times," she wrote, "indeed in all my walks, and in the night, with unspeakable tenderness . . . ." Emerson responded: "Gladly I received & read twice through today your letter. You know best of all living how to flatter your friend, both directly & by finest indirections." Margaret's reply was a challenge tinged with scorn: "It is to be hoped, my best one, that the experiences of life will yet correct your vocabulary, and that you will not always answer the burst of frank affection by the use of such a word as 'flattery.' "

Three years later, when in New York she was preparing *Woman in the Nineteenth Century,* she asked "dear Waldo" to write the introduction. He agreed most courteously; but somehow he never seemed to take the task in hand. Actually Margaret had anticipated that he would dissemble; she was not surprised, but disappointed. She no longer breathed that rarefied atmosphere of the ethereal regions where Emerson liked to dwell. So far had she moved from Transcendentalism that she was capable of shrugging her emotional shoulders: "Leave him in his cell affirming absolute truth; protesting against humanity, if so he appears to do; the calm observer of the course of things."

Then in New York occurred the unfulfilled affair with James Nathan, which brought her one step closer to the possibility of a flesh-and-blood relationship with a man of flesh and blood.

IO

Once she had written wistfully, "Could but love, like knowledge, be its own reward!" Now wistfully she stood at the window gazing down at the promenading crowd on the Via del Corso, and suddenly she recognized the lithe, graceful figure of Giovanni Angelo Ossoli. He stood apart, gazing upward, as if seeking her image. It was if some miracle had provided an answer to a prayer she had not dared utter. Without thought she threw on all that was necessary for the street—bonnet, light shawl, gloves—and raced down the stairs. Once she had written of herself in the third person, "Her proper speech was dance or song." That was how she felt now.

He was still waiting. He smiled, and the melancholy in his eyes disappeared. It would be a pleasure, he said, to show her all the sights of Rome.

Thus began one of the most intense and shortest of the Platonic love episodes in Margaret's life. She introduced Ossoli to the Springs, and explained to him that within six weeks their party planned to leave. They would work their way slowly through the Italian cities of the north, then Switzerland, and on to Germany and home. Ossoli looked first disbelieving and then pained. Two months in a city aged more than two millennia were nothing. Moreover, the city was astir with political ferment. If she wished to write . . .

She silenced his remonstrances, and they began a tour of Rome to see the little things inside the great. In reality they were looking into each other, and the more they looked, the finer was their pleasure. Yet it was Margaret and not he who was keenly conscious of the difference in their ages (he was born January 17, 1821). How could he explain to her—had he been aware of the necessity of explanation—that Italian men regarded girls as girls, and women as women; that Italian men had the most rewarding affairs with women of some maturity. There was nothing the least unusual about a young man's becoming the lover of a middle-aged woman of charm and beauty. How amazed he would have been had she attempted to delineate the Puritan conscience. So he spoke and acted as if he fully intended to become her lover, and as if she fully understood this from the beginning. But if she understood, she did not admit it to herself. She betrayed her perplexity only in the way she hesitated before the luscious female nude in Titian's painting titled "Sacred and Profane Love," when viewing the collection at the Villa Borghese. Once she had remarked of herself: "I am very destitute of what is commonly called modesty."

From Paris Mickiewicz had replied promptly to her letter, urging her to make the most of her opportunities. "You ought to have stayed longer at Naples," he said. "Don't leave too hurriedly the places where you feel well; one is rarely free to return. Prolong your good moments! Don't leave lightly those who would remain close to you. In this I refer to that young Italian whom you met in the church . . . . Absorb from Italy all that you are able to take, in joy, and in health. It's not worth while to take anything else!"

She was seeing "that young Italian" frequently, and prolonging the good moments—up to a point. Oddly, she was at a loss to know what to call him. Contrary to the custom of the times, she called all her friends by their first names. But *Giovanni* or *Angelo* did not strike the right note. *Signor Ossoli* seemed stilted, and *Marchese*—for that indeed was his title—seemed much too formal. His family called him *Giovanangelo*—difficult for the English-speaking mouth. *Dear Ossoli* was a compromise, and sounded right in Italian. But there was another salutation she slipped into, *Caro Giovane* (Dear Youth), meant tacitly to remind him of her more advanced age, while speaking with tenderness. As for Ossoli, he was content with whatever she called him, and responded with *Cara Amica* (Dear Friend) or simply *Cara*.

Gradually she learned much more about him. She noticed the little scar on his face, and he told her, "It was made by a jealous dog when my mother was caressing me as an infant." He prized the blemish, for it was visible proof of the dead mother's love. When he spoke of his mother, the words were tender, and a note of longing invariably entered his voice.

Margaret was astonished at the paucity of his education. He had studied at a *collegio* run by priests who had stressed only the lives of the saints, with a smattering of Latin and French. He had acquired somehow a background in Roman and Italian history; but of books he was hardly aware. To any one of the transcendentalists in Boston he would have seemed illiterate. But he was not. He had a store of knowledge of practical things, of absorbed values of art and architecture and music, and the behavioral patterns of a gentleman. He knew, of course, those things any young nobleman needed to know—estate management, upkeep of buildings, riding and care of horses, use and care of arms, and so forth. He was equipped like all the male members of the family to serve the pope as if an emperor, receiving his blessings and financial rewards.

The stem and the full name of the family, Ossoli della Torre, was recorded in the Golden Book of Italian Nobility. They had originated in the north near Lake Garda in the early Middle Ages, but had not transferred to Rome and the papal service until 1685. They then had acquired the great castle of Pietraforte, in the Sabine country, and a *palazzo* in Rome on the medieval Via Tor di Specchi, near the Campidoglio designed by Michelangelo.

It was in this palazzo that Giovanni Angelo lived with his father, the Marchese Filippo, who was over seventy and lay sick and helpless. And to the youngest, unmarried, son had fallen the lot of caring for the father. It was not this, however, which created the tension between Angelo and his older brothers, Giuseppe, Alessandro, and Ottavio. Giuseppe, especially, as the eldest (he was twenty-one years Angelo's senior), bore down on Angelo because he did not approve of the ideas that Angelo had acquired. Giuseppe was haughty, hard, and grasping, and sought what remained of the family wealth all for himself. Alessandro and Ottavio, as officers, ordered Angelo about like a private. The elder sister, Angela, was married to the Marchese de Andreis, and lived in the spacious first floor of the Palazzo Ossoli, which had been given her as a dowry. She was disorganized as a person, frightened of Giuseppe, but secretly had allied herself with Angelo, trying to protect him from Giuseppe's wrath. Of younger sister Matilde little was heard except an occasional letter from Ireland. Angelo, then, was alone—as he had been alone emotionally since childhood and the loss of his mother. Indeed he was taciturn and "without enthusiasm of character," as Margaret said, for he had thus defended himself throughout his life.

Along with the burden of his brothers, the weight of family tradition lay heavily on Angelo. The Ossoli, as lords of the great castle of Pietraforte ("Strongrock"), were not content to bury their dead in the country, but brought them down to Rome. The Italian family chapel made evident to all the world the status of the family, and the Ossoli chose to construct theirs in the fifteenth-century Church of the Maddalena, near the Pantheon.

The Church of the Maddalena is significant by its absence from the list of the innumerable churches visited by Margaret in Rome. Such a complete omission of mention was one of Margaret's typical tricks for concealing any intimate matter concerned with Angelo. It is unthinkable that she did not stand with him before the altar of the Ossoli family chapel—an altar richly endowed with candlesticks of gold and flanked on either side by lofty corinthian columns of green marble. Unthinkable, too, that she did not study the fine seventeenth-century painting by Baciccia representing the Virgin and Saint Nicholas—the patron saint of the Ossoli.

The dedicatory inscription Angelo might well have read aloud in that soft and glowing Latin of the Italians, giving a cadence and pronunciation like a living language:

D(eo) O(ptimo) M(aximo)
ARAM HANC S. NICOLAO EPIS(copo) SACRAM CLEMENS XIII PONT(ifex) MAX(imus) JOSEPHO DE OSSOLIS PETRAEFORTIS ET OFFLANI MARCHIONE PRO SE SUSQ(ue) CONSANGUINEIS ET AFFINIBUS VITA FUNCTIS AC BEATAM SPEM EXPECTANTIBUS POSTULANTE PERPETUO PRIVILEGIO DITAVIT VII ID(us) APRILIS MDCCLXVII

And as Angelo read, Margaret, standing beside him, would have translated silently: "Almighty God—To this altar, sacred to Saint Nicolas, Bishop, Clement XIII, Highest Pontiff, granted perpetual privilege, being requested to do so by Joseph de Ossolis of Petrafortis, Marquis of Offlauum, on his behalf and that of his relatives by blood and marriage who have departed life and are awaiting the blessed hope. On the 7th day before the Ides of April 1767."

Proudly carved above each door were the Ossoli della Torre arms: In the left field of azure, three human bones (*osso* means "bone") in a line, surmounted by two human eyes and eyebrows; in the right field of azure, a tower (*torre*) of silver, sustained by two golden lions, surmounted by a black eagle crowned in gold. Topping the entire crest was the coronet appropriate to a marchese—Angelo's by feudal right to wear.

But if the young Marchese Giovanni Angelo Ossoli introduced Margaret to the family dead, he most certainly did not introduce her to the family living. Had he at first thought seriously of marriage, this would have been the first step. Nobody in the family cared in the least how many affairs he had, or with whom. An American woman no longer young? That did not matter. Poor? That did not matter. Protestant? What difference did it make in a nonconjugal bed. Republican—friend of Mazzini? Ah—that was a different matter. Here was danger of subversion, even though the objective of marriage was not involved. Contamination, infection—those were the words the family males would have used. Radical women had ideas, which made them unreliable. One did not make mistresses of radical women—much less wives. In a sense Margaret herself had anticipated their reaction when she wrote, ironically, in *Woman in the Nineteenth Century,* about "guardians who think that nothing is so much to be dreaded for a woman as originality of thought or character."

Very carefully Angelo avoided letting the family know anything about his association with Margaret. And Margaret acquiesced, accepting family nonrecognition, because marriage to Angelo was not her objective. She wanted to make Angelo her soul mate, as she had those others when her affection had been alchemized into love. She and Angelo had a day in the country, alone together. In her stumbling Italian she attempted to get through to the inner Ossoli. When he failed to understand, she could only blame the inadequacy of her tongue. So she gave her pen a chance, and the Italian words seemed to flow more smoothly.

"Dear Youth," she wrote, "you are the only one I see in Rome in whom I recognize my kin. I want to know and love you and have you love me. How can you let me pass you by? You say you have no friendliness of nature but that is not true—you are the very one to need the music and the recognition of kindred minds. Soon I must leave here. Do not let me go without giving some of your life in exchange for some of mine. I feel I have something precious to give and that you are not unaware of this. Am I mistaken? Yet the day we were together I could not meet you as I wished; I wished to speak in frank affection and I could not. Something prevents. What is it? Answer!"

Ossoli must have been stupefied on receipt of this letter. "Kindred minds . . . something precious to give . . . have you love me . . . some of your life in exchange for mine . . . ." It would be difficult for any Italian to believe that even Puritans could accomplish all that through kindred minds. Certainly any Italian male would raise his eyebrows and shrug his shoulders at such a prospect. Indeed Angelo wished to give some of his life in exchange for some of hers, but she did not seem to understand just how he wished to give it. As a virgin her attractiveness was increased for him—for the cult of the Virgin Mother is as deep rooted in Italy as an ancient olive tree. The more elderly Margaret now fulfilled for him perfectly his profoundest emotional needs: He could love her as both virgin and mother and also make her his wife. To Margaret's amazement his response, without consulting his family, was an offer of marriage. A special dispensation to marry a Protestant could be secured from the Vatican, with his father's help.

Her reply was No.

Much later Margaret wrote to her sister Ellen, "I loved him, and felt very unhappy to leave him; but the connection seemed so every way unfit, I did not hesitate a moment."

The "dear youth," so gentle and tender, was deeply hurt. Nevertheless he did not sulk, but kept Margaret constantly with him. To Caroline Sturgis she wrote of "those last glorious nights, in which I [we] wandered about amid the old walls and columns, or sat by the fountains in the Piazza del Popolo, or by the river, were worth an age of pain—only one hates pain in Italy."

And it was she who had inflicted pain on Ossoli.

Though melancholy, he was unwilling to accept defeat. "You will return," he said, "—to me."

I I

On schedule, Margaret left Rome with the Springs in early
June; though after so many months of enforced intimacy, patience had become short and tempers frayed. Margaret felt a
"wicked irritation" with the Springs. "I was always *out* of the
body, and they were always *in* it." Even little Eddie was not in
tune.

Perhaps the true irritation she felt was with herself. Once she
had written prophetically in her journal: "I have no real hold
on life—no real, permanent connection with any soul." Perhaps she feared that in Rome she had rejected her last chance.

Nevertheless, in Rome something had changed. As she had
written, also prophetically, in her journal a few years before:
"Once I was almost all intellect; now I am almost all feeling.
Nature vindicates her rights, and I feel all Italy glowing beneath the Saxon crust. This cannot last long; I shall burn to
ashes if all this smoulders here much longer. I must die if I do
not burst forth in genius or heroism." Or love, she might have
added. Rome had relighted the fires that glowed beneath the
Saxon crust.

In Florence Margaret moved naturally into that high society which in Rome ironically had been denied her because of her preoccupation with the Marchese Angelo Ossoli. Her mentor was the Marchesa Costanza Arconati Visconti, an outstanding woman who bore one of the outstanding names of all Italy and all Europe. Not only were the Arconati a distinguished family, but Costanza had married (at the age of seventeen) the Marchese Giuseppe Visconti—those Visconti who had been known since the twelfth century for their brilliance, treachery, and splendor. As dukes of Milan they had built the greatest palace, begun the greatest cathedral, collected the greatest library, and held the most sumptuous court in Europe. Kings of England and Holy Roman Emperors had been dazzled by them, and had been eager to betroth Visconti daughters.

Now the Marchese Giuseppe Visconti and his wife were lately returned to Italy after twenty-six years of exile, imposed on them by the Austrian invaders because of their efforts for Italian independence. And had their name been other than Visconti, they might well have been imprisoned or executed. They were not, however, followers of Mazzini, whom they felt responsible for "deplorable disorders," but followers of Abbot Gioberti, "the polar star for those of us who are not Republicans." Had they been Mazzinians, probably they would not have received an amnesty—such was the vindictiveness of the Austrian authorities.

Actually Margaret had met the Marchesa Arconati briefly in Rome, making a profound impression. From Florence the marchesa wrote in French, "The moments which I passed with you in Rome inspired in me the most vivid sympathy and real admiration for you," and urged Margaret to call as soon as possible.

Margaret, for her part, detailed her impression of Costanza Arconati in a letter to Elizabeth Hoar: "She is a specimen of the really high-bred lady, such as I have not known. Without any physical beauty, the grace and harmony of her manners produce all the impression of beauty. She has also a mind strong, clear, precise, and much cultivated. She has a modest nobleness that you would dearly love. She is intimate with many of the first men. She seems to love me much, and to wish I should have whatever is hers. I take great pleasure in her friendship."

But in spite of having entrée into the great houses, Margaret did not like Florence as much as Rome, because it was "more in its spirit like Boston," and the people were "busy and intellectual"—rather astonishing observations from a busy Boston intellectual. To Emerson she wrote: "There is less to excite . . . I feel as if I needed to sleep all the time." In Florence she spoke French constantly, but to Emerson she confided, "To know the common people, and to feel truly in Italy, I ought to speak and understand the spoken Italian well, and I am now cultivating this sedulously. If I remain, I shall have, for many reasons, advantages for observation and enjoyment, such as are seldom permitted to a foreigner."

It was the twentieth of June that the phrase "if I remain" appeared. By the first of July she had come to a firm conclusion. To her brother Richard she wrote, "I should always suffer the pain of Tantalus thinking of Rome, if I could not see it more thoroughly than I have yet begun to." She would leave the Springs in Switzerland, as Germany held no charms for her now, and return to Rome for the autumn, "perhaps the winter." Did she write to Ossoli telling her decision? Surely she must have, but no record exists. As July and August in Rome were the "fever months," and everyone escaped the city who could, it was logical that she should wait until autumn to return. For the moment she chose to disregard the serious economic struggle she would face.

Her travel diary was succinct, avoiding those verbose passages that sometimes trapped her in her formal writings. As usual she noted everything in the utmost detail: "Women braiding each other's hair, walking in large straw hats . . . shoemaker that wept about the Pope's amnesty . . . the Pitti Gallery—the apartments of the Grand Duke . . . house of Michaelangelo —white magnolia in a glass in parlor." It did not occur to her that the Buonarroti family might have been astonished at having their *salone* described as a "parlor."

Settling down to work, she began her article for the *Tribune.* She described the trip from Rome to Florence, by way of Assisi, Perugia, and Arezzo. She commented on the red poppies and the vineyards, the "light-colored oxen Shelley so much admired," and the *Viva Pio IX!* scrawled on the walls of Assisi. She visited an Etruscan tomb: "In it were several female figures, very dignified and calm, as the dim lamp-light fell on them by turns. The expression of these figures shows that the position of women in these states was noble." She stood by a spot where Goethe met with a little adventure, and observed, "Who can ever be alone for a moment in Italy? Every stone has a voice, every grain of dust seems instilled with spirit from the past."

Discussing Florence, she deviated from art and architecture for a moment and dipped into politics, describing the repressive rule of the Grand Duke Leopold: "the people are still and glum as death. This is all on the outside; within, Tuscany burns." From politics she jumped to the American sculptors in Florence, Horatio Greenough and Hiram Powers. It was essential that she see Greenough's unfinished model of *David,* and Powers' already famous *Eve Before the Fall* and the *Greek Slave.* She took time to describe Powers' statue of John C. Calhoun in some detail, as "full of power, simple, and majestic in attitude and expression." This marble, by one of the oddest quirks of Margaret's destiny, was to play a part in Margaret's fate.

She was bored with Florence. She saw the festivals of San Giovanni, "but they are poor affairs to one who has seen the Neapolitan and Roman people on such occasions."

She leapt ahead. Bologna, oldest University in Europe, which greatly honored women, even displaying the portrait bust of a woman professor of anatomy; Ravenna, fifth century mosaics, where the hotels were so bad that she was invited to stay in the palace of the Conte Pasolini, at the intervention of her friend Costanza Arconati; Venice, lagoons, where she melted emotionally—"Of Venice and its enchanted life I could not speak; it should only be echoed back in music."

In Venice she announced the change in plans which secretly had been maturing within her. Politely she parted company with the Springs, explaining that she could not possibly leave Italy now that she had just begun to know it. She wanted to remain in Venice for a while. She needed more time to study the art and architecture, more time on the lagoons. To Caroline she wrote: "In the first week, floating alone in a gondola, I seemed to find myself again." She was dreaming—of Rome.

But she could not remain forever in a gondola. She must complete her self-packaged tour of the North. There was Vicenza, with its Palladian prototypes copied in the Georgian–Early American architecture she knew so well at home; Verona, with its Roman amphitheater; Mantova, with its Gonzaga palace containing apartments for dwarfs; Lake Garda, with its island where Byron loved to go. At Brescia she became ill, and the tour abruptly ended. She felt keenly the lack of all those little aids and comforts Marcus Spring so adroitly had arranged, and in addition she was being cheated outrageously for every service. With chills and fever, and taking nothing but water, she had a bed made in a carriage and was driven to Milan. She was convinced that her brain was being affected. Nevertheless she recovered quickly, as she was so impatient at being sick.

Now she was on territory where many young men had been condemned to death for their patriotic ideas, and many more had been sentenced for years to the most dreaded prison in Europe, the Spielberg—where no Strauss waltzes ever played. For the first time in her experience she met men to whom instruments of torture had been applied—the red-hot brands, the "Spanish shoes" of iron, the iron glove to squeeze and break the fingers. One such was Gaetano De Castillia, who had been condemned to death by the Austrians. After vigorous protests by leading Italians, the sentence had been commuted to twenty years in the Spielberg—considered by everyone worse than death. But De Castillia had managed somehow to survive, and at the end of fifteen years the Austrians had deported him, a human hulk, to the United States. At last he had been allowed to return to Milan, as he was now considered harmless. No wonder that Margaret wrote in her dispatch to the *Tribune,* "The Austrian rule is . . . hated, and time, instead of melting away differences, only makes them more glaring."

She met other "radicals, young, and interested in ideas." Some were friends of Mazzini, others were friends of the Marchesa Arconati Visconti. It was through the Marchesa that she met the famed romantic radical of the past, Alessandro Manzoni, more handsome than Byron, and author of the already classic *I Promessi Sposi* (*The Betrothed*). To Emerson she wrote, "Manzoni has spiritual efficacy in his looks; his eyes glow still with delicate tenderness . . . . His manners are very engaging, frank, expansive; every word betokens the habitual elevation of his thoughts." But to the *Tribune* she stated, "Young Italy rejects Manzoni, though not irreverently; Young Italy prizes his works, but feels that the doctrine of 'Pray and wait' is not for her at this moment—that she needs a more fervent hope, a more active faith. She is right."

Milan in August was hot and humid, so Margaret resumed her tour. She paused for cooling breezes off the limpid waters of Lake Maggiore, reflecting the blue sky and the high Alps, then went on to Switzerland. Returning, she was invited to visit the Marchesa Arconati at Bellaggio, on the shores of the dulcet Lake Como, where she moved once more among the aristocracy. Notable was the Polish Princess Radziwill, whom she found both "fair and brilliant." To Caroline Sturgis she wrote, "The life here is precisely what we once imagined as being so pleasant. These people have charming villas and gardens on the lake, adorned with fine works of art. They go to see one another in boats. You can be all the time in a boat, if you like; if you want more excitement, or wild flowers, you climb the mountains. . . . I have found soft repose here." And charmingly, "The pretty girls of Bellaggio, with their coral necklaces, brought flowers to the 'American countess,' and 'hoped she would be as happy as she deserved.' " Then Margaret added, like a murmur, "Now, I am to return to Rome."

First, however, to Milan once again, to witness the entry of the new archbishop, with parades and panoply. The new prelate, an Italian in Italy with an Italian parish, was, unlike his predecessor, pro-Italian. Thus some youths sought to sing, in his honor, the *Hymn to Pius IX*. At this the Austrian police took affront and charged the crowd, wounding many persons in the back. It was, indeed, a most ingenious paradox. Not long since, an Austrian army had occupied by pretext the papal town of Ferrara. Catholic Austria, with its Catholic emperor, the mentally deficient Ferdinand I, and his Catholic minister Prince Metternich, found themselves opposed not only to the Catholic Italians but to the Pontifex Maximus, His Holiness the Pope, as subversive. And for the pope the dilemma was equally real: Was he to support his Italian flock, or his Austrian flock to clear his name? Margaret saw it all, and her report to the *Tribune* seethed with outrage. With every continuing moment of her stay in Italy she was becoming increasingly involved, increasingly partisan, as only a foreigner could be involved, could be partisan. *Pazienza* for her became a disgusting word.

On the return trip to Florence she paused to inspect the architectural marvels of the Visconti-built Certosa in Pavia, and the paintings in Parma and Modena. Of the pictures she said nothing, commenting merely that in those states "the poor, ignorant sovereigns skulk in corners, hoping to hide from the coming storm." She was cross, for among other irritations she had lost her gold pencil in the coach.

In Florence she collapsed from physical and emotional fatigue. Fortunately she was taken in by Joseph Mozier and his wife, and restored to health. Mozier was an Ohio merchant who had decided to become a sculptor. Apparently his greatest talent was for quarreling with his fellow sculptors, but for Margaret he was a godsend.

She was pleased and stimulated by a letter from "brother Adam," insinuating that Eve should eat the apple: " . . . You ought not to confine your life to books and reveries. You have pleaded the liberty of women in a masculine and frank style. Live and act as you write . . . . I have seen you, with all your learning, and all your imagination, and all your literary reputation, living in a bondage harder than that of a servant . . . .

78

The relationships which suit you are those which develop and free your spirit, responding to the legitimate needs of your body and leaving you free at all times. You are the sole judge of these needs."

Toward the end of September in Florence, as she prepared for the final leg of her private Hegira, she wrote to that stalwart virgin Elizabeth Hoar in Concord, "Now I begin to be in Italy! but I wish to drink deep of this cup before I speak my enamored words. Enough to say, Italy receives me as a long-lost child. . . ."

The truth of the matter was that in *Woman in the Nineteenth Century* she had foreseen herself when she wrote, "Woman is born for love, and it is impossible to turn her from seeking it."

12

Due to her Florentine illness, and subsequent side trips to Fiesole, Settignano, and Siena (which she found enchanting), she did not reach Rome until the thirteenth of October. Shortly thereafter she wrote to Marcus Spring, "All mean things were forgotten in the joy that rushed over me like a flood . . . . All other places faded away, now that I again saw St. Peter's, and heard the music of the fountains." Her choice of St. Peter's as an illustration was hardly accidental; the incident there had become the focal point of her life. No description exists of her reunion with Ossoli—but surely that was the source of her flood of joy.

A scattering of news had arrived from home, from her mother and friends—news which proved only slightly distracting and very unreal. Boston seemed to be receding. Emerson was planning a trip to England, and Thoreau and Alcott were building a Concord summerhouse for The Sage. Ellery Channing had published a book on Rome, of all subjects; also he and Ellen seemed unable to find happiness together. Mrs. Fuller's letters were full of chitchat: marriages, births, suicides, and Mrs. Farrar's sallow appearances after taking the water cure. Mrs. Fuller was in turns visiting her children—now son William Henry, a successful merchant in Cincinnati, and next Eugene in New Orleans. Sometimes she struck a somber note, a full Puritan resignation to the will of God.

"I try to look on the fair and beautiful side of things," she wrote, "and to submit to the chastisement needed as well as to cherish gratitude for my many blessings, but I am very weak—when Arthur wrote me that they had put my poor Lloyd into the Asylum in Brattleborough for the insane, I wished to die. He has been a child of so many prayers that I was sure this affliction would never come to me. He acquiesced, in the good he might receive from going there. His brothers feel sure that the habit which has grown from a solitary life, and early companionship with one vicious person, is the cause of his present melancholy condition."

Poor Lloyd, with the "habit" which grew from early companionship with one vicious person. Poor Lloyd, who felt at so early an age so great a burden of guilt that much of his youth was spent singing hymns in expiation. They had tried to improve him by sending him to Brook Farm; but he had proved intractable. He developed the malicious trick of writing unfavorable things in his diary about persons he did not like, and then scattering the pages to be found and read. At one time a sudden crisis involving one of the brothers had occurred in the Fuller family —a crisis which required urgently a considerable sum of money, a crisis so scandalous that even in letters among themselves it was referred to obliquely. Only poor Lloyd, involved probably in something considered deviate sexually, could have been the author of such panic among them.

But if now Margaret seemed hardly touched by the news of Lloyd's tragedy, her mother's report on the Greeley child, Pickie, pressed sensitive nerves. For Margaret, Pickie—like the precocious little boy Waldo Emerson, Jr.—had been one of "her" children. They adored each other. Recently Mrs. Fuller had passed through New York during one of Pickie's illnesses, and had called at the Greeley farm.

"Pickie is as beautiful as ever," she reported, "but his will grows with his strength, and his conflicts with his mother are dreadful. The day after I was there he refused to be bathed, and his mother was violent and he hit her, and his father could hardly command his voice to tell me the frightful scene. She always says when I talk with her about Pickie—'I am keeping him for Margaret, as no other person can take care of Pickie.' All that I can foresee is that her management of Pickie will end in his driving her mad, for they act upon each other like wild fire. Poor Mr. Greeley, I pity him from my soul, while I blame his weak submission to her."

And, unwittingly, it was Pickie who linked Margaret to the past love which now left her totally numb: "Pickie selected two pale carnelians given him by Mr. Nathan, and, his lovely hand open, said, 'Mrs. Fuller, I wish to give these pretty stones to you because they are so pretty.' Mrs. G. says Mr. Nathan married his wife for her love and knowledge of musick, and that he wishes her to teach after she recovers from the birth of her child."

Yes, that was typical of Nathan. Hers was an old love, a vestigial remnant, like a figment, really, of someone she had never known. She received the news coldly, without interest. Yet, the letters. Nathan still held, locked away in some musty trunk, tied with an already fading ribbon, the love letters of Margaret Fuller. Perhaps it was fortunate, after all, that Ossoli did not read English.

One painful subject was recurrent in nearly all Margaret's communications with her family: money. Uncle Abraham, her father's eldest brother, had died not long before, wealthy and unmarried, raising hopes of a bequest for Margaret. From the time of her father's passing, Uncle Abraham, a lawyer, had been the sharpest thorn in the family flesh, attempting to run the family finances, attempting to halt the education of the younger children, attempting to boss Margaret. Like all the Fullers, he had a vigorous personality, and was not averse, among other things, to advising the ladies on how to mend and darn. Margaret had packed her microscope and accepted a teaching job at the Greene Street School in Providence, Rhode Island, at the age of twenty-six, partially to free herself from the domination of Uncle Abraham. She called him "that sordid man"—advising her mother not to be affected by his "vulgar insults."

The bequest turned out to be a mirage. In a letter to Miss Mary Rotch of New Bedford, called always "Aunt" Mary, Margaret fully expressed her feelings in the matter: "I am rather sore at constantly being congratulated about my Uncle's legacy. My friends are [laboring] under some mistake, I fancy. My Uncle died as he had lived, hard-hearted against me. For eleven years that I had struggled amid so many difficulties and ill health, he, far from aiding, wished to see me fall, because I had acted against his opinion in giving my family advantages he thought, with his narrow views, useless, and defended my mother against his rude tyranny. When I came to escape, he, a little ashamed perhaps, said he 'had thought of making me a present, but was short of cash just then.' In his will he left me no legacy. *After the legacies were paid,* I came in with 62 other heirs for my share of what was left . . . ." Margaret's share amounted to less than one thousand dollars.

To her mother she wailed: "Grateful as I am for Uncle A's bequest, and for its coming just when needed to save me from a check in all my plans, which would have been so bitter, it was not enough. If he had left me ten or even five thousand dollars, I should have been so happy."

She was planning, in fact, to live six months in Rome on four hundred dollars. On the third day of her return she found "permanent" lodgings on the second floor of 519 Via del Corso, not far from the Piazza del Popolo—so that, she said, "I see all that goes on in Rome." The new apartment was ideally suited to her purposes, and she became enthusiastic in her description to her mother: "The rooms are elegantly furnished, everything in the house so neat, more like England than Italy, service excellent, everything arranged with reasonable economy . . . . The only drawback is a little danger from the character and position of my hostess. She is a most insinuating creature and disposed to pet me too much . . . . She was formerly the mistress of a man of quality who loved her so much that she made him marry her before his death, so that she is a Marchioness, but not received into society . . . . She has black eyes and hair like Aunt Martha, a pretty color and fair skin, very graceful manners, and speaks Italian beautifully, which is good practice for me. She has introduced me to her present lover. He is a distinguised Italian artist, who has been devoted to her for some years. He is an officer of note in the newly organized Civic Guard, and will bring all the news to the house. He is also very agreeable. Of course I seem to ignore all these circumstances; he appears here merely as a friend and visitor, and if she observes strict good sense and propriety in her relations with me, all will go well."

Rereading the letter, Margaret realized that she had taken for granted a situation which in American eyes would seem shocking, so she hastened to add a postscript to avoid upsetting her mother: "I ought to observe to give you a clearer idea of my position with the Marchioness that the custom of Rome is to take your own apartment, and live entirely separate from the family to whom the house belongs. The house is divided into suites: they occupy one, each tenant another. I did not expect ever to see them except when I paid my bills. But it is her pleasure to come in and arrange my flowers, and serve me at table . . . . I think she will do this less when I cease to be a new toy."

Then, apparently, occurred another uneasy afterthought: her own position was almost identical with that of her *padrona*. Here was a house where Ossoli could come "merely as a friend and visitor," and the landlady would "seem to ignore" the circumstances. Margaret had written in such detail because, in reality, she was writing about her own circumstances only slightly disguised. Even the matter of a lover who was a member of the civic guard was parallel—and perhaps the artist-officer was a friend of Ossoli, or at least they must have been acquainted. Perhaps thus Margaret had learned of the availability of the rooms.

Ossoli was not yet, however, a member of the guard, though the decision to join must have been an immediate subject of his conversations with Margaret. Formation of the guard had been granted reluctantly by the clerical authorities in July, in response to insistent demands from the Roman people, led by Angelo Brunetti. He was a *popolano,* a wine and horse dealer, a giant who wore an earring in his left ear and was nicknamed *"Ciceruacchio"* (Big-boy) for his girth. He alternated good-natured and fiery speeches, and swayed the people with ease.

In any case, by the fifteenth of November the decision for Ossoli to enroll was taken, for on that date the nobleman Giovanni Angelo Ossoli became a sergeant in the people's militia, entitled to wear the dark blue and red-corded uniform and the rakish little kepi for a cap. All the Americans, according to one of them, thought he looked very handsome in the uniform; but Margaret probably encouraged him to wear it as a sign of his identification with the people. The reaction of his officer brothers in the papal *Guardia Nobile* must have been another matter, and surely they berated him for the step.

Margaret quickly surrounded herself with books and papers for the study of the contemporary Italian situation. The idea of a history of Italy during its revolutionary period was beginning to take shape in her mind. She set up a careful schedule. On Monday evenings she received her American acquaintances (though she was too poor to provide refreshments); the rest of the week she kept free for herself. Untruthfully she wrote to Emerson, "I live alone, eat alone, walk alone . . . . just for happiness Rome is sufficient."

Frequent visitors were the painter Christopher Cranch and his wife, and a little later, William Wetmore Story and his wife and baby boy. Cranch was an intellectual friend dating from transcendentalist days, an "escapee" from Brook Farm. Story had circulated merely on the fringe of the movement, though he had attended Margaret's "Conversation on Greek Mythology" and had been greatly stimulated by it. William was the son of Supreme Court Justice Joseph Story, a descendant of one of the Boston Tea Party "Indians," and had been trained in the law. He was wealthy, cultivated, and full of wit, enthusiasm, and gaiety. He sported a long flowing moustache and a little patch of chin whiskers. Graced with both literary and artistic talent, he was seeking to find in sculpture a life more satisfactory to him than that of a Boston lawyer. "How shall I ever again endure the restraint and bondage of Boston?" he wrote to his friend James Russell Lowell. "There is no such thing as flesh and blood . . . . We love nothing . . . . We criticize everything . . . . The sky itself is hard and distant. The heart grows into stone."

Story's wife, Emelyn, was a pretty, plump young woman who wore her abundant dark hair parted in the middle, with long curls dangling on either side of her face. She was charming, intelligent, and far from a rigid Puritan. Eventually she became Margaret's closest American confidant in Rome.

Story and Ossoli were about the same age, and though of different temperaments, Story got to know Ossoli better than did any other American who appeared in Margaret's little salon. Mrs. Story wrote afterward: "We soon became acquainted with the young Marquis Ossoli, and met him frequently at Margaret's rooms. He appeared to be of a reserved and gentle nature, with quiet, gentleman-like manners, and there was something melancholy in the expression of his face, which made one desire to know more of him." But Ossoli was too taciturn for intimate friendship with foreigners, even friends of Margaret.

Nor was Margaret in a mood for close association with Americans. Her imagination had taken flight in fields apart. Such was the state of her Italo-euphoria that she declaimed to her mother: "The Italians sympathize with my character and understand my organization as no other people ever did. They admire the ready eloquence of my nature, and highly prize my intelligent sympathy (such as they do not often find in foreigners) with their sufferings in the past and their hopes for the future."

For "they" read "he." Certainly one Italian understood her perfectly. Ossoli's prediction that she would return to him was indeed fulfilled.

She wrote eventually to her sister Ellen, "I acted upon a strong impulse. I could not analyze at all what passed in my mind. I neither rejoice nor grieve. For bad or for good, I acted out my character."

13

It was a dreamy autumn. The countryside was "sere and brown," but the light was golden and the weather fine. Margaret was constantly with Ossoli. "Two days I have been at the Villa Borghese. There are races, balloons, and, above all, the private gardens are open, and good music on the little lake." There were rides in the *campagna,* to see the grape harvest, and once they met the pope "on foot, taking exercise, flanked by two young priests in spotless purple." There was a visit to the cemetery of the Santo Spirito on the Day of the Dead, to see the mourners, the flickering candles, the heaps of chrysanthemums, and the hordes of professional beggars who lined the road. There were expeditions to the Castelli Romani, the near-by castle-towns in the hills—little picnics, with a basket of food and wine. They lay together on some hillside, viewing the serene grandeur of Rome at sunset.

There were military reviews. "This morning I was out, with half Rome, to see the Civic Guard maneuvering in that great field near the tomb of Cecilia Metella, which is full of ruins. The effect was noble, as the band played the Bolognese march, and six thousand Romans passed in battle array amid these fragments of the great time." There were the late October festas, especially in Trastevere—the old settlement across the Tiber (tras-Tevere), at the foot of the Janiculum Hill on the right bank, the only part of Rome continually inhabited since ancient times. Featured were illuminations with oil lamps, bands, bazaars, fireworks, and above all, the handsome Trasteverini dancing the saltarello in their brilliant costumes. "The *Saltarello* enchants me," Margaret said, "in this is really the Italian wine, the Italian sun."

And Margaret, following Adam Mickiewicz's advice, permitted the magic of Rome to have its effect, and became beautiful.

The change in her appearance and character was obvious even to casual friends. "To me she seemed so unlike what I had thought her to be in America," remarked Emelyn Story, "that I continually said, 'How have I misjudged you—you are not at all such a person as I took you to be.' To this she replied, 'I am not the same person, but in many respects another; my life has new channels now, and how thankful I am that I have been able to come out into larger interests—but, partly, you did not know me at home in the true light.' It was true that I had not known her much personally, when in Boston; but through her friends, who were mine also, I had learned to think of her as a person on intellectual stilts, with a large share of arrogance, and little sweetness of temper. How unlike to this was she now!—so delicate, so simple, confiding, and affectionate; with a true womanly heart and soul, sensitive and generous, and, what was to me a still greater surprise, possessed of so broad a charity, that she could cover with its mantle the faults and defects of all about her."

After a few months the new friendship was to be interrupted, for the restless Storys drifted to the south. They did not lose touch with Margaret, however, and their admiration for her grew. They told friends all about her kindness and generosity, using a certain incident as an illustration: She had lent an indigent artist her last fifty dollars, when she herself had hardly enough to eat.

But Margaret's thoughts turned less and less to her old friends. The seriousness of her approach to the developing revolutionary situation became apparent with her first totally political dispatch to the *Tribune*, written shortly after her return to Rome. In Piedmont, ruled by the House of Savoy, the dyspeptic King Carlo Alberto had just shown momentary democratic weakness in liberalizing censorship of the press. Immediate advantage of this opportunity was taken by Count Camillo Cavour, an aristocrat who was to become the chief architect of the Kingdom of Italy. He founded a newspaper called *Il Risorgimento* (The Re-arising or The Revival). It was this term that was to be given to the political reawakening of all Italy and the long-delayed drive for national unity. And it was this term that encompassed the full scope of Margaret's journalism and the history she planned to write.

With Ossoli an ever-present companion, she undertook to attend the meetings of all groups and parties, that she might sample all points of view. Her Mazzinian contacts gave access to the Republicans, the Marchesa Arconati Visconti equally opened liberal doors, and Ossoli was an invaluable guide through the mazes of papal policies. Systematically she accumulated documents as though preparing a display for a museum, and no item seemed too small for her attention. But it was in her ability to correlate facts and make intelligent judgments that she really shone. Indeed her political awareness, her shrewd insights, seem almost incredible for someone so lately arrived on the scene. Rarely did this astuteness fail her.

Well in advance of events that proved her right, she stigmatized King Carlo Alberto as "a worthless man, in whom nobody puts any trust so far as regards his heart or honor; but the stress of things seems likely to keep him on the right side." Nor could Margaret forget that it had been the House of Savoy that had condemned Mazzini to death for "treason."

Well in advance of events that again confirmed her judgments, she foresaw the fatal indecisions of Pius IX. She noted with pleasure "the childlike joy and trust" of the Roman people in the first tentative measures of reform undertaken by the pope, "who has not in his expression the signs of intellectual greatness so much as of nobleness and tenderness of heart, of large and liberal sympathies . . . ." Still, doubts were always present whether all this joy was not premature. The task undertaken by the pope seemed to present insuperable difficulties. "Our age is one where all things tend to a great crisis; not merely to revolution, but to radical reform. From the people themselves the help must come, and not from princes. Rome, to resume her glory, must cease to be an ecclesiastical capital; must renounce all this gorgeous mummery, whose poetry, whose picture, charms no one more than myself, but whose meaning is all of the past, and finds no echo in the future."

Margaret must many times have discussed the economic and social situation of Rome with William Story, for when he came to write his *Roba di Roma* he seemed to echo her words. "The number of beggars in Rome is large. They grow here as noxious weeds in a hot-bed. The government neither fosters commerce nor stimulates industry. The policy of the Church everywhere is conservative, and this is specially the case in Rome, where the Church is the State. Founded on ancient ideas and dogmas, consolidated by long established forms and usages, its evident duty is to defend them and conserve them. It naturally opposes itself to all innovations. It distrusts and dislikes changes. Its aim is piety, submission, and obedience among the people, rather than prosperity in business and increase of trade. Its primary duties and interests are ecclesiastical, and to these all other duties and interests are secondary. It restricts education, [only 2 percent of the rural population and only 10 percent of the population of Rome could read] and subjects literature to censorship through fear that the development of new ideas may lead to revolution or to atheism. If piety be developed by it, life and thought languish, trade stagnates, industry decays, and the people, ceasing to work and to think, have grown indolent and supine. Poverty is a necessary consequence."

Other disturbing consequences arose as well. In such closed states secret societies inevitably flourish, and the pontifical domains were no exception. To promote ideas of reform, and to circulate forbidden literature, the liberal Carbonari were organized—so-called from the conception of blackening the face with carbon to pass unseen in the night. And to combat the Carbonari, the San Fedists arose. They appeared in bands devoted to the protection of Holy Faith by use of club, dagger, and pistol against any person suspected of liberal tendencies. They supplemented, sometimes openly but usually secretly, the conventional punishments of prison or enrollment in chain-gangs as galley slaves. (W. W. Story describes seeing the monument to the Virgin in the Piazza di Spagna erected by a gang of prisoners condemned to the galleys.)

It was in such an atmosphere that the pope, under pressure, granted the formation of a council of state, whose members were not to be ecclesiastics. The council, Margaret noted for the *Tribune,* would deal with such practical problems as "gaslights, introduction of machinery, etc."—problems long since resolved in the other major cities of Europe. The inauguration of the council was greeted with a celebration, and the pope made a speech, wrote Margaret, "implying that he meant only to improve, *not* to *reform,* and should keep things *in status quo,* safe locked with the keys of St. Peter. This little speech was made, no doubt, more to reassure czars, emperors, and kings, than from the promptings of the spirit. But the fact of its necessity . . . seems to say that the pontifical government, though from the accident of this one man's accession it has taken the initiative to better times, yet may not, after a while, from its very nature, be able to keep in the vanguard."

The Americans in Rome showed "a warm interest" in the new council, said Margaret, and prepared to display the United States flag for the occasion. As they found that not one existed in the city, the gentlemen subscribed the money for purchase of cloth, and the ladies met to make it. The sewing went well, and the Stars and Stripes appeared in silk. But at the last moment an ordinance was passed barring all flags except that of papal

Rome from the streets—for the authorities feared that the flags of the other parts of dismembered Italy might appear draped in black, and offense be given to royal heads of state.

The repetition of this Betsy Ross flag-making scene appeared to turn Margaret's thoughts to Americans and American problems. She had confessed at about this date, to an unknown person, "Since I have experienced the different atmosphere of the European mind, nay, mingled in the bonds of love, I suffer more than ever from that which is peculiarly American or English. I should like to cease hearing the language for a time."

She was thoroughly aware of the long list of Americans who had preceded her to Italy ever since the mid-eighteenth century. She knew and referred to the classic anecdote about the portrait painter Benjamin West, who in 1760 shocked a distinguished Roman audience by exclaiming of the nude Apollo Belvedere, "How like a Mohawk warrior!" West was followed by almost all the leading American painters and sculptors: John Singleton Copley, Rembrandt Peale, Washington Allston, Henry Benbridge, Thomas Cole, Samuel F. B. Morse (inventor of the telegraph). Among the writers were Washington Irving, James Fenimore Cooper, Thomas Jefferson (who both spoke and wrote Italian), and Henry Wadsworth Longfellow. And her three immediate successors, James Russell Lowell, Herman Melville, Nathaniel Hawthorne,* were well known to her.

She had gone out of her way to congratulate, in a recent article, her contemporaries, the sculptors Horatio Greenough and Thomas Crawford, for their active participation in Italian affairs—Greenough by joining the Tuscan National Guard in Florence, and Crawford by joining the civic guard in Rome. In contrast, she had blasted the slugs: "I am sorry to say that a large portion of my countrymen here take the same slothful and prejudiced view as the English, and, after many years' sojourn, betray entire ignorance of Italian literature and Italian life . . . . they talk about the corrupt and degenerate state of Italy

---

* Hawthorne allegedly described her as his heroine in his novel *The Blithedale Romance*. In his later years he attacked her bitterly, unkindly, and inaccurately.

as they do about that of our slaves at home. They come ready trained to that mode of reasoning which affirms that, because men are degraded by bad institutions, they are not fit for better . . . . The people learn as they advance."

She prepared a special letter to the *Tribune*, to be printed on New Year's Day, about her countrymen abroad and at home. She said what she thought, without apologies, and it was not equivocation when she stated, "The American in Europe, if a thinking mind, can only become more American." And of Americans in Europe there are three species. "First, the servile American—a being utterly shallow, thoughtless, worthless. He comes abroad to spend his money and indulge his tastes. His object in Europe is to have fashionable clothes, good foreign cookery, to know some titled persons, and furnish himself with coffee-house gossip . . . .

"Then there is the conceited American, instinctively bristling and proud of—he knows not what. He does not see, not he, that the history of Humanity for many centuries is likely to have produced results it requires some training, some devotion, to appreciate and profit by . . . . to him the etiquettes of courts and camps, the ritual of the Church, seem simply silly—and no wonder, profoundly ignorant as he is of their origin and meaning. Just so the legends which are the subjects of pictures, the profound myths which are represented in the antique marbles, amaze and revolt him; as, indeed, such things need to be judged of by another standard than that of the Connecticut Blue-Laws . . . .

"The third . . . is that of the thinking American—a man who, recognizing the immense advantage of being born to a new world and on a virgin soil, yet does not wish one seed from the past to be lost. He is anxious to gather and carry back with him every plant that will bear a new climate and a new culture . . . . He wishes to give them a fair trial in this new world."

America, indeed, Margaret declared, was fated to be "the advance-guard of humanity, the herald of all progress . . . . But we must stammer and blush when we speak of many things." Worst of all is "this cancer of slavery, and the wicked war [the Mexican War] which has grown out of it. How dare I speak of these things here? I listen to the same arguments against the emancipation of Italy that are used against the emancipation of our blacks; the same arguments in favor of the spoilation of Poland as for the conquest of Mexico. I find the cause of tyranny and wrong everywhere the same—and lo! my country! the darkest offender, because with the least excuse . . . . How it pleases me here to think of the Abolitionists! I could never endure to be with them at home, they were so tedious, often so narrow, always so rabid and exaggerated in their tone. But, after all . . . it was really something worth living and dying for, to free a great nation from such a terrible blot, such a threatening plague. God strengthen them . . . !"

Finally, "It is to the youth that hope addresses itself . . . the American youth, who I trust will yet expand, and help to give soul to the huge, over-fed, too hastily grown-up body."

It was a rich and meaningful autumn. Everything that Margaret wrote was full of vigor, full of purpose. She was gulping life, quenching the deep thirst that for so long had parched her truest self. The petty irritations hardly troubled her. It was nothing that her charming *padrona* had turned out to be "the greatest liar I ever knew . . . the most self-interested, heartless creature."

The dulcet days were seriously marred only by the lack of money. "A little money would have enabled me to come here long ago, and find those that belong to me, or at least try my experiments; then my health would never have sunk, nor the best years of my life been wasted in useless friction." Still, all was not lost. She *had* come to Rome—she *had* found the one who belonged to her.

To her mother on December sixteenth she wrote: "My life in Rome is thus far all I hoped. I have not been so well since I was a child, nor so happy ever, as during the last six weeks."

14

Two days later the winter rains began, continuous, cold, dreary, from skies heavily overcast. The thick stone houses were dank, bone-chilling. The dampness penetrated everywhere. Margaret, invariably subjective, was affected by the weather. "The ruins and other great objects, always solemn," she observed, "appear terribly gloomy, steeped in black rain and cloud; and my apartment, in a street of high houses, is dark all day."

But there was another reason for her depression.

In her journal she had once written: "I have no child, and the woman in me has so craved this experience that it has seemed the want of it must paralyze me." And once, in the hush of night, she had scribbled: "My Child! O, Father, give me a bud on my tree of life, so scathed by the lightning and bound by the frost! Surely a being born wholly of my being would not let me lie so still and cold in lonely sadness."

The prayer at last was to be answered. Her response was not joy but panic and despair.

Four days after the "happiness" letter to her mother, she

wrote to Emerson: "Nothing less than two or three years, free from care and forced labor, would heal all my hurts and renew my life-blood at its source. Since Destiny will not grant me that, I hope she will not leave me long in the world, for I am tired of keeping myself up in the water without corks, and without strength to swim. I should like to go to sleep, and be born again into a state where my young life should not be permanently taxed. Italy has been glorious to me, and there have been hours in which I received the full benefits of the vision. In Rome I have known some blessed, quiet days, when I could yield myself to be soothed and instructed by the great thoughts and memories of the place. But those days are swiftly passing. Soon I must begin to exert myself, for there is this incubus of the future, and none to help me, if I am not prudent to face it."

On December 30, writing for the *Tribune* with rain falling "incessantly," she confessed publicly, "At the end of this fortnight without exercise or light, and in such a damp atmosphere, I find myself without strength, without appetite, almost without spirits."

Shortly thereafter she wrote to Caroline Sturgis: "I have known some happy hours, but they all lead to sorrow; and not only the cups of wine, but of milk, seem drugged with poison for me. It does not *seem* to be my fault, this Destiny. I do not court these things—they come. I am a poor magnet, with power to be wounded by the bodies I attract . . . . When I arrived in Rome, I was at first intoxicated to be here. The weather was beautiful, and many circumstances combined to place me in a kind of passive, childlike well-being. That is all over now, and with this year I enter upon a sphere of my destiny so difficult that at present I see no way out except through the gate of death. It is useless to write of it. You are at a distance and cannot help me—whether accident or angel will, I have no intimation. I have no reason to hope I shall not reap what I have sown, and do not. Yet how I shall endure it I cannot guess; it is all a dark, sad enigma. The beautiful forms of art charm no more, and a love in which there is all fondness but no help, flatters in vain. I am all alone; nobody around me sees any of this."

She was describing the essential state of human loneliness in the two great crises: birth and death—the great alonenesses. Conception was another crisis, but not felt as such. It was, instead, a soaring unrecognized—a flowing from that rare moment when two human beings are able to feel almost as one. But Margaret, in shock, forgot the ecstasy. Ossoli must have sensed Margaret's conflicts—but only Ossoli.

As always with illegitimate pregnancies, the immediate question was: "What is to be done?" Abortion? Or marriage? Or nothing? No record indicates whether they thought or spoke of abortion; but the question of marriage seems to have been under constant discussion. Emelyn Story wrote in retrospect, "We saw Ossoli pale, dejected, and unhappy. He was always with her, but in a sort of hopeless, desperate manner . . . telling her that he must marry her or be miserable."

Had they secretly married at this time, as Mrs. Story later believed, no reason would have existed for the future secrecy with which the entire affair was shrouded by Margaret and her family. When eventually she wrote to her sister about her relationship to Ossoli, she remarked, "As to marriage, I think the intercourse of heart and mind may be fully enjoyed without entering into this partnership of daily life." Margaret in fact was adamant in refusing marriage to Ossoli—she seemed to feel that it would be meaningless, or be made meaningless either by her own death or the death of the child. Profound, too, had been the impact of Mickiewicz's injunction to "free your spirit, responding to the legitimate needs of your body, and leaving you free at all times."

It is true that every aspect of such a marriage seemed hopeless. Disparate in background and age, penniless, diverse in language, how could they anticipate any long-term successful solution? Yet these were as nothing compared to the most serious problem threatening them: the political. Margaret, by conversion to Catholicism, could have become religiously acceptable to Ossoli's family. But Margaret the Republican, the radical, the Mazzinian, could never become acceptable. The essential requisite to marry a Protestant—a special papal dispensation

—very probably could have been blocked by Angelo's brothers. They would have thought that—in a milieu so tense with suspicions and spies—she might jeopardize their position at the Vatican.

However marriage to Margaret might be arranged, Angelo, once married, would be forever at odds with his family—and in Italy the family was not lightly tossed aside. The family, as name, entity, tradition, property, existed through the generations and the centuries, with the same attitudes, on the same land, in the same houses. Marriages were not made for love, but to strengthen the family. Divorce was unthinkable. The family was real, the nation nothing. The first loyalty of every individual was to the family, as structured and blessed by the Church. A certain sentimental loyalty was attached to the area of origin; no other loyalty really counted, except of course to the Church.

Yet in spite of all this, Angelo Ossoli apparently urged Margaret to marry him. For both their sakes, she would not.

Gradually she managed to face the fact of her pregnancy, for she had no alternative but to go on with her work. As it was obvious that she would be increasingly in need of money, she began to turn out dispatches to the *Tribune* at intervals of ten days to a fortnight. The frantic pace of the letters reflected both current events and the author's emotions. She reported sadly on a lovely young woman taking the veil; on a performance of Giuseppe Verdi's *Attila* at the opera, and the wild applause which greeted the Roman leader's line, ". . . let the shades of our ancestors arise!"; on the unrest in Naples, with the comment, "The King alone remains inflexible in his stupidity." She spoke of the death of the Archduchess Maria Louisa of Parma, of the marriage of the Countess Guiccioli, and of how the boy duke of Reichstadt withered under the mean, cold influence of his grandfather—without giving sufficient explanation for Americans to understand what on earth she was talking about. No doubt her readers were puzzled at why the usually lucid Margaret Fuller began to chatter like a lady attending a church supper.

Perfectly clear, however, was her description of her Christmas

Eve activities. "I set out for the Quirinal to see the Pope return from that noble church, Santa Maria Maggiore, where he officiated this night. I reached the mount just as he was returning. A few torches gleamed before his door; perhaps a hundred people were gathered together round the fountain. Last year an immense multitude waited for him to express their affection in one grand good-night . . . . Just as he returned, the moon looked palely out from amid the wet clouds, and shone upon the fountain, and the noble figures [statues] above it, and the long white cloaks of the *Guardia Nobile* who followed his carriage on horseback; darker objects could scarcely be seen, except by the flickering light of the torches, much blown by the wind." But some facts remained unreported. Certainly her companion was Ossoli, as she would not have been alone in the streets at that hour of the night; and certainly his brothers rode in their white cloaks and swords with the *Guardia Nobile,* for that was their function. There was no need to fear; in the feeble light of wind-blown torches, Angelo was safe from recognition.

By now she had begun to sort out her impressions of the city. "I begin to see and feel the real Rome," she wrote. "As one becomes familiar, Ancient and Modern Rome, at first so painfully and discordantly jumbled together, are drawn apart to the mental vision. One sees where objects and limits anciently were; the superstructures vanish, and you recognize the local habitation of so many thoughts. When this begins to happen, one feels first truly at ease in Rome. Then the old kings, the consuls and tribunes, the emperors, drunk with blood and gold, the warriors of eagle sight and remorseless beak, return for us, and the togated procession finds room to sweep across the scene; the seven hills tower, the innumerable temples glitter, and the Via Sacra swarms with triumphal life once more.

" . . . Then the later Papal Rome: it requires much acquaintance, much thought, much reference to books, for the child of Protestant Republican America to see where belong the legends illustrated by rite and picture, the sense of all the rich tapestry, where it has a united and poetic meaning, where it is broken by some accident of history.

99

" . . . Then Modern Rome—still ecclesiastical, still darkened and damp in the shadow of the Vatican, but where bright hopes gleam now amid the ashes! Never was a people who have had more to corrupt them—bloody tyranny, and incubus of priestcraft, the invasions, first of Goths, then of trampling emperors and kings, then of sight-seeing foreigners—everything to turn them from a sincere, hopeful, fruitful life; and they are much corrupted, but still a fine race."

She had begun to "exert" herself, as foreseen. All was hasty, sometimes more than a little disconnected. If the sentences would not parse, it was no matter; they were more vivid for having come so glowing though unformed from the forge. Under the chatter was the burden of gloom and dismay; under the travelog the increasing throb of revolution.

And the rains continued, without cease.

15

Even before the multitudinous church bells of Rome tolled in the New Year, it was evident that 1848 would mark a crest in the ever-increasing European revolutionary surge. Whether the crest would sweep away the moorings of the old order, or break on the hard rocks of reaction, was the question. Nowhere was the tide felt more strongly than in Italy, where the political patience of the people was beginning to give way to exhaustion, the exhaustion to anger, and the anger to violence.

Shortly before Christmas Margaret wrote to Emerson in England: "I don't know whether you take an interest in the present state of things in Italy, but you would if you were here. It is a fine time to see the people. As to the Pope, it is as difficult here as elsewhere to put new wine into old bottles, and there is something false as well as ludicrous in the spectacle of the people first driving their princes to do a little justice, and then *evviva*-ing them at such a rate."

As a Christmas present to the people the pope revised his council of ministers to include only one cardinal, as the secretary of state. He did not, however, specify to the curia that the other posts were to be occupied by lay persons, and as a result the new council was entirely composed of ecclesiastics.

Two days after Christmas, "Big-boy" Ciceruacchio, whose popular stature was steadily growing to match his girth, presented a long list of demands to the pope, including the immediate suppresion of the Jesuits. On New Year's Day a huge crowd sought to demonstrate before the pope, and to receive his blessing. This was denied by the cardinal in charge, and access to the Palazzo Quirinale was blocked by soldiers. A riot was on the verge of erupting, but Ciceruacchio convinced the people to send an emissary to the pope. The pope was ill; he had been informed of neither demands nor demonstrations and was distressed at the emissary's news. Pius thereupon promised to appear in public.

"Accordingly, the next day, though rainy and of a searching cold like that of Scotch mist," wrote Margaret in her newspaper dispatch, "we had all our windows thrown open, and the red and yellow tapestries [Rome's official colors] hung out. He passed through the principal parts of the city, the people throwing themselves on their knees and crying out, 'O Holy Father, don't desert us! don't forget us! don't listen to our enemies!' The Pope wept often, and replied, 'Fear nothing, my people, my heart is yours.' At last, seeing how ill he was, they begged him to go in, and he returned to the Quirinale; the present Tribune of the People, as far as rule in the heart is concerned, Ciceruacchio, following his carriage." Ciceruacchio held in his hands a pontifical banner, across which had been written: "Courage, Holy Father, trust the people." And as Ciceruacchio passed, many cried out, "Viva Pius IX alone. Death to the Jesuits!"

Margaret correctly estimated the blocking of access to the Quirinale as a provocation. "The influence of the Oscurantist foe [the Jesuits] has shown itself more and more plainly in Rome," she commented. "A false miracle is devised: the Madonna del Popolo (who has her handsome house very near me), has cured a paralytic youth (who, in fact was never diseased), and, appearing to him in a vision, takes occasion to criticise severely the measures of the Pope. Rumors of tumult in one quarter are circulated, to excite it in another. Inflammatory handbills are put up in the night. But the Romans thus far resist all intrigues of the foe to excite them to bad conduct.

" . . . For the moment, the difficulties are healed, as they will be whenever the Pope directly shows himself to the people. Then his generous, affectionate heart will always act . . . dissipating the clouds which others have been toiling to darken."

At about this time Margaret had been reading *Il Gesuita Moderno* (The Modern Jesuit), a fiery indictment of the company's politics, ethics, and teachings by the devout, mild-mannered Abbot Gioberti. The Jesuits were feared by the people, intellectuals, and large sections of the ordinary clergy, because they had succeeded in establishing themselves as controlling elements at the highest level of government, not only in Italy, but in many other Catholic countries, including Austria. Margaret felt no hesitation in writing for the *Tribune* that she was "satisfied, from the very nature of their [the Jesuit] institutions, that the current prejudice against them must be correct."

Of the Jesuits she could speak intellectually; but certain practices of the Church roused the old Puritan indignation of her forebears: "This afternoon (January 10) I went to the Quirinal Palace to see the Pope receive the new municipal officers. He was today in his robes of white and gold, with his usual corps of attendants in pure red and white, or violet and white. The new officers were in black velvet dresses, with broad white collars. They took the oath of office, and then actually kissed his foot. I had supposed this was never really done, but only a very low obeisance made; the act seemed to me disgustingly abject. A Heavenly Father does not want his children at his feet, but in his arms, on a level with his heart."

Due to the slowness of the mails (six weeks to two months for a New York-Rome letter, depending on the steamship), the news of a New York mass meeting *pro Italia* had just reached her. The meeting no doubt was the result of the impassioned words on Italy with which Margaret had bombarded her readers. That old warrior, Horace Greeley, who considered himself as well as his *Tribune* a Tribune of the people (like Ciceruacchio in Rome), had called a rally at the Broadway Tabernacle, the largest hall in New York, to demonstrate American support for the pope's progressive policies. On November 29 the Tabernacle was jammed, and more than seven hundred people signed an address to the pope. Letters were read from the ex-President of the United States Martin Van Buren, current Secretary of State James Buchanan, and many other important people, including the mayor of New York City. The statement praised Pius IX for his "political enlightenment" and "liberal measures," condemned Austria for its barbarities, and declared that "the emancipation of Italy would be the signal for the liberation of Europe from slavery." The document plunged on, heedless of the fact that certain words were anathema in Rome. Tribute was offered the pope, "not as Catholics, but as republicans." Applauded were "the efforts of the Italian people to achieve national independence and constitutional liberty." So great, indeed, was the enthusiasm that hardly a week later the current President of the United States, James K. Polk, recommended to Congress that diplomatic relations be established with the Papal States.

But in the Papal States the statement of the mass meeting was met by almost total indifference. It seems to have been more widely reprinted in France than in the tightly censored Italian press. Where it appeared, no comment was added. Margaret was deeply wounded that such an expression of sympathy for Italy should have been given so little public attention in Italy, though "the private expressions of pleasure have been very warm." She was fully aware that "republican" and "constitutional liberty" were favored words in the lexicon of neither popes nor kings. The pope in fact must have been acutely embarrassed at finding himself the hero of citizens of the nation generally looked upon as the most radical in the world. He feared, wrote Margaret, "lest he should be called a Protestant Pope."

In her column of January 10, Margaret repeated in full another address to the pope, that of Giuseppe Mazzini. Its aim was also the unity and independence of Italy. It was first printed in Paris, then distributed throughout Italy as a leaflet. Copies were flung into the pope's carriage, though the original letter had reached him through other channels. To Margaret a copy must have been sent direct, because Mazzini later asked if she had received it. Not surprisingly, Margaret, in her translation, managed to make Mazzini sound like Margaret Fuller:

"I am not a subverter, nor a communist, nor a man of blood, nor a hater, nor intolerant, nor exclusive adorer of a system, or of a form imagined by my mind. I adore God, and an idea which seems to me of God—Italy an angel of moral unity and of progressive civilization for the nations of Europe . . . . If the people should rise in violent attack against the selfishness and bad government of their rulers, I, while rendering homage to the right of the people, shall be among the first to prevent the excesses and the vengeance which long slavery has prepared.

" . . . I believe you good. There is no man this day, I will not say in Italy, but in all Europe, more powerful than you; you then have, most Holy Father, vast duties. God measures these according to the means which he has granted to his creatures.

"Europe is in a tremendous crisis of doubts and desires. Through the work of time, accelerated by your predecessors of the hierarchy of the Church, faith is dead, Catholicism is lost in despotism; Protestantism is lost in anarchy. Look around you. You will find superstition and hypocrites, but not believers. The intellect travels in a void . . . nobody *believes*.

" . . . Take no counsel except from God, from the inspirations of your own heart, and from the necessity of rebuilding a temple to truth, to justice, to faith . . . . Unify Italy, your country . . . . It will be fulfilled, with you or without you."

Shortly thereafter, Mazzini said that he had composed his letter to the pope "in a moment of enthusiasm and youthful illusion." To Margaret he declared: " . . . All great hopes of the Pope have failed . . . . Pius the IX is evidently a good man, a charitable Christian, a zealous administrator of the material interests of his two millions of subjects. *Un buon curator;* that is all. As a king he has neither genius nor energy; he fears the Jesuits and fears us. As a Pope he has been sent to give the last *blow to the Papacy;* and it will be seen when he dies. He is the Louis XVI of the Papal Rome."

Mazzini would have been both amused and saddened had he been informed of the pope's anguished exclamation in a private talk with the French ambassador (Pelligrino Rossi): "They want to make a Napoleon of me, who am only a poor priest!"

Mazzini, in this letter to Margaret as in so many others, leavened his political message with personal items. He had been in France (illegally) and in Switzerland, and had considered a visit to his mother, but "it could not be ventured without making her frantic with terror." Terror for him, not for herself. At Mazzini's suggestion, Margaret and the Springs, on first reaching Italy, had paused in Genoa to visit Maria Mazzini, a small, courageous woman with great dark sad eyes and a white lace mantilla draped over ink-dark hair. She had been delighted with Margaret, and had said so to her son.

"Your letter made me very happy," he replied to his mother, "because of the report you give me of Miss Fuller, the affectionate ways she had with you, the cordial welcome she received, and everything." Thereupon Maria Mazzini wrote to her son that she wished his American friend would settle in London and take care of him. Immediately Giuseppe rejected the idea of marriage to Margaret, for, not to be diverted from his revolutionary aims, he had taken the vow of celibacy in the early days of his exile. The friendship with Margaret nevertheless flourished; he could give her warm affection if not love. "I have often been thinking of you and of your friendship as a strengthening blessing," he told her.

Recently she again had identified herself publicly with Mazzini and his movement. An article attacking his "sanguinary schemes" had appeared in the London *Times,* and had been reprinted in *Galignani's Messenger,* which was printed in English in Paris and distributed in Italy. She wrote a scathing rebuttal to the *Messenger,* calling it a paper which, "by a base instinct, delights to copy into its columns whatever is adverse to the cause of progress." As for the *Times,* the author of the article showed "a love of falsehood or a vindictive spirit . . . . To couple the epithet *sanguinary* with the name of Mazzini would be simply absurd, as to speak of the darkness of light."

They had been having trouble with their correspondence, as Mazzini was under constant surveillance. One of Margaret's letters had reached him open, obviously read by the papal police. He sought to make use of her banker's address as a letter drop, but he preferred a direct courier, as he now wrote, "one whose Christian name is Scipione . . . . He will call."

Then suddenly from this world of low conspiracy and high politics, Mazzini's letter flung her back into that vacuous transcendental world from which she had fled, and which to her seemed increasingly vague. "Emerson is out of town lecturing," Mazzini wrote, "but he is soon coming back to London. I will see him and tell you my impressions. I [word missing, paper eaten by mice] very much, of course, but feel fearful that he leads or will lead man to too much contemplation. His work, I think, is very greatly needed in America, but in our own old world we stand in need of one who will, like Peter the Hermit, inflame us to the Holy Crusade and appeal to the collective influences and inspiring sources, more than to individual self-improvement."

The thought of Emerson's gangling figure at the lectern, preaching to the English and the Scots on Nature, Representative Men, and the Over-Soul, was almost too much to bear. The unbridgeable gap between Mazzini and Emerson had become the unbridgeable gap between Margaret and Dear Waldo—in only one short year and a half.

The cause: Mazzini himself . . . Mazzini and the revolution.

16

"This month, no day, scarcely an hour, has passed unmarked by some showy spectacle or some exciting piece of news," Margaret informed her *Tribune* readers in her dispatch at the end of January. She did not inform them that it was only this excitement that buoyed her up, kept her functioning at all. She seemed, in fact, to be seeking distraction, almost desperately, from the physical and financial realities of her situation. For diversion she chose politics and circuses.

Like a string of firecrackers linked together, revolutionary explosions occurred all over Italy, none yet a big bang, but all loud enough to be heard, feared, and immediately reacted to by the protectors of royalty's law and order. The standard calming device was to grant a constitution, and observe it—for awhile.

The month and year led off, on the second, third, and fourth, with the so-called "tobacco riots" in Milan, in which many of Margaret's friends were involved. As tobacco was a monopoly of the Austrian overlords, the Lombard patriots decided to boycott tobacco as an economic weapon and a means of popular protest. The device was eminently successful, so much so that the Austrian authorities retaliated with a comic-opera scheme which quickly turned to tragedy. They furnished their officers and a claque of paid provocateurs with abundant supplies of cigars, and instructed them to smoke on the streets and in the caffes and blow smoke in the faces of the Italian men who were abstaining. There were of course many who could not contain themselves under such direct insult, and attacks were made on the Austrian officers. This, declared Margaret in the *Tribune*, was "an attempt to rouse the people to revolt, with a view to arrests, and other measures calculated to stifle the spirit of independence . . . . In this iniquitous attempt they murdered eighty persons; yet the citizens, on their guard, refused them the desired means of ruin." Margaret was right that revolt in Milan was premature; but the Austrians, by their tactics, had alienated themselves from the last vestige of any sympathy from any class of the Lombard population.

In Palermo, on the birthday of the Bourbon King Ferdinando II (January 12), the population began an insurrection which quickly flared throughout all Sicily and then in Naples. Rumor (untrue) spread that Ferdinando had taken refuge in Rome. Margaret was delighted. "There was a report, day before yesterday," she wrote, "that the poor, stupid King was already here, and had taken cheap chambers at the Hotel d'Allemagne, as, indeed, it is said he has always a turn for economy, when he cannot live at the expense of his suffering people. Every carriage that the people saw with a stupid-looking man in it they did not know, they looked to see if it was not the royal runaway . . . .

"This morning authentic news is received from Naples. The King, when assured by his own brother that Sicily was in a state of irresistible revolt, and that even the women quelled the troops—showering on them stones, furniture, boiling oil, such means of warfare as the household may easily furnish to a thoughtful matron—had, first, a stroke of apoplexy, from which the loss of a good deal of bad blood revived him. His mind apparently having become clearer thereby, he has offered his subjects an amnesty and terms of reform, which, it is hoped, will arrive before his troops have begun to bombard the cities in response to earlier orders . . . . There is news that the revolution has now broken out in Naples; that neither Sicilians nor Neapolitans will trust the king, but demand his abdication nevertheless." Ferdinando II, frightened and uneasy, did not abdicate, but offered a constitution—a kind of political lollipop.

Thus it went throughout Italy. In Piedmont, soon thereafter, shrewd Count Camillo Cavour made an address demanding a constitution from King Carlo Alberto, and aroused such public pressure that the king was forced to yield. The Grand Duke Leopold of Tuscany followed with a similar grant. These constitutions, for all their "popular" aspects, permitted no democratic nonsense on two essential points, as made clear by King Ferdinando: (1) "The sole religion permitted by the State shall be the Roman Catholic Apostolic, and no other cults will be tolerated." (2) "The person of the King shall be forever sacred, inviolable, and not subject to responsibility."

True, minor variations did appear. King Carlo Alberto's constitution stated that other cults would be "tolerated according to the laws," and that his ministers "are responsible." The great concessions were that two governmental chambers were to be established, one consisting of members appointed by the royal head of state, the other to be elected on the basis of an enfranchisement plan to be decided by the king. As for the press, as Carlo Alberto neatly put it in his Article 11: "The press shall be free, but subject to repressive laws."

These events were not unnoticed in the Vatican. The atmosphere in Rome was feverish, despite the chilling *tramontana,* the winter wind. The pope was moved to further reform of his council, and made the first lay appointment. Margaret's comment was succinct: "We must hope these men of straw will serve as thatch to keep out the rain, and not be exposed to the assaults of a devouring flame."

During this period Margaret was in constant correspondence with the Marchesa Costanza Arconati Visconti, on the intimate level of first names. They discussed, in French, the Abbot Gioberti, the Brownings, current books and plays, gossip, Mazzini's letter to the pope—which the marchesa found "presumptuous," though it had the "accent of truth." To this Margaret bluntly replied, without losing the friendship of Costanza: "What black and foolish calumnies are these on Mazzini! It is as much for his interest as his honor to let things take their course, at present. I do not wonder that you were annoyed at his manner of addressing the pope; but to me it seems that he speaks as he should—near God and beyond the tomb; not from power to power, but from soul to soul, without regard for temporal dignities. It must be admitted that the etiquette, Most Holy Father, etc., jars with this."

They discussed, too, the friends whom Margaret had met in Lombardy, and the sanguinary scenes in Milan. "The massacres at Milan were premeditated," the marchesa wrote. "Marshal Radetsky thrust his hordes of soldiers into the streets to provoke and insult the inhabitants, and had prepared the cavalry . . . . He will repeat this horrible enterprise. The league against tobacco was in imitation of the Americans [the Boston 'Tea Party']."

The marchesa continued to send Margaret notes of introduction to important people in Rome. When she herself was unable to perform this function, she suggested other ways. So it happened that it was the Marchesa Arconati who informed Margaret that the Principessa Belgioioso was in Rome, and that she would not prove difficult to meet. "She has probably heard a great deal of you, since she is in correspondence with Mazzini." It was to be one of the strangely fortuitous meetings of Margaret's life.

Cristina Trivulzio, born into a privileged, aristocratic family, was one of the most extraordinary women among the large gallery of extraordinary women in Italian history—very much on a par with her most famous predecessors in antiquity and the Renaissance. At first glance her married name, Belgioioso, is forbidding to the English eye, and appears unpronounceable. But when analyzed—*bel* and *gioioso*—it becomes "beautiful" and "joyous." And she was one of the most beautiful of the long line of Italian beauties, and at times could be one of the most

Ralph Waldo Emerson—Margaret's "Dear Wise One"—as he appeared at about the time she broke away from his influence. (Concord Library, Mass.)

An 1847 map of Italy. The Papal States (Stato Ecclesiastico), stretching from
Ferrara in the north to Terracina in the south, and from sea to sea, effec-
tively cut the peninsula in two. It was a "divide and rule" papal policy
effective for more than a thousand years. (*Museo Centrale del Risorgimento, Rome*)

The young Italian Republican nobleman, the Marchese Giovanni Angelo Ossoli, who approached Margaret in St. Peter's during Easter week of 1847. The decade difference in their ages did not prevent their being immediately attracted to one another. (*Harvard University Library*)

The Ossoli nobles built their family chapel in the fifteenth-century Church of the Maddalena in Rome. The entire chapel is paneled in marble, and the ornate altar is flanked by four green marble corinthian columns. Above the altar is a distinguished seventeenth-century painting by Biciccia depicting the Virgin Mary and St. Nicholas—the patron saint of the Ossoli. (*The Herziana Library, Rome*)

The Ossoli coat of arms is topped by the coronet of a marchese. A pair of human eyes with eyebrows, and three human bones (*osso* means "bone") rest in the left field of azure. In the right field of azure a silver tower supported by two golden lions is surmounted by a black eagle with a gold crown. (*Photo by Felbermeyer, Rome*)

Pope Pius IX, as temporal ruler of the Papal States, won boundless support both in Italy and abroad for his apparent liberality in the early days of his reign. After his refusal to support the movement for Italian unity, and his failure to oppose the Austrian invaders of Italy, the people turned against him. He chose to flee from his palace in Rome to the protection of the Bourbon king of Naples. (*Museo Centrale del Risorgimento, Rome*)

Ferdinando II, the Bourbon king of Naples and Sicily, was dubbed "King Bomba" by his people because of his frequent use of cannon against them. Disguised as Harlequin in this satirical cartoon, he shows Piux IX how to bombard his subjects. (*From "Don Pirlone"*)

After twenty-six years of exile imposed by the Austrians for her efforts in behalf of Italian independence, the Marchesa Costanza Arconati Visconti —of the famed and ancient Visconti family—returned to Italy and became one of Margaret's closest friends. It was she who opened the doors of the aristocracy for Margaret in Lombardy, Florence, and Rome. (*Museo del Risorgimento, Milan*)

passionately joyous. With this, she was an intellectual, a scholar, a writer, a revolutionary conspirator, an activist, a princess, and immensely wealthy. But she was also an epileptic.

Though she was two years older than Margaret, she had not lost her youthful beauty, which was legendary. She had delicately cut features, like an oval cameo, framed by black hair brushed back tight and circled with a braid. Her eyes were very large and dark, lustrous like those of a night animal, and set widely apart under long, dark, arched eyebrows. Her complexion was pale, almost pallid—the romantic requirement of the day. Her normal expression was one of quizzical languor, of cynical amusement at life. She wore only the simplest but finest jewels, and tended to ignore fashion, designing for herself garments of sumptuous fabrics having the graceful lines of antiquity. She was an omnivorous reader, and her intellectual attitudes had been set by Voltaire, especially *Candide,* by the time she was fifteen.

At sixteen she was married to the twenty-four-year-old Principe Emilio Belgioioso, of a family as ancient and renowned as her own. He was a Carbonaro, a conspirator for a united Italy under a constitutional monarch, though for all his sentiment, so frivolous and so volatile that it was difficult for him to persevere in a single course. Within a few months of the wedding this couple, so brilliant and so favored, had chosen separate paths, though the marriage, in Catholic rite, was indissoluble. The principe was gifted with a glorious voice, and would have become a leading opera star had he not been a prince. He had come close to a death sentence for conspiracy, but was saved by an amnesty. Ordered to attend the salon of Prince Metternich, who was visiting Milan, he was invited to sing. "What a voice!" exclaimed the Princess Metternich. "And what a loss to music if your husband had ordered my execution!" Belgioioso answered, to the acute embarrassment of the Austrians.

The active participation of the principessa and her husband in the subversive anti-Austrian movement soon led to orders for their expulsion from Italy, and thenceforth the principessa was followed constantly by spies. Their reports were filed in the secret police archives in Milan, and provided a day-to-day, almost hour-by-hour account of her doings. Her salon in exile, in Paris, was attended by the leading musicians, writers, and politicians of the day, including Frédéric Chopin, Vincenzo Bellini, Franz Liszt, Gioacchino Rossini, the aging General Lafayette (who was infatuated by her), Adolphe Thiers (future president of the French Republic), Heinrich Heine, Théophile Gautier, Alexis de Tocqueville (whose *Démocratie en Amérique* was enjoying a great success), George Sand, Victor Hugo, Alexandre Dumas the elder, the Contessa Guiccioli (mistress of Lord Byron and whose marriage Margaret had reported in the *Tribune*), Alfred de Musset (who first loved the Principessa Belgioioso and then hated her), and Stendhal. Inevitably there were rumors of many lovers.

The Austrians thought to curtail the principessa's political activities by confiscating her estates. She scorned the action. Though she underwent a period of extreme poverty, she never ceased her activities against the Austrian invaders. Through political influence she managed to have her estates restored, and she introduced a kind of simple communal living and property sharing to improve the lot of the poverty-ridden peasants. As she acquired political experience, she gravitated toward the Republican cause and Mazzini—a shockingly radical orientation, which alienated many of her former friends.

She was, in short, a personality to stimulate and challenge a Margaret Fuller—a person who had moved in the very highest echelons of power and intellect throughout the whole of her life. She was, in a sense, a sophisticated, aristocratic, strangely beautiful, European Margaret Fuller. Or, alternatively, she was the fantasy Margaret Fuller of the real Margaret Fuller, the embodiment of those dreams of long ago, in Cambridgeport, when the overimaginative child Margaret had believed herself to be a changeling, a princess left by some mischance in a dour and difficult Puritan house, instead of the castle which was hers by birthright.

To her brother Richard, Margaret remarked in a letter, "I have lately seen a good deal of a very celebrated woman, the

Princess Belgioioso . . . . She is a woman of gallantry, which the Sand is not. She also has had several lovers, no doubt, but her public life has been truly energetic and beneficient." Margaret's journal entries describing her first encounter with the Principessa Belgioioso are lost. Lost, too, is the letter she sent to the Marchesa Arconati describing the fervent enthusiasm the principessa aroused in her. The Marchesa replied with perhaps a touch of prudery or of jealousy: "I understand Madame Belgioioso's attraction for you. She is a woman of superior intelligence and who has the art of captivating. I have been taken like you—but morally she has little worth." Events would prove, however, how strong was the principessa's "moral" fiber, and how valuable it might be in a crisis, which she and Margaret would face together.

17

Apart from excursions and alarms in politics, Margaret continued to race through Rome's normal life at a fantastic pace. With Ossoli always at her side she attended a state funeral, describing "the long files of armed men, the rich coaches, and liveried retinues of the princes." She went to an exhibition in honor of the Magi, arranged by the College for the Propagation of the Faith. She watched the blessing of the animals, the lambs in the church of St. Agnes and the horses in the church of St. Anthony. She participated in the *festa* of the Bambino, "the most venerated doll of Rome."

For the *Tribune* she described the event in detail. "This is the famous image of the infant Jesus . . . which, being taken away from its present abode—the Church of Ara Coeli—returned by itself, making the bells ring as it sought admittance at the door. It is this which is carried in extreme cases to the bedside of the sick. It has received more splendid gifts than any other idol.

"The church of Ara Coeli is on or near the site of the temple of Capitoline Jove, which certainly saw nothing more idolatrous than these ceremonies. For about a week the Bambino is exhibited in an illuminated chapel, in the arms of a splendidly dressed Madonna doll. Behind, a transparency represents the shepherds, by moonlight, at the time the birth was announced, and, above, God the Father, with many angels hailing the event . . . . The ceremonies begin with splendid music from the organ, pealing sweetly long and repeated invocations. As if answering to this call, the world came in, many dignitaries . . . and did homage to the image; then men in white and gold, with candles . . . uplifted high above themselves the baby, with its gilded robes and crown, and made twice the tour of the church, passing twice the column labelled 'From the Home of Augustus,' while the band played—what?—the *Hymn to Pius IX* and *Sons of Rome, Awake!* Never was a crueller comment upon the irreconcilableness of these two things. Rome seeks to reconcile reform and priestcraft."

Indeed, the reconciliation was somewhat long in coming; when W. W. Story published, in his *Roba di Roma,* a decade later, an account of the Bambino Gesú very similar to Margaret's description, the book was banned in Rome by the papal censor, on the grounds of "disrespect" to the Bambino.

Margaret's disbelief in "the ugly little doll" was motivated by personal indignation. "An orphan by my side [Ossoli], now struggling with difficulties, showed me on its breast a splendid jewel, which a doting grandmother thought more likely to benefit her soul if given to the Bambino, than if turned into money to give her grandchildren education and prospects in life. The same old lady left her vineyard, not to these children, but to her confessor, a well-endowed Monsignor, who occasionally asks this youth, his godson, to dinner!"

And there was another factor: nerves. "What a Rome!" she wrote in her last January dispatch. "The fortieth day of rain, and damp, and abominable reeking odors . . . . It has been dark all day, though the lamp has only been lit half an hour. The music of the day has been, first, the atrocious *arias,* which last in the Corso till near noon, though certainly less in virulence on rainy days. Then came the wicked organ-grinder, who, apart from the horror of the noise, grinds exactly the same obsolete abominations as at home or in England—the *Copenhagen Waltz, Home Sweet Home,* and all that! . . . Within, the three pet dogs of my landlady, bereft of their walk, unable to employ their miserable legs and eyes, exercise themselves by a continual barking, which is answered by all the dogs in the neighborhood. An urchin returning from the laundress, delighted with the symphony, lays down his white bundle in the gutter, seats himself on the curbstone, and attempts an imitation of the music of cats as a tribute to the concert. The door-bell rings. *Chi è?* 'Who is it?' cries the handmaid, with unweariable senselessness, as if anyone would answer, *Rogue,* or *Enemy,* instead of the traditional *Amico, Friend.* Can it be, perchance, a letter, news of home . . . or some ray of hope to break the clouds of the difficult future? Far from it. Enter a man poisoning me at once with the smell of the worst possible cigars, not to be driven out, insisting I shall look upon frightful, ill-cut cameos, and worse-designed mosaics, made by some friend of his . . . and will sell so cheap!"

Apparently the nausea of pregnancy already had begun to assault her. "As to eating, that is a bygone thing; wine, coffee, meat, I have resigned; vegetables are few and hard to have, except horrible cabbage, in which the Romans delight."

And the rain continued steadily to fall. "Pour, pour, pour again, dark as night . . . this atmosphere is so heavy, I seem to carry the weight of the world on my head and feel unfitted for every exertion."

The "orphan by my side" was indeed an orphan, for February began with a new source of depression—the death of Angelo's father. For the first time Margaret saw Angelo weep. What little defense he had against his elder brother Giuseppe was now removed. Worse, Giuseppe became the titular head of the family, with all its legal prerogatives. Uncle Abraham had been easy to combat, in comparison with the situation in which Angelo found himself. Now marriage to Margaret, with its necessity for a special papal dispensation, became unthinkable. Or even if the dispensation could be secured, Giuseppe would use it as an excuse to disinherit and drive Angelo out of the family.

Other lesser consequences were immediate. Angelo was evicted from his father's rooms in the palazzo. As he had no other place to go, he moved in with Angela on the first floor. Giuseppe seized all the furniture and household objects, the silver, the paintings, everything attachable, claiming they were his by right. As he lived elsewhere, he then rented the suite to an attorney. This was particularly disturbing to Angelo, for one of the rooms was the library. As a boy he had dreamed three times that a treasure lay behind a certain panel. After the third dream he had smashed the panel and found nothing. Now the attorney's sudden emergence in opulence, immediately after moving into the Palazzo Ossoli, convinced Angelo that the dream had been true. He felt all the more abandoned, all the more distressed at the irony of his poverty. In his loneliness he could turn to Margaret, and to Margaret alone. They clung to one another.

Though the Marchesa Arconati was uninformed of the pregnancy, she was well informed of Margaret's poverty. She wrote from Florence at the end of the first week of February, "I am very saddened at learning what you have suffered. Relax, I beg you, and put your spirit in repose about your affairs. To make my advice easier to take, I am sending you some money, which you can repay whenever you wish."

Ten days later the marchesa tried again. "On the 8th of this month I wrote to you, and later I sent you a book and a sum of money. I have received no response from you, no acknowledgement that what I sent came into your hands. I am uneasy . . . drop me a word which will reassure me . . . . We are continually in alarm for Milan, which is under a reign of terror. Adieu, my dear friend, write me or have someone write. Your affectionate Constance."

There was no reply.

18

Two months passed before she was able to summon her latent energy, despite her urgent need of funds, and begin to write again for the *Tribune*. "Now this long dark dream—to me the most idle and most suffering season of my life—seems past . . . . My health entirely gave way beneath the Roman winter. The rain was constant, commonly falling in torrents from the 16th of December to the 19th of March. Nothing could surpass the dirt, the gloom, the desolation of Rome . . . . I have had constant nervous headaches without strength to bear it, nightly fever, want of appetite. Some constitutions bear it better, but the complaint of weakness and extreme dejection of spirits is general among foreigners in the wet season."

If, to the public, she made an effort to excuse and generalize her depression, with her friends she was candid about her depression if not about her pregnancy—the root reason. In a letter concerning *Carnevale* she said, "In all the descriptions of the Roman Carnival, the fact has been omitted of daily rain. I felt, indeed, ashamed to perceive it, when no one else seemed to, whilst the open window caused me convulsive cough and headache. The carriages with their cargoes of happy women dressed in their ball costumes drove up and down, even in the pouring rain. The two handsome *contadine* who serve me took off their woolen gowns and sat five hours at a time in the street, in white cambric dresses and straw hats turned up with roses. I never saw anything like the merry good-humor of these people.

"I should always be ashamed to complain of anything here. But I had always looked forward to the Roman Carnival as a time when I could play too; and it even surpassed my expectations, with its exhuberant gayety and innocent frolic, but I was unable to take much part. The others threw flowers all day and went to masked balls all night; but I went out only once, in a carriage, and was more exhausted with the storm of flowers and sweet looks than I could be by a storm of hail. I went to the German Artists' Ball, where were some pretty costumes and beautiful music; and the Italian masked ball, where the interest lies in intrigue.

"I have scarcely gone to the galleries, damp and cold as tombs; or to the mouldy old splendor of churches—where, by the way, they are just now wailing over the theft of St. Andrew's head, for the sake of the jewels. It is quite a new era for this population to plunder the churches; but they are suffering terribly, and Pio's municipality does, as yet, nothing."

Margaret did not attempt to explain the apparent inconsistency between the *carnevale* gaiety of the people and their poverty—but in fact the poorest of all, the Trastevereni, like the Napolitani, were the gayest of all. Perhaps it was because they became forgetful of poverty; perhaps because they lived their lives from moment to moment, meal to meal, day to day, love to love, like pagans. In spite of misery and tyranny they laughed and played, and their high spirits almost drew Margaret out of the deep despair that had settled upon her. No Puritan had laughed and played this way since the beginning of the Reformation. For Margaret it would have been a triumph of life over Luther *and* Lucifer—but the release was denied her.

On Washington's birthday the Americans in Rome held their own prim little *carnevale,* with a poem from William Story, a speech by Margaret's old friend the Reverend Henry Hedge of Bangor, Maine, and other items. Margaret was too ill to attend. Hedge's presence, though he was a trusted friend, did exactly nothing to cheer her. If anything, she was afraid that he might divine the secret concealed under her flowing dress.

The gloom of Rome was pierced by one bright ray from Paris. "The news of the dethronement of Louis Philippe reached us just after the close of the Carnival," Margaret wrote for the *Tribune.* "It was just a year from my leaving Paris. I did not think, as I looked with such disgust on the empire of sham he had established in France, and saw the soul of the people imprisoned and held fast as in an iron vice, that it would burst its chains so soon."

The pleasure of this good news was shared by Adam Mickiewicz, who had come to Rome early in February to recruit a legion from the Poles living in exile. Margaret had found space for him in her small lodgings. Apparently Ossoli made no objection, for they shared Margaret's one evening out during *carnevale.* To Emerson, still in England, Margaret wrote, "Mickiewicz is with me here, and will remain some time. It was he that I wanted to see, more than any other person, in going back to Paris, and I have him much better here. France itself I should like to see [during the revolution], but remain undecided on account of my health, which has suffered so much this winter that I must make it the first object in moving for the summer. One physician thinks it will of itself revive, when once the rains have passed . . . . At present, I am not able to leave the fire, or exert myself at all."

Evidently she confided her secret to "brother Adam," as is clear from the letters he wrote her a month or two later. He must at the time have spoken in very much the same terms as the letters: "My dear, guard yourself from anxieties and melancholy reveries. Don't preoccupy yourself with the future pessimistically, and above all stop worrying. Think of the future with optimism." And, a trifle sharply: "I see little amelioration in your moral state. You are frightened at a very natural, very common ailment, and you exaggerate it in an extravagant manner. It depends on you whether you want to suffer more or less . . . . You can still regain your health and live robust and gay. Believe it."

She accepted his newest advice but slowly, improving and then worsening, backsliding like a true Puritan into a morass of guilt and self-abnegation. For a Puritan woman it was so difficult to believe that a baby was not simply and solely a punishment for her sexual joy, her sin. And so long as Margaret could not free herself of this conception, she could not recover.

There were other personal preoccupations, but none sufficient to change her emotional direction. Hurtfully, not from Caroline but from other sources came news of Caroline Sturgis's marriage, in December, to William Tappan of New York. Now suddenly Margaret must have felt estranged from Caroline as she thought of her as Mrs. Tappan, properly and legally married—someone she did not know, sleeping in a strange man's bed. Could Caroline have failed to write, or, as so often, was the letter lost? The question must have plagued her. It was evident that if only she could have told the truth to Caroline, as to Adam, she might have been purged of the guilt incubus—because to share it was to disperse it. She considered writing to Caroline, confessing; but as yet she was afraid.

All this must have been totally incomprehensible to Ossoli, who as an Italian nobleman would have seen nothing in the least unusual about conceiving an illegitimate child, with a woman on his own social level or any other. He was not preparing to abandon either mother or child, so why should the mother flagellate herself? True, they were not married. But Italian men had clandestine families and lived with the families for years, without the sacrament of matrimony. Angelo preferred matrimony, but if he could not have it, he was willing to take his woman—this particular woman—as his wife without it. No doubt his attitude seemed as strange to Margaret as her attitude seemed strange to him.

Only to political events did Margaret respond with a semblance of the old fire. Eagerly she watched every development in Rome and in Italy. The pope, responding to the object lesson implicit in the barricades of Paris, prepared for the proclamation of a constitution. He did not entrust the drafting to his new ministry, which included laymen, but to a special commission composed entirely of clerics. Thus authority over all ecclesiastical and "mixed" affairs was withheld from the newly elected chamber of deputies, and "the profession of the Catholic religion" was the "condition necessary for the enjoyment of political rights." The final decision on all new laws was allocated to the secret consistory of cardinals; and to the cardinals was reserved the right of veto, absolute and without appeal.

As in any theocratic state it was impossible to tell where religion left off and civil affairs began, confusion was inevitable in every aspect of administration. Only to the people did matters seem clear: They cheered the happy gift of any constitution at all. And, to their street cries of "Viva l'Italia," added "Death to the Jesuit, the friend of Austria."

Margaret was less easily gulled. She snorted in disdain: "He [the pope] acted wiselier than he intended; as for instance, three weeks after declaring he would not give a constitution, he gave it . . . a poor vamped up thing that will by and by have to give place to something more legitimate, but which served its purpose at the time as a declaration of rights for the people."

It was in Milan, not Rome, that the firecrackers first set off the powder keg. Late on March seventeenth it became known that Hungary was in revolt against the Austrians, that the Viennese themselves had risen against their feeble emperor (who immediately promised a constitution), and that the hated Prince Metternich had fled. And in Prussia an insurrection against King Friedrich Wilhelm IV had begun. Almost any one of these items would have been enough to pour the Milanese into the streets against their oppressors, but the combination was irresistible. Within five days Marshal Radetsky and fifteen thousand soldiers had been put to full flight by an unarmed citizenry, and a provisional government had been established.

At Venice, under the astute leadership of Daniele Manin, freshly sprung from prison, the Austrians were ejected and the

Republic of St. Mark proclaimed. The people of the duchies of Modena and Parma hissed away their princelings. Thus almost all of northern Italy momentarily had secured freedom. Its stability depended on the Piedmont ruler, King Carlo Alberto, who had a first-rate professional army, and on the pope, who could with a word unite all Italy to drive the Austrians across the Alps.

Margaret gave an eyewitness account of the mass reaction: "With indescribable rapture these tidings were received in Rome. Men were seen dancing, women weeping with joy along the street. The youth rushed to enroll themselves in regiments to go to the frontier. In the Colosseum their names were received . . . . I have seen the Austrian arms dragged through the streets of Rome and burned in the Piazza del Popolo. The Italians embraced one another, and cried, *Miracolo! Providenza!* The modern tribune Ciceruacchio fed the flames with faggots; Adam Mickiewicz, the great poet of Poland, long exiled from his country, looked on . . . . When the double-headed eagle was pulled down from above the lofty portal of the Palazzo Venezia, the people placed there in its stead one of white and gold, inscribed with ALTA ITALIA [northern Italy]."

Pius IX himself made a public declaration about the situation, taking an appropriately lofty tone and ignoring the acts of the people: "The events which these two months past have seen rush after one another in rapid sucession, are no human work. Woe to him who, in this wind, which shakes and tears up alike the lofty cedars and the humble shrubs, hears not the voice of God! Woe to human pride, if to the fault or merit of any man whatsoever it refer these wonderful changes, instead of adoring the mysterious designs of Providence." This too Margaret reported.

Whatever the mysterious designs of Providence, the Principessa Belgioioso took matters into her own hands. When King Ferdinando II so reluctantly had granted a constitution, she had gone at once to Naples to lend her talents to the movement against the Bourbons. When word of the events in Milan reached Naples, she promptly chartered a steamship and let it be known that she would accept volunteers to go to Lombardy to fight the Austrians. She was overwhelmed with takers, of all social classes. "Ten thousand Neapolitans were ready to follow me," she wrote, "but my steamer could carry only two hundred passengers. The whole population seemed to awake unexpectedly from a long lethargy, aroused by the sole incentives of war and devotion."

One evening at sunset the little ship puffed out of the Bay of Naples, surrounded by skiffs filled with cheering well-wishers. The principessa, the only woman on board other than her maids, stood among the arms piled on deck and waved the red, white, and green tricolor flag of the Italian nation yet to be born. The expedition anticipated by a dozen years Garibaldi's amazing "voyage of the thousand" from Genoa to Sicily. Of course Margaret was brimming with admiration. The principessa's adventure, Margaret commented in the *Tribune,* "showed her usual energy and truly princely heart." No reader could doubt that Margaret would have thrilled to be a part of the expedition, to be cheered in the streets of Milan, and eventually to be decimated by the phlegmatic but better-armed Austrian conscripts.

At the end of March Margaret wrote to kindly old William Henry Channing: "I have been engrossed, stunned almost, by the public events that have succeeded one another with such rapidity and grandeur. It is a time such as I always dreamed of, and for long secretly hoped to see. I rejoice to be in Europe at this time, and shall return possessed of a great history. Perhaps I shall be called on to act. At present I know not where to go, what to do. War is everywhere. I cannot leave Rome, and the men of Rome are marching every day into Lombardy. The citadel of Milan is in the hands of my friends, Guerriere, etc., but there may be need to spill much blood yet in Italy . . . . A glorious flame burns higher and higher in the heart of the nation."

It was the first specific mention of the great history-to-be; already it was gestating in her mind—helping to divert attention from her womb.

19

April was at hand. With Ossoli, Margaret attempted to resume their idyll of the autumn. They went by carriage to the sea, to Ostia, the ancient port of Rome, and to Castel Fusano, a terrain of rolling sand dunes, scrub oak, berry bushes, and pines, not unlike a terrain so familiar to Margaret at home—the bay side of Cape Cod. But the man beside her was unlike any she had ever known, and for at least a little while his presence gave her peace.

"A million birds sang," she wrote, "the woods teemed with blossoms; the sod grew green hourly over the graves of the mighty Past; the surf rushed in on a fair shore; the Tiber majestically retreated to carry inland her share from the treasures of the deep; the sea-breezes burnt my face, but revived my heart. I felt the calm of thought, the sublime hopes of the future, nature, man—so great, though so little—so dear, though incomplete."

Mickiewicz had gone, off to Florence with his squadron—furious exiles spurring their horses, clattering sabres, and shouting—to be received as "the Dante of Poland." And from

Florence, on to Milan, where he made contact with the Marchesa Arconati at Margaret's behest. Correspondence with the Marchesa was at last resumed. She was not offended that Margaret had not acknowledged her gift of money, saying only that she was very happy to have finally an explanation of "a mystery which had weighed upon my heart." Then she asked, chiding gently, why no friend had written to say "Margaret Fuller is sick, she cannot write."

In the north Mazzini ended seventeen years of exile, and as Margaret said, quoting Wordsworth's great man, returned "to see what he foresaw." He returned as the head of an influential party, publicly, and not as an underground revolutionary with a price on his head. He was welcomed, and to some extent flattered, by the provisional government of Milan, though the majority of its members were far from being Republicans in their sentiments. Obviously Piedmont's King Carlo Alberto, who had condemned him to death, viewed his return to Italy with mixed emotions. The king, who already had earned for himself the title of *Re Tentenna* (King Wobble), was an old-fashioned royalist, absolutist, and a religious mystic very much at the disposition of his confessor. While Mazzini was pressing for allied military action against the disorganized Austrians, the king hesitated, sniffing republicanism on every hand like the sulphurous fumes of the devil, with Mazzini himself playing the role. The king wanted to annex Lombardy to Piedmont, and then take action against the common enemy. Mazzini wanted action, and then a plebescite to choose between annexation or the establishment of a republic. Discord was the result. Meanwhile the precious sands slipped through the hourglass, as the Austrians regrouped and gathered reinforcements.

Mazzini had become for all Italy a great and contentious figure. The Marchesa Arconati Visconti and Adam Mickiewicz symbolized the contrasting points of view. On almost the same date they were writing Margaret their opinions, he as a guest in the marchesa's house. "There is an unbreachable wall between Mazzini and my group," said the marchesa. "He is too convinced to modify his opinions, and we believe that Mazzini and his party are the ruin of Italy." Said Mickiewicz: "I have seen Mazzini, the only man who has the political energy necessary for the moment. You have not deceived yourself on his account." Astonishingly, it was Margaret Fuller, political amateur, non-European, and passionate partisan of Mazzini, whose positive-negative insights outstripped them all. "Mazzini has a mind far in advance of his time in general, and his nation in particular . . . . And yet Mazzini sees not all: he aims at political emancipation; but he sees not, perhaps would deny, the bearing of some events which even now begin to work their way . . . . I allude to that of which the cry of Communism, the systems of Fourier, etc., are but forerunners." And while Margaret was writing for the *Tribune* this fundamental critique of Mazzini's republicanism as being all politics and no economics, Marx and Engels, in one of history's coincidences, were publishing *The Communist Manifesto*. The "specter haunting Europe" indeed had been let out of Pandora's capitalist box. And Margaret understood.

While the revolution in the north was momentarily marking time, in the south it moved in agitated jerks. The newly elected parliament of Sicily met in Palermo and proclaimed unanimously the deposition of the Bourbon dynasty from the throne of Sicily. Ferdinando II replied that the deposition was illegal, null and void, and began to deploy his armies and his fleet. In Naples massive demonstrations against the Jesuits illustrated the mood of the people. Street fighting broke out, which the king used as a pretext for a bloody coup d'etat on May 15 against the constitution and the newly elected chamber of deputies, employing his Swiss regiments to crush the poorly armed people. The plump king, puffing, wiped the sweat of temporary victory from his brow, reaffirmed his absolutism, and began to load his cannons for the next round. All the major developments were duly reported by Margaret, though she could not be bodily on the scene.

In Rome Margaret had not only eyewitness advantage but the advantage of "informed sources" of information—Mazzini's and Ossoli's friends. The pope's political position had become ever more contradictory: in the north, armed volunteer units of the papal forces were menacing the Catholic Austrian armies; in the south, ecclesiastical units of the papal forces were intriguing to support the tottering Catholic Bourbon throne. Among the pope's counselors, liberals and Austro-Jesuits strove for supremacy; those who would give a little in response to the people contended with those who would give nothing. For awhile the liberals had secured ascendancy, and the image of a progressive, reformist pope had been propagated to the world. But from the beginning of his reign Pius IX had been in fact unwilling to accede to the popular demands made upon him. Margaret increasingly drew the conclusion that the liberal Pius IX was a myth. It was the famous "Allocution" of the pope (April 29) that confirmed Margaret's opinion of his role—an opinion that placed her, as time has proved, in the front rank of political analysts.

In the *Tribune* she wrote of the pope: "The problem he had to solve was one of such difficulty that only one of those minds, the rare product of ages for the redemption of mankind, could be equal to its solution. The question that inevitably rose on seeing him was, 'Is he such a one?' The answer was immediately negative. But at the same time, he had such an aspect of true benevolence and piety that a hope arose that Heaven would act through him, and impel him to measures wise beyond his knowledge . . . . His name was in every form invoked as the chosen instrument of God to inspire Italy to throw off the oppressive yoke of the foreigner, and recover her rights in the civilized world.

"However, the Pope was seen to act with great blindness in the affair of the Jesuits. The other states of Italy drove them out by main force, resolved not to have in the midst of the war a foe and spy in the camp. Rome wished to do the same, but the Pope rose in their defence. He talked as if they were assailed as a *religious* body, when he could not fail, like everybody else, to be aware that they were dreaded and hated solely as agents of despotism. He demanded that they should be assailed only by legal means, when none such were available. The end was in half-measures, always the worst possible. He would not entirely yield, and the people not at all. The Order was ostensibly dissolved; but the great part of the Jesuits really remain here in disguise, a constant source of irritation and mischief.

" . . . Thus affairs went on from day to day . . . when the report that one of the Roman Civic Guard, a well-known artist engaged in the war in Lombardy, had been taken and hung by the Austrians as a brigand, roused the people . . . and they went to the Pope to demand that he should take a decisive stand, and declare war against the Austrians.

"The Pope summoned a consistory; the people waited anxiously . . . . The speech of the Pope declared that he had never had any thought of the great results which had followed his actions; that he had only intended local reforms, such as had previously been suggested by the potentates of Europe; that he regretted the *mis*use which had been made of his name; and wound up by lamenting over the war . . . which he would fain see hushed up, and its motives smoothed out and ironed over.

"A momentary stupefaction followed this astounding performance, succeeded by a passion of indignation, in which the words *traitor* and *imbecile* were associated with the name that had been so dear to his people. This again yielded to a settled grief: they felt that he was betrayed, but no traitor; timid and weak, but still a sovereign whom they adored, and a man who had brought them much good, which could not be quite destroyed by his wishing to disown it.

" . . . These events made indeed a crisis. The work begun by Napoleon is finished. There will never more be really a Pope, but only the effigy or simulacrum of one.

"I cannot repress my admiration at the gentleness, clearness, and good sense with which the Roman people acted under these most difficult circumstances. It was astonishing to see the clear understanding which animated the crowd as one man, and the decision with which they acted to effect their purpose. Wonderfully has this people been developed within a year!

" . . . The responsibility of events now lies wholly with the people, and that wave of thought which has begun to pervade them. Sovereigns and statesmen will go where they are carried."

Pio Nono's anxiety could be judged from the fact that the Castel Sant'Angelo—fortress refuge of the popes for more than a thousand years—was suddenly garrisoned with soldiers. Rumors spread that the castle's guns were turned against the people's quarters. Not since the ignominious flight of Clement VII to the shelter of the walls in 1527 had a pope revealed himself so timorous.

On these events the Marchesa Arconati Visconti also had her say—a rather surprising say: "I believe truly with Mickiewicz that the first man of Rome is Ciceruacchio," she wrote Margaret. "One is ungrateful toward Pius IX when one has no more need of him; yet he has spoken in his Allocution the language which he has always spoken when he had the freedom to do so. Only one interprets his words according to their seasonableness. His reign is finished but he is neither a traitor nor an apostate."

For once, with the political opinion of the aristocratic Marchesa Arconati Visconti, the plebian Margaret Fuller was totally in accord.

20

It was entirely in character for Margaret to draw conclusions
for America from all she had seen and heard in Italy. Gradually
she had come to the opinion that certain political constants
were the same in old Europe and new America—that the class
structures, for all their superficial differences, had much in
common.

In the *Tribune* she sounded a Fuller trumpet blast: "To you,
people of America, it may perhaps be given to look on and learn
in time for a preventive wisdom. You may learn the real meaning of the words FRATERNITY, EQUALITY: you may, despite the
apes of the past who strive to tutor you, learn the needs of a true
democracy. You may in time learn to reverence, learn to guard,
the true aristocracy of a nation, the only real nobles—the
LABORING CLASSES."

For her audience, whose minds were full of the Mexican War
and the discovery of gold in California, she played again and
again the same tune, but in different keys: "My friends write to
urge my return; they talk of our country as the land of the future. It is so, but that spirit which made it all it is of value in my

eyes, which gave all of hope with which I can sympathize for that future, is more alive here at present than in America. My country is at present spoiled by prosperity, stupid with the lust of gain, soiled by crime in its willing perpetuation of slavery, shamed by an unjust war, noble sentiment much forgotten even by individuals, the aims of politicians selfish or petty, the literature frivolous and venal. In Europe, amid the teachings of adversity, a nobler spirit is struggling—a spirit which cheers and animates mine . . . . Here things are before my eyes worth recording, and, if I cannot help this work, I would gladly be its historian."

Just as a decisive turning point had come in the history of Rome, so a decisive turning point had come in the history of Margaret's own life. Soon she must hide, or reveal her secret. Even under the loose bodice and flowing skirt of contemporary fashion, her girth was beginning to show. Separation from Ossoli was at hand, for he could not leave his post in the civic guard. They had a last fling together, a brief tour of the little towns in the hills near Rome—Mount Albano, where a great temple to Jupiter had stood; Subiaco, where the Emperor Nero once reveled in believable vice and unbelievable luxury; Tivoli, where the Renaissance fountains of the Villa d'Este still played by gravity, and the ruins of Hadrian's vast architectural complex, called a "villa," amazed the eye and saddened the heart. Perhaps they were looking for a suitable place for Margaret to hide, but these towns were too close to Rome, and attractions for tourists. In any case the tour was a last farewell, a leave-taking of history and of a certain phase of love.

Returning, the hazy Roman plain filled her eyes with melancholy. All seemed uncertain, all insecure. Letters from home were wellsprings of old emotions. Brother Eugene was married, and very happy after "a luscious honeymoon." Arthur was not content with his pastorate, as younger men than he were being called to more important pulpits. Early in March Emerson had written to his "dear compatriot, sister and friend" that "I mean yet to coax you into Mrs. Brown's little house opposite my gate."

Fear of revolution was thinning the attendance at his lectures, he said, and he had earned not so much as a pound. From London, at the end of April, he offered advice: "You are imprudent to stay there any longer. Can you not safely take the first steamer to Marseilles, come to Paris, & go home with me?"

She must have imagined the expression on Emerson's face had she met him in Paris bulging with child. "I should like to return with you," she replied, "but I have much to do and learn in Europe yet. I am deeply interested in this public drama, and wish to see it *played out*. Methinks I have *my part* therein, either as actor or historian." Of the private drama she said not a word, but there was the history again.

In a letter to "Aunt" Mary Rotch, at the end of May, she could not resist phrases approaching childish pathos and self-pity: "You must always love me, whatever I do. I depend on that . . . . I am now hoping in the silence and retirement of the country to write more at length on the subjects that have engaged my attention for some time back. But who knows! The disturbances of the times or an unfavorable state of my health may mar my purpose, as has happened before.

". . . I hear often from Waldo. He sees much, learns much always, but loves not Europe. There is no danger of the idle intimations of other minds altering his course, more than the moving star. He knows himself and his vocation. Goodbye, dear Aunt Mary. If I live, you will always hear from me now and then."

Into her letters crept an undertone of fatalism—the acceptance that she might soon die. But she never added "in childbirth." This was the curse of being an old maid pregnant—she had lost the intuitive feeling of physical immortality which characterizes the very young. She realized that in giving life her own might be taken.

She had been sending gifts to the people she had loved, trinkets only, things of trifling value, because she was desperately poor. To sister Ellen she sent a cameo, to Ellen's daughter Greta a little cross made of coral, and to her mother a small mosaic. Writing to her mother, she came as close to the truth as she dared: "If you were here, I would confide romantic chapters of my sad life."

Of all the members of her family only Richard was proving troublesome. She had commissioned him to sell what was left of her property, and pay two hundred dollars of her debt to the Springs. Now remained to her only six hundred dollars, with no immediate prospect of any income. Richard offered five hundred dollars, contributed by himself, Eugene, Arthur, and their mother, for her return trip to America. He proposed that she come to live with him, for at the age of twenty-three he had become disillusioned with women, and determined never to marry. She hedged with a gentle refusal. "I should like to live with you where Nature was beautiful . . . . But I have no idea you will be content without marrying, nor am I so selfish as to wish it." Nevertheless Richard persisted. "Dear and beautiful sister, your presence inspires others but your efforts for yourself have been as yet but fragmentary. My plan would be for you to concoct your own books and reap the harvest of your ripening." Now it became necessary for her reply to be more precise: "There are reasons why I cannot answer positively till the autumn . . . . There are circumstances and influences now at work in my life not likely to find their issue till then. If you still wish it, I think I shall be able to answer by October."

Had she been married to Ossoli at this time, it seems improbable that she would have replied to Richard with such a commitment—surely she would never have dreamed of leaving Ossoli to live with her brother Richard. As she prepared her flight from Rome, she wrote again to Richard, closing her letter on a note like someone preparing for death: ". . . I must not write any more. Only 3 days remain and I wish to write a letter to the *Tribune* and close up many others. This done, I shall probably go out of town for a time, the hire of my chamber being up. It is cheaper out of town and I need for a time exercise and freer air. The mountain air does me good; that of Rome is always heavy and I have too little appetite here: change does me good. Farewell, my dear Richard. Receive whatever I have written in the spirit you have always known in me. You know that, while I viewed you with the sympathy of a sister and acted towards you with the good-will of a parent, I always left you to yourself . . . . That you may lead a peaceful, aspiring, and generous life was ever and must ever be [word obscured] from the soul of your sister."

Scores of things remained to be done before she could leave. She took a bundle of papers to the painter Thomas Hicks, for transmission to her family if she should die. Among her last wishes was the statement: "I have wished to be natural and true, but the world was not in harmony with me—nothing came right for me. I think that the spirit that governs the universe must have in reserve for me a sphere where I can develop more freely and be happier."

Meanwhile, at her insistence, Angelo, not in uniform, had a daguerrotype made by the photographer Latilla. This she prepared to take with her in her wicker basket of treasures. There had been no time and no money for a miniature painting, nor were any of the Ossoli family portraits available to her. She packed, too, her already bulky collection of government documents, pamphlets, leaflets, posters, newspaper clippings and satirical cartoons. This was the raw material of the book-to-be.

A good-bye note to Costanza Arconati had to be written, as again she was derelict in corresponding. "This is my last day at Rome," she scribbled hastily on May 27. "I have been passing several days at Subiaco and Tivoli, and return to the country tomorrow. These scenes of natural beauty have filled my heart, and increased, if possible, my desire that the people who have this rich inheritance may no longer be deprived of its benefits by bad institutions . . . . An illumination took place last night, in honor of the 'Illustrious Gioberti.' He is received here with great triumph, his carriage followed with shuts of '*Viva Gioberti, morte ai Gesuiti!*' . . . I sit in my obscure corner and watch the progress of events. It is the position that pleases me best, and, I believe, the most favorable one. Everything confirms me in my radicalism; and, without any desire to hasten matters, indeed with surprise to see them rush so like a torrent, I seem to see them all tending to realize my own hopes."

The transcendental idealist had become a radical; the old maid, an impending mother. She might have added to her letter to Costanza the same postscript as to her just-completed *Tribune* dispatch: "Meanwhile the nightingales sing; every tree and plant is in flower, and the sun and moon shine as if paradise were already re-established on earth. I go to one of the villas to dream it is so, beneath the pale light of the stars."

It was to be her last letter to the *Tribune* for many months to come.

21

Remote from the haunts of tourists, the town of Aquila (Eagle) nestles among the high Apennine mountains of the forest region called the "Abruzzi." It was founded in the thirteenth century by the King of Sicily (and Naples) Federico Secondo ("Wonder of the World"), who was also the Holy Roman Emperor Friedrich II of Hohenstaufen. Its purpose was to serve as a border fortress against threatened and actual invasion of the kingdom by papal armies. Many times the tranquility of the town had been shattered by the clash of arms.

It was this site that Angelo and Margaret chose as her hideaway. Her presence in the town was carefully concealed from her American friends, most of whom thought she had gone to Subiaco. For an address she gave only the name of her banker in Rome, and no letters from America were sent to her direct. Angelo collected her mail, and forwarded it to her in packets. He accompanied her to Aquila, then returned hurriedly to Rome.

Margaret's first reaction to the village was almost ecstatic, so great had been her fear in Rome that her condition might be discovered. "I am in the midst of a theatre of glorious, snow-crowned mountains, whose pedestals are garlanded with the olive and mulberry, and along whose sides run bridle-paths, fringed with almond groves and vineyards. The valleys are yellow with saffron flowers; the grain fields enamelled with the brilliant blue corn-flower and red poppy. They are of intoxicating beauty, and like nothing in America. The old genius of Europe has so mellowed even the marbles here, that one cannot have the feeling of holy virgin loneliness, as in the New World. The spirits of the dead crowd me in most solitary places.

"Here and there, gleam churches or shrines. The little town, much ruined, lies on the slope of a hill, with the houses of the barons gone to decay, and unused churches, over whose arched portals are faded frescoes, with the open belfry, and stone wheel-windows, always so beautiful. Sweet little paths lead away through the fields to convents—one of the Passionists, another of Capuchins; and the draped figures of the monks, pacing up and down the hills, look very peaceful. In the churches still open, are pictures, not by great masters, but of quiet, domestic style, which please me much, especially one of the Virgin offering her breast to the child Jesus. There is often sweet music in these churches; they are dressed with fresh flowers, and the incense is not oppressive, so freely sweeps through them the mountain breeze."

The repetition of the word *virgin* seems to indicate that Margaret in fantasy was making that female identification with the Madonna, both humble and exalted, which had given the Madonna such preeminence among all the goddesses in the long pantheon of Italian history. If so, Margaret was rudely shaken by one of the first letters received in Aquila.

In the haste of her last-minute letter to Costanza Arconati from Rome, she had scribbled some ambiguous sentences. Now she had the marchesa's reply. "What mystery is there in your last lines? Yes, I am faithful and capable of sympathy without regard to the opinions of others—but what is this? Someone has told me that you had a lover in Rome, a Roman in the Civic

Guard. I did not wish to believe it, but your mysterious words make doubt enter my heart."

So the secret was out, at least among the Italians, and she was no virgin mother but merely a *ragazza-madre*—rather undignified, at the least, for one of her age to be called a "girl-mother." Had Mickiewicz been that "someone" who told? And if so—why? Perhaps he assumed that the marchesa already knew. Or perhaps he wished to shake Margaret into accepting the reality of her position, give her a foretaste of the gossip that was to come. She could only have been enormously distressed by the revelation in the marchesa's letter, perhaps alternately blushing with shame and defiantly defending her right to live according to her own nature. But alas, with no one in Aquila could she carry on a polemic, and all this tumultuous debate must have taken place in the silence of her mind. Perhaps she remembered the curious opposites she had once chosen to hang beside her writing desk at home: Andrea del Sarto's *Madonna,* and a *Silenus Holding the Infant Pan.*

On the heels of the marchesa's postal courier came another, bearing a letter from Emerson in Paris. He refused to accept as final her decision not to return with him. It was very upsetting that he should be so insistent: "I go to London tomorrow . . . . You will not wait but will come to London immediately and sail home with me! Write immediately on receiving this . . . . They write me the most amiable letters from home. Elizabeth's [Hoar] last letter I am half tempted to send you as a leaf from Concord woods. Lidian and the children send me almost weekly all the chat of the nursery. Henry Thoreau is there."

If homesickness had ever assailed her in Italy, it assailed her now. Alone, periodically ill, nearly penniless, pregnant, unmarried, and for all practical purposes jobless, the question before her was: What had Italy to offer, other than pain and disgrace? Death alone could now change the situation. Otherwise, she must wait for nature to relieve her of the physical burden she was carrying. Only then could she begin to exercise choice. She could then, perhaps, if she wished, go back to America—back to New York and the *Tribune,* back to Boston and the "Conversations," back to Concord and Emerson's transcendentalism.

None was forward; all were backward. Now, if ever, she might well ask: Transcendentalism—what did it mean? The truth was that no one really knew. The transcendentalists themselves could not agree. Its definition varied according to the definer. It lacked precision. It was elastic according to the wishes of the wisher. The transcendentalists could not even accept totally the definition offered in the *Dial* by their high priest, Emerson: "What is popularly called Transcendentalism among us, is Idealism . . . . The materialist insists on facts, on history, on the force of circumstances and the animal wants of man; the idealist on the power of Thought and of Will, on inspiration, on miracle, on individual culture . . . . Mind is the only reality, of which men and all other natures are better or worse reflectors. Nature, literature, history, are only subjective phenomena . . . . The Transcendentalist adopts the whole connection of spiritual doctrine. He believes in miracles, in the perpetual openness of the human mind to new influx of light and power; he believes in inspiration, and in ecstasy."

If Emerson was, as he said, "A transparent eyeball," he should also, as he said, "see all." He claimed that "the currents of the Universal Being circulate through me." Yet he did not see or understand the profound turbulence that was shaking all Europe and would one day shake the world. He felt only that it was "imprudent" to expose oneself to these tremendous currents of history which were so clear to Margaret's own Universal Eye. The history through which she and Ossoli were living seemed unlike a subjective phenomenon—though perhaps if she were five thousand miles away it would seem less real, and perhaps she herself would be more objective. Indeed she had felt inspiration and also ecstasy, but the result of the latter was, as Mickiewicz had said, a very natural phenomenon, which had recurred some billions of times. And the miracle that might save her steadfastly refused to occur.

Writing again to Emerson, she spoke of her spiritual experiences of earlier days and hinted at the way she had changed.

"Those were glorious hours, and angels certainly visited me; but there must have been too much earth—too much taint of weakness and folly, so that baptism did not suffice. I know now those same things, but at present they are words, not living spells."

With Costanza Arconati she returned to politics, the subject that now primarily interested her, ignoring the unsettling letter and carefully avoiding her private condition. "I am no bigoted Republican, yet I think that form of government will eventually pervade the civilized world. Italy may not be ripe for it yet, but I doubt if she finds peace earlier."

In a letter home she was more candid: "I am as ardent a Socialist as W. Channing himself—that is to say as firm a believer in the next form Society must take to remedy its ills."

It meant, in essence, that she was prepared to part company permanently with Emerson. Years ago he had taken his stand, when the Transcendental Club split over George Ripley's "socialistic" experiment in communal living at Brook Farm. Said Emerson: "I am not bitten by this madness of Socialism. I urge the sacredness of private integrity, the paramount duty of Self-Reliance." It was obvious now that Emerson—for all his scorn of money-grubbing merchants, tight-fisted bankers, slave drivers, insatiable land grabbers, exploitive manufacturers— spoke for a raw and expanding frontier country where the virtues of private initiative and self-reliance had real meaning. But in Europe, as feudalism died, capitalism had been born, and the historical context of its rise was vastly different from America. Socialism would not develp first in virginal America, but in exhausted Europe, where the structure of society and the conflict of interests more forcefully demanded it. Margaret was preparing to write her history on a new level, interweaving politics and economics—a European history, seen through fresh, analytical, American eyes.

All the same, to Emerson she confessed that she had passed far from her native orientation: "I never see any English or Americans, and now think wholly in Italian." And to Costanza she explained: "I am here, in a lonely mountain home, writing the narrative of my European experience. To this I devote a great part of the day. Three or four hours I pass in the open air, on donkey or on foot . . . . Apply as I may, it will take three months, at least, to finish my book. It grows upon me."

And, like the book, the child grew within her. She was paraphrasing *book* with *babe,* for it was due in three months' time.

22

To Angelo she wrote every third day, in accord with the schedule of the post, and he to her. She addressed her letters properly to "Il Nobiluomo [the Nobleman] Signor Marchese Giovanni Angelo Ossoli." But he in reply addressed his letters merely to the "Signora M. Ossoli." Had they been married, he would have written the name "Signora Marchesa Margherita Ossoli."

Astonishingly—or perhaps not so astonishingly—Margaret's handwriting changed as she wrote in Italian to Angelo. When she wrote not of problems but of love, the hurried, tight, parallel lines of her English script gave way to rounded, softer, slower characters, which seemed almost to have been formed by a different personality.

At first she and Angelo used the rather formal salutations, *Cara Amica* and *Caro Amico.* In closing, each would say, "Your affectionate friend"—with Angelo almost always signing his full name or his full initials. Gradually the salutations changed to "My Dear," then to "My Dearest," then to "Beloved." In closing, each became simply "Yours," in the familiar form, though frequently with "I hug you and kiss you." Absence had made each realize anew the other's worth.

Margaret's letters to Angelo Ossoli had nothing in common with the rarefied romanticism of her letters to James Nathan. She was of course hampered by writing in a non-native language, which she had by no means mastered; but the abstractions disappeared, the soulful ambiguities were no more. True, she wrote as a lover, but along with the love went practical details of health and finance, travel and politics. Very careful were the efforts to elude or confuse the eye of the censor. Margaret followed the pattern Ossoli set for her when he wrote such information and instructions as: "I met the Hungarian and the Priest, and they send their regards. He [the priest] doesn't want to go back to Naples . . . . Always inspect carefully the newspapers I send you, for it's easy to enclose something in them."

Ossoli's first letter (8 June 1848), after leaving Margaret in Aquila, was typical of his frequent brief correspondence, though at times he wrote at great length. "My Dear Friend—I arrived in Rome this morning at 7, after having spent two entire nights in travel, which left me very tired. The trip from Aquila to Rieti was quite eventful. When I am able to come to you I will tell you all that happened and how we proceeded to Rieti, where we arrived at 3 in the morning—but I was much pleased to find that also arriving was the celebrated Romeo [probably a cover name] of Naples, whom the people of Rieti welcomed very warmly. I stayed a long time at his house, where I had luncheon, and it was a great pleasure to get to know the famous man in person . . . . I hope you are well and take heart, and that the small apartment suits your needs and you are happy. I embrace you lovingly and send you a kiss. Your affectionate friend, G. A. Ossoli. PS—Everything is calm in Rome. From the papers, you will see how affairs in Naples are going."

A week later he was writing: "This morning Rome is in great agitation because of rumors of the surrender of Vicenza to the Austrians by General Durando. This news has caused groups to assemble on the Corso to await more official reports. Twice the post has come without any letter from you. I don't understand your silence since you are aware of the fact that I am always anxious to hear from you. Conduct yourself accordingly . . . . I salute you, and believe me always yours, G.A.O."

Immediately Margaret replied: "This· morning I received your letter, my love, but I am sorry that you don't write of yourself. I will write no more if you act this way. I want news of *you.* Otherwise I wrote you three times last week. It's not my fault if you don't hear from me—it's the fault of this accursed postal service which seems to torment us. I have the newspapers, but not the medicine as yet; nevertheless I thank you very much . . . . I have decided that it is finally necessary to write about the money question . . . . At present I am unable. I was very ill last night. But don't be disturbed by this; I think it has passed, but today am too weak to write more than is necessary. I embrace you with unchanged affections. Yours, M."

Angelo had chosen for her as servants two young women, Giuditta and Maria Bernani, who apparently were family retainers or dependent on him in some way. Their function was to care for Margaret and for the baby when it arrived. But from the very first days friction developed between Margaret and Giuditta, and Margaret implied in a letter to Angelo that Giuditta caused problems. She was always imposing herself: dreaming that money would arrive for her from a mysterious source, fretting because she heard nothing from a former lover, weeping hysterically over an old man's death. Margaret expressed the hope that she would become more tranquil.

Angelo answered that he was pleased to hear "that Giuditta has learned how you think, so you will be more content during these months of solitude. They will be shorter. Meanwhile, try to be courageous, thereby making me happier. You can imagine how sad I am, aware that I cannot be near you my dear to take care of all your needs. I hope on the first of the coming month to come to your arms for a day. Keep this in mind when writing me. My affairs are going as before. Here the weather is good but very hot. I salute you and embrace you an infinite number of times. Affectionately, G.A.O."

At this point Margaret received a pressing invitation from

Emelyn Story to come to Sorrento for a visit. William had leased a commodious villa, and had drawn a circle of friends into a kind of court. Margaret replied that she must remain in the mountains and devote all her energies to her book, but "perhaps I may join you in some place for the autumn." After sharing gossip and news, Margaret complained, "From my family no letter for two months!"

Increasingly, except for Ossoli and now infrequent letters from home, she seemed abandoned by the world. She therefore concentrated all her emotions in her communications with Angelo. Toward the end of June he sent her a large packet of newspapers, and she replied at once that she had found his secret note hidden in the pages of *Epoca*.

"A week has passed since I last heard from you, but I am resolved to let it bother me no longer. I yearn to see you immediately. It is impossible for me to express my desire to have you once again at my side . . . . If it is convenient for you, I wish you would go to Lowe in the Piazza di Spagna and see if they have a bottle of their *best* Eau de Cologne (priced 5 paoli). Addio, *caro mio*. I await your coming with great joy. If only it were possible to remain closer to you . . . because, apart from the health-giving air and the security, I don't like this place at all."

This letter did not reach Angelo until after his visit to Aquila, along with another dated three days earlier. It was evident that their mail was being delayed by the censor. Angelo's letters became, if anything, more cautious. His assent to Margaret's idea of changing hideouts was indicated in his report of arriving in Rome after a fatiguing trip. "If things are not going well for you in Aquila, I urge you to consider moving to Rieti at once. It may be easy to find adequate lodgings for you."

But Margaret deferred the decision to leave Aquila, and commented merely, "Your visit, though too short, did me much good. I am calmer, apart from having frequent toothaches. The midwife says that one must have patience, and wait, and suffer for now these things."

It was at about this time that the papers were full of the landing of Giuseppe Garibaldi at Nizza (Nice), his birthplace and still Italian soil. He returned (June 21) from South America with a band of his already famous "Italian Legion." He was forty and had amassed twelve years of unmatched experience in guerrilla warfare in Uruguay during fourteen years of political exile. He, like Mazzini, had been condemned to death for participating in Mazzini's abortive 1834 revolt against the absolute monarchy of Savoy. He had been greatly influenced by Mazzini's "Young Italy" movement; he joined and with total willingness risked his life. As a sailor and son of a sailor it was natural that he should enlist in the Piedmontese fleet. This he did with the sole object of fomenting rebellion. When the revolt failed, he jumped ship, and after a day or two read the sentence on his head. Now, home at last, he offered his services to King Carlo Alberto to help drive the Austrians from Italy. He was curtly rebuffed as a Republican, and was able to fight only because the provisional government of Milan gave him a post in its hastily organized forces.

Margaret, for all the acuteness of her political judgment, was much too busy with her own affairs to analyze or even recognize the political significance of this event. Or perhaps, unlike the Italians, she was not aware of Garibaldi's exploits in South America—though Mazzini's organization had carefully fostered from the very beginning the Garibaldi legend, and she should have known.

Toward mid-July came word from her family. "They are fine," she wrote Angelo, "but the letters made me cry, by begging my return. They were not letters enclosing money, so now it would be well if I could have the 200 francs from Greene & Co., Paris. If that is not possible, and I don't receive the other bank draft within a few days, I shall write to some friends. More soldiers [Bourbon] arrive, and people say that a great many are quartered in the Città Ducale. It's uncertain whether I may be forced to flee from here and go to Rieti. I ask every day, but I hear nothing sure." Two days later she reported that the soldiers "had picked out six persons from the village and imprisoned them in the castle, and disarmed the local guard."

A week later she was still unable to make up her mind about moving to Rieti, and no news had been received from the banker; but in spite of frequent headaches she was thinking politically again. "This is certainly a terrible time that Rome is going through. I can't imagine the end. The deplorable weakness of the Pope has done Italy more harm than the King of Naples' treason."

Then she passed on to an item which was to produce a totally unexpected reaction in Ossoli. "By accident I met the Marchesi di Torres, two brothers who are the most important signori here. It was not very prudent for several reasons, but now the thing is done. If I wish to leave, I shall ask their advice."

This incident she afterward described: "I made one of those accidental acquaintances . . . which may be called romantic: two brothers, elderly men, the last of a very noble family; formerly lords of many castles and still of more than one; both unmarried, men of great polish and culture. None of the consequences ensued that would in romances. They did not in any way adopt me, nor give me caskets of diamonds, nor any of their pictures, nor their rich cabinets, nor miniatures on agate, nor carvings in wood and ivory. They only showed me their things, and their family archives of more than a hundred volumes, manuscript letters from Tasso, and the like. With comments and legendary lore enough to furnish Cooper or Walter Scott with a thousand romances, they enriched me." But for all Margaret's pleasure, the contact truly was not very prudent, because the world of the aristocracy was small, and rumors made rapid headway within it.

Nor had she made herself clear in her note to Angelo. Misunderstanding her use of the word *prudente,* he responded vigorously in a typically Italian manner: "It disturbed me to learn that these Marchesi whom you met are not at all prudent . . . . I am anxious to know in what way they were not prudent? I suppose it was towards Maria or Giuditta—and I dare not think otherwise. If this is not the case, let me know precisely what happened, and I will come immediately to meet these nobles of Aquila."

Margaret's reply is lost.

On July 27 she was writing, "It's my plan, dear, to move to Rieti on Saturday. I'll write you as soon as I arrive there, enclosing an order on my banker, who has confirmed that I can get the money I need from him. You take this, and I hope that you will be able to come to me on *Saturday August 5th,* and stay two or three days. I shall go to the Rienzi locanda [lodging house] in Rieti, and look for an apartment from there. I won't write any more, though I'm not ill, but because writing tires me. I'll tell you everything when I see you."

The two months of isolation in Aquila had proved more than Margaret could endure. In contrast, Rieti seemed like a suburb of Rome. Later, in a letter to Caroline Sturgis Tappan, she described her new locale: "Rieti—not only an old classic town of Italy, but one founded by what are now called the aborigines— is a hive of very ancient dwellings with soft-colored red-brown roofs, a citadel and several towers. It is in a plain twelve miles in diameter one way, not much less the other, entirely encircled with mountains. Small villas and hermitages gleam here and there on the lower slopes. The plain is almost the richest in Italy and full of vineyards. Rieti is near the foot of the hills on one side, and the rapid Velino makes almost the circuit of its walls."

She found an attractive apartment overlooking the river with its Roman bridge. The Via Salaria was the road that led on to Rome. She could watch the swallows dart over the tile rooftops, dipping and diving, just as she had once described her feminine habit of "ducking, diving, or flying for truth." After a fortnight she wrote her brother Richard from the vague "mountains of Southern Italy," giving some details of her lodging: "The house is upon a rapid river. I occupy its upper apartment, containing a chamber for my servant, a little room for eating, and mine—a large brick-paved room of the simplest finish and furniture, but with a loggia upon the river with its whispering willows. This loggia, a wooden terrace, is long enough for my evening walk. On these glorious moonlight nights I pass many hours there, uninterrupted by a sound except the rush of the stream and occasionally a soft bell from a convent . . . . I never in my life had a room I liked as I do this." But to Caroline she confessed that the loggia was a place "where I walked most of the night, for I could not sleep at all in those months. I do not know how I lived."

With Richard it was also necessary to discuss the perennial problem of money, for no word from her mother had been received in nearly four months. "Now I do not know what will become of me if I do not in the course of September receive money either from you or Mr. G. I shall not have means to leave Italy nor even to return to Rome, if indeed I could still have food and lodging here . . . . As to Mr. Greeley, he shows no disposition to further my plans. Liberality on the part of the *Tribune* would have made my path easy . . . . I trusted for the expenses of the summer to a remittance from Mr. Greeley, which up to now has never arrived."

She had in fact done nothing for the *Tribune,* probably because of Greeley's suddenly fatuous attitude. Perhaps he had heard rumors about Margaret's way of life that displeased him. In any case, the abrupt termination of her newspaper correspondence, without public explanation, must have seemed strange to friends and readers alike—and set the stage for later scandal.

23

To Angelo she wrote immediately, saying that she had reached Rieti, and urging him to come to her at once. Henceforth they wrote each other almost every day. His hours were now even more occupied than before, as he had found some sort of estate-administration job, evidently part-time, with his uncle. And it paid little, for he was invariably short of cash. Once again Margaret gave instructions to him about the bank, and added: "Take some money for your trip."

While Margaret was moving, the opposing Austrian and Piedmontese armies in the north went into action. Due to the vacillation of King Carlo Alberto and the incompetence of his generals, the Austrians under Radetsky defeated the Italians, and forced the king to retreat to Milan.

Angelo, already aware that Margaret was on the way to Rieti, wrote in considerable excitement on the first of August: "Here in Rome, late on Sunday the 30th, a bulletin was published on the war, giving news of the victory of Carlo Alberto—information more detailed than in the newspapers. The news caused great joy in Rome. At nightime the masses gathered and went to the Minister to enquire if this rumor was true, and he confirmed it. Then the people went to the Campidoglio to ring the great bell (it was midnight). All the other bells in the churches rang and rifles were fired off continuously, lasting until daybreak."

Margaret was appropriately skeptical of the victory attributed to King Carlo Alberto, which was in fact a grave defeat. She replied at once, saying that she was pleased to hear of a victory, "but I am surprised that *Epoca* dated 31st July doesn't speak of the bulletin. I am anxiously awaiting another newspaper." Then, after more bank directions—for by now she was urgently in need of money—she returned to her uppermost thought. "Don't fail me on Sunday. You should arrive early and I will see the diligence as it crosses the bridge. I am staying in the house of a certain Papetti, in Bondara Street. This man is the Bishop's chancellor. If you don't find me, ask for the Campana Hotel, and come quickly to your loving Margherita."

Happily, all went according to plan. But the happiness was of short duration, for the first news from Rome after Angelo's return cast them both into despair. Angelo's letter (August 11) was so short and tightly phrased as to be almost telegraphic: "C.A. [Cara Amica] I arrived in Rome at 6 A.M. The first news I received gave the impression that all was calm; then a messenger came with news of fighting in Bologna. The same in Milan for the last three days. I find that in Rome the people are ready to move immediately. You will learn the details shortly. I am fine and hope you are the same. Addio. G.A.O."

The Austrians, scorning the flabbiness of the pope, had provocatively attacked Bologna, though it was within the papal domains, and were driven back only because the infuriated people dreaded the Austrian eagle more than the papal tiara. The Milanese, however, were given no such chance to defend themselves, for on August fifth King Carlo Alberto delivered the city to the Austrians, negating the Milanese triumph so painfully won in their famous Five Days of street fighting. The despairing masses would have assassinated the king had they been able to reach him. The royal failures, contrasted with the Republican successes, reduced the prestige of the House of

Savoy to the pit, and raised Mazzini and his party to the heights. Only Venice still held out against the invader—Venice, and Garibaldi, who fought with a handful of followers (Mazzini carried his battle flag) until driven across the Swiss border.

But the fate of Bologna remained uncertain. Not only the chanceries of Europe but the people of Rome waited suspensefully to see what the pope would do. From Angelo again came a letter-telegram: "I fear that it will be difficult for us to see each other, because Pio IX today wants all the Civic Guard to go to the frontiers to defend Bologna. I hope to slip away to visit and embrace you once more, but I can't tell you anything definite. I enclose another newspaper so that you can keep up with the latest news of Bologna and Milan."

For Margaret this was the last blow. Nevertheless she remained calm, concealing the true extent of her anxiety. "It appears incredible how everything goes against us," she wrote (Sunday, August 13). "That Bologna has resisted is good, but this makes probable your departure—at just this moment! But do what is best for you, love. I don't really believe that the pope will decide to send the guard, but if this occurs and you feel it necessary to leave for your honor, I shall be able to take care of myself. Your visit did me good, and I was more tranquil afterwards. At least we managed to spend a few peaceful hours together—even if all has ended now. Addio, love. I embrace you always and pray for your welfare."

From Rome came a barely coherent letter even more disturbing than Angelo's initial note that the pope might muster the civic guard: "My present state is the most deplorable it would be possible to find, because I am engaged in an extraordinary self-conflict. Ah! if only you were not in such a condition I could be more decisive, but at this time I can't leave you alone, I can't go away from you, my dear love. Oh, how cruel is my destiny! In this sort of emergency, it is true my friends do not counsel me to leave, always hoping for me a better fortune. Therefore I must keep on hoping, while staying among my hated brothers, when by leaving I could get them out of my sight. The heart cannot resolve one's duty. From your dear last of the 13th I well understand how ready you are to make sacrifices for me, and I am immensely grateful for this, but I can decide nothing as yet."

Stunned, Margaret replied soberly: "On our behalf, my love, I will be very grateful if you are not obliged to depart. But oh! How unworthy a Pope! He now seems a man without a heart; and this traitor Carlo Alberto—they will be damned for centuries to come . . . . I see in the paper that the Pope is delaying the troops' departure. He is behaving as I expected, and I would like very much for you not to volunteer again. Soon these matters will be more certain; you will be able to find a more advantageous solution than at the moment. See if you can get details of Milan—wouldn't it be possible at the Caffè delle Belle Arti? I am terribly sorry about our dear friends; how they must be suffering now. I also am thinking much of you. I hope that you are less tormented. If we were together it would be a consolation, though everything is going badly now. But it's impossible to continue so always, always. Goodby my love. I am sorry that we must pass so many days until you come; but I am glad I have the small portrait, which I look at often."

She waited eagerly for his reply, which was delayed by the *Ferragosto* holiday, and hearing nothing, she penned a brief note which stressed the lines: "I only want to hear from you always and to see you again."

On the same day his laconic note was noncommital, saying merely "I am pleased to hear that you are in good health; but I would have been more pleased to learn that you are freed of your burden."

Now even more agitated, she decided on another appeal: "My love, I feel for you and your problems, but don't think I am able to advise you wisely. However, I do think this is a bad moment to take up arms unless your duty or honor compels you. The Pope is so cold, his ministers so indecisive, that nothing will be done well or successfully. Since it is hoped that France and England will intervene, it is not at all certain that the war will continue. If it doesn't go on, you would leave Rome and your job at your uncle's for nothing. If possible, wait a few weeks. But the public state of affairs and mine will be decided by then, and you will be in a better position to make a decision. I will say no more and will leave to your judgment what course of action to take. Only one thing—if you go, come here first. We must see each other one more time. I am sorry not to give you particular news of myself, but I am still the same and am still waiting. I had a bad night and have a headache this morning. I had a nosebleed, and it is difficult for me to write. Don't ask your uncle's permission, if it is so trying. We can take care of things without it."

Angelo's reply was immediate, but avoided a commitment: "I received this morning your dear letter . . . . The banker sent a message that the documents didn't come, because Mazzini had escaped from Milan. I am very disturbed at hearing you had such a bad night. But what can we do? One must suffer, and I hope you will always be courageous. I will be waiting for a sign to come straight into your arms, before they deprive us of even this pleasure . . . . Meanwhile I salute you and believe me am always yours."

Probably without Angelo's letter yet in hand, she wrote the next day (August 20), which was Sunday, concealing the depth of her disappointment: "I expected you a little this morning, and had your coffee ready. But I think you are right to wait. If you have no objections, come next Saturday night. My nights become more and more disturbed, and this morning it was necessary to bleed me; now I feel better but weak and unable to write anything more than that I am always your loving M."

The old dominant and commanding Margaret had completely disappeared. In a postscript she included another order to the banker, as she was not sure that she could write many days more. Then the letter concluded, "I hug you."

Angelo still parried the central problem, the question of his departure for the war. "I am very sorry not to have been there for breakfast," he replied, "but I am waiting for a sign from you to come immediately . . . . You say that it is difficult for you to write and I quite understand; but when you feel tired, ask the owner of the house to write, if nothing else, a short description of your health. This would much relieve me, but please put your seal on the letter with your ring. That is enough for me."

Then, abruptly, came the precise word from Angelo that Margaret so fearfully had awaited: "As concerns the departure of the Civic Guard, popular feeling has cooled down considerably. The Guard was summoned to Monte Cavallo on Sunday, and the general expectation was that the Pope would speak in favor of the defense of his State and arouse the people to this end. But, after giving the Benediction and signaling the people to rise, he made only the following statement: 'At present I have nothing to tell you except that I can repeat the Holy Benediction.' Then the people left in a cold and sad mood, angry and disappointed at not having received encouragement. Therefore I shall not march from Rome unless conditions change. So I hope to see you again on Saturday. Among those who had offered to go, many have decided against it; but I am grateful for what you wrote me."

In the wisdom of her love-induced strategy, Margaret did not labor the point. She passed over Angelo's crisis, and dwelt on the importance of his presence at the birth of his child. She was better, she said, but " . . . we must wait some more. Wait!! How boring always . . . . If I were sure of being all right, I would want very much to pass through this trial before your arrival. But—when I think that I could die alone, without being able to touch a dear hand, I want to wait some more."

Next day he replied in his normal tone: "How happy I am at receiving news of your dear self so often, and to be able to find consolation in hearing that you feel a bit better. I tried to go to the Caffè delle Belle Arti to learn something about Milan. But . . . at said Caffè, when they see persons who don't usually go there, one is very likely to receive some insults instead of information. I have never frequented the Caffè in question . . . . I hug you and give you a kiss."

On the twenty-fifth Margaret again displayed anxiety: "My love, I received this morning your letter of Wednesday. You don't say whether you are coming Saturday evening or not, but I certainly hope so. I couldn't in any case wait any longer, if it hadn't been necessary for your affairs . . . there is a beautiful place near here where we can go together, if I am able, when you come. I will expect you on Sunday and have your coffee ready once again."

On the same day he was writing, "Dear—Tomorrow I leave Rome, and I hope to have you in my arms Sunday . . . . Addio until then."

He remained at her side until, on Tuesday, September 5, a boy was born. The birth was difficult. The parents named the baby Angelo Eugenio Filippo Ossoli. The father was twenty-seven years old, the mother thirty-eight. The future of their child seemed anything but promising.

24

The unwanted baby proved to be the true alchemist in Margaret's life. From the moment she first held him in her arms, and felt him snuffling toward her breast, the glow of the Italian Madonnas suffused her face. She experienced the full emotion of motherhood, the unique emotion no male could ever feel, the envied emotion she had so wanted and then so feared. Gradually fear gave way to love, and pain to delight. Afterward, people remarked on the change in her expression, and the rich new warmth in her personality. The lover as lover had not proved enough; his gift to her had completed the transformation.

Much later she wrote to her sister Ellen: "The great novelty, the immense gain, to me, is my relation with my child. I thought the mother's heart lived in me before, but it did not—I knew nothing about it. Yet before his birth I dreaded it. I thought I should not survive; but if I did and my child did, was I not cruel to bring another into this terrible world? I could not at that time get any other view. When he was born, that deep melancholy changed at once into rapture, but did not last long. Then came the prudential motherhood . . . . I became a coward . . . . I seemed wicked to have brought the little tender thing into the midst of cares and perplexities we had not feared in the least for ourselves."

On the evening of the baby's birth Margaret was left alone by her lover. But the baby remained, a part of him, cuddled against her. For the moment she forgot or ignored all that was going on in the world outside, and lived serenely in the microcosm of herself and her child. Angelo continued to write about politics, but for awhile she could write only about the marvel in her arms. It was in this week of the baby's birth that King Ferdinando II earned his new title, "King Bomba," by bombarding for six days without mercy the civilian population of Messina. For Margaret, however, Messina seemed remote as the city of Boston.

She and Ossoli took to a new mode of address, calling each other "Dear Consort." Thus they implied marriage, without using the specific Italian words for husband (*marito*) and wife (*moglie*). And a kind of marital coziness developed in their letters as they discussed the baby, his appearance, his ways.

On the day after the baby's birth Angelo reported hurriedly that he had been late reaching Rome and that he had forgotten what to do with the letter she had given him, adding: "I am well, but you can imagine in what a state at having left you in such a condition. I beg you to take care of yourself and our dear little boy." On the seventh Margaret dictated her first note, managing only to sign it herself. "Dear Consort, I am well, better than I had hoped. The child is well too, though he still cries much. I hope he will be calmer when you come. I want you to be at rest about me, and I will give you news, writing often and soon."

"Dear Consort," Angelo replied, "I am very happy to hear of your good health and that of our dear child. If he cries, it's only his habit. I hope he will calm down as he grows up. I'll send you the Roman paper No. 23 when you let me know you are more able to take pleasure in reading—soon, I hope . . . . While I am writing, the Pope has gone to the sanctuary for his service as usual, but what silence in the streets where he passed! The Civic

Guard had been called to do the honors, but few were there, which shows clearly they are not following the orders received . . . . Hugging you and the dear child sincerely, give him a kiss from me."

Next day from Margaret came the unsettling news that she had developed a fever and the baby was rejecting her milk. Later she told Caroline Tappan that the fever was due to the evil actions of the people around her, and she became seriously upset —but she did not detail the actions. To Angelo she commented merely, "Today I have to send Giuditta to Rome. She can't do anything more now." By the following day she was too ill to write, and was forced to resume dictation: "Now I am better and much calmer since I made Giuditta leave. I told her not to look for you in Rome because I don't want anything more to do with her . . . . I am enjoying seeing you reflected in our dear boy, who is always near me, and giving him a kiss from you."

A wet nurse was found, and this, like the fever, Angelo dismissed as not unusual; but about the maid he was curious: "I am sorry to hear about Giuditta, and that you had to deal with such a woman. I am anxious to know some particulars on the subject of Giuditta. I am very pleased that our child is so handsome; it consoles me greatly."

Angelo was not in the least vain about his good looks; he merely took for granted that if the baby reflected him, it would be handsome. But he was denied seeing his child, for as sergeant he was assigned two special stints of guard duty, and was unable to return to Rieti before October. He sent Margaret new batches of newspapers, and urged her to resume her interest in public events. She thanked him and said that she was eagerly waiting to hear more. But the subject of her greatest attention was the fact that the wet nurse's child was ill, and this might prove a threat to the new baby. Then, in a concession to the censorship, she said, "I am leaving this letter open, so that it will be more certain to reach you."

Angelo continued to talk politics, but she replied: "The wet nurse's child is better, and I am relieved. One must have courage, but it is a big thing staying alone and ignorant with a baby in the first days of its life. When he is a month old I will feel more relaxed; then he will be better able to withstand the changes he will have to undergo. Now he is beginning to sleep well, and he is very handsome for his age. Everyone around here, without knowing what name I thought of giving him, called him Angiolino [little Angel] because he is so pretty. He has your mouth, hands, and feet. I think his eyes will be turquoise. For the rest, he is altogether an imp. He understands well, and is very obstinate about having his own way. I will have much to tell you when you come . . . . "

To this rush of sentiment about the baby from Margaret, Angelo replied tersely, "I am glad to know he is so handsome and begins to be a bit better . . . . With the new ministry I am afraid that what has never happened may happen, because new orders are much feared which the people will not like." Angelo was alluding to the pope's appointment of the Count Pellegrino Rossi, two days previously, as his chief minister. This was the same Rossi, once a scholar, who had served as French ambassador to the Holy See, and who now returned to the Papal States to serve the pope. He was a cold and contemptuous man, detested equally by liberals and conservatives because he did not go the whole way with either the one or the other. His mission was to preserve the temporal power of the papacy, with minimum reforms but without the restoration of the total absolutism of the past. He announced publicly that he intended to combat both revolution and reaction, and that he intended to use the full powers of the police to do so.

Margaret ignored totally the ominous political remarks in Angelo's letter, commenting that the wet nurse's child was well now, and "this wet nurse would be happy to go to Rome to stay with her brother, keeping our baby, and hoping to get work as a dressmaker afterwards. I like her very much, but there are a few difficulties in the picture. Ask about wet nurses as much as you can, and their wages."

It was evident that Margaret was beginning to plot as to how she might smuggle Angelino into Rome, having him close at hand, and yet concealing the baby's existence.

It was a plan totally disfavored by Ossoli, who wrote immediately: "As regards the wet nurse, don't decide anything, as we will have a great deal to discuss when I arrive . . . . The greatest caution imaginable is needed, because I think we should leave the baby out of Rome in order to keep things more secret."

So it was Angelo and not Margaret who was the most insistent on secrecy. Her response was mild: "I will wait to consult with you about everything. Just remember that if the baby is out of Rome you won't be able to see him often; on the other hand, the country air would be better, beyond a doubt, for his health. He is so dear. Sometimes, it seems to me amongst all the difficulties and mishaps that if he lives and is well, he can become a treasure for both of us and a compensation for everything. I greatly want you to see him again but you must be patient at hearing him scream often . . . . The weather is good now and I go out on the terrace. Ser Giovanni [the master of the house] is nice to me, but his sisters are detestable, prying into everything, and so avaricious and calculating. They want to save me money —they want to take it for themselves. But I try to keep peace with them. You find bad people everywhere, and these women, though calculating and vulgar, at least aren't perfidious like Giuditta."

Angelo remarked in reply, "I am very glad to hear you are taking into consideration my advice." He had developed a cough which he dismissed as nothing, but Margaret was alarmed. "If you aren't well, don't come here at night in that wretched trotting cart, wait for the diligence." But now the baby was uppermost in her thoughts: "He is always such a darling. How will I ever be able to leave him? I wake up at night, and look at him and think: Ah! I can't leave him." Her letter two days later was merely a continuation of the same theme: "The baby does not grow much, but he is always so lovely—has really delicate little ways, like a dancer."

One month to the day after Angelino's birth, the father managed a visit. Apparently the chief topic of conversation at this meeting was the matter of baptism—a problem that previously had not occurred to Margaret. Angelo was very much agitated that the baptism already had been delayed so long.

The act of baptism in Italy assumed a special importance not only from a religious but from a civil aspect, for it was the equivalent not only of a passport to heaven but a mundane birth certificate as well. Every state in Italy required its subjects to carry full documentation at all times, and if one had never been baptized, he was in effect stateless. Or, worse still, he did not exist, and therefore was subject to all sorts of damaging circumstances.

So Angelo's concern was entirely with the practical aspects of the situation. He was not unduly troubled by the fact that the child was illegitimate, for he had decided to give the baby his name. In Italy it was possible (as now) for a father to acknowledge an illegitimate child, and without marrying the mother, give the child not only his name but full rights to inheritance of property and title. When the time was auspicious, Ossoli could present the boy to his family, and Angelino would be accepted without question or stigma as his son. A child who bore the mother's name alone was labeled (but not doomed) as a bastard. Once a child bore the father's name, he could be wholly legitimized if the father chose later to marry the mother.

For Margaret, however, other issues were involved. Her ideas and beliefs had been formed in a church-going, praying, devoutly Puritan community, at a time when the Bible was accepted literally as divine writ and man was believed to have been made in the image of God. Her own ideas were mirrored in reverse, as gradually she rejected the conventional religious values she found around her. In frank self-appraisal Margaret had been forced to admit that her efforts at neither transcendentalism nor mysticism had been successful, for as she said of herself, her tendency was "rather to a great natural than a deep religious life." She had, in fact, reacted negatively to church-going from her earliest years, for as early as the age of eight she found church a place "where I heard nothing that had any connection with my inward life, and . . . gave me associations with empty formalities and arbitrary restrictions." Candidly she admitted to her journal, "I almost always suffered much in church from a feeling of disunion with the hearers and dissent from the preacher."

At nineteen, she confided to a friend, "You ask about my religion. I have not formed an opinion. I have determined not to form settled opinions at present. Loving or feeble natures need a positive religion, a visible refuge, a protection, as much in the passionate season of youth as in those stages nearer to the grave. But mine is not such . . . . I believe in Eternal Progression. I believe in a God, a Beauty and Perfection to which I am to strive all my life for assimilation . . . . At present my soul is intent on this life." By the time she was twenty-four, she had developed a critical approach: "My object is to examine thoroughly, as far as my time and abilities wll permit, the evidences of the Christian religion . . . . It seems best that I should go through these conflicts alone. The process will be slower, more irksome, more distressing, but the results will be my own, and I shall feel greater confidence in them."

She observed, too, that a study of the classics tended to create negative reactions to Christian doctrine. "I have always thought all that was said about the anti-religious tendency of a classical education to be old-wives' tales. But their puzzles about Vergil's notions of heaven and virtue, and his gracefully described gods and goddesses, have led me to alter my opinions . . . . I well remember what reflections arose in my childish mind from a comparison of the Hebrew history, where every moral obliquity is shown with such naivete, and the Greek history, full of sparkling deeds and brilliant sayings, and their gods and goddesses, the types of beauty and power, with the dazzling veil of flowery language and poetical imagery cast over their vices and failings." Later she confessed, "My priests have been very generally of the Pagan greatness, revering nature and seeking excellence, but in the path of progress, not of renunciation." Finally she summed up by saying, "Ourselves are all we know of heaven."

Now suddenly she was faced by the practical necessity of committing her child to the Christian religion through baptism. Indeed, not only to Christianity, but to Catholicism—baptism as a Protestant was one thing, and baptism as a Roman Catholic quite another. Catholic baptism was a lifetime commitment to the dogmas of the Church. Long before she had come to Italy, she had drawn the conclusion, from her extensive reading, that "Catholicism loads and infects as all dead forms do, however beautiful and noble during their lives." And, after her experiences in Rome, she had written boldly in the *Tribune,* "How anyone can remain a Catholic—I mean who has ever been aroused to think, and is not biased by the partialities of childish years—after seeing Catholicism here in Italy, I cannot conceive. There was once a soul in the religion, while the blood of its martyrs was yet fresh upon the ground, but . . . that soul is now quite fled elsewhere."

How then did she reconcile the outspokenness of her ideas on religion, and in particular the vigor of her opposition to the Roman Church, with the fact that she had entangled her life irretrievably with a Roman Catholic? For Ossoli was, and still remained, despite his pragmatic anticlericalism, a practicing member of the Church. However much they agreed on many things, on this they were disparate; but Margaret, in the wisdom of a woman who loved her man, never made the slightest effort to convert Angelo to any other point of view. A year later, in writing of Ossoli to her sister, she remarked, "I should be glad if he disengaged himself entirely from the Roman ritual, but I doubt he ever will. His habitual attachment to it is strong, and I do not trouble myself about it as no priest has any influence over his mind."

It was in this spirit, then, that she approached the problem of baptism and was willing to yield her child to the practice, which seemed to her Catholic anti-Catholic lover no more than a mechanical formality . . . a bureaucratic ritual presided over by parish priests instead of minor lay officials. But for all her resignation, the problem was not so simple, as during the coming weeks she and Angelo were to learn with dismay.

25

With the autumn solstice, the weather in Rieti seemed to reflect the turbulent inner life of the lovers. Margaret wrote afterward: "In the wild autumn storms the stream became a roaring torrent, constantly lit up by lightning flashes, and the sound of its rush was very sublime. I see it yet, as it swept away on its dark green current the heaps of burning straw which the children let down from the bridge."

Again like their internal life, there were moments of tranquility: "Opposite my window was a vineyard. It was pretty to watch the vintage—the asses and wagons loaded with this wealth of amber and rubies; the naked boys singing . . . as they cut the grapes; the nut brown maids and matrons in their red corsets and white head-cloths; the babies and little children frolicking in the grass."

But Angelo's first letter after his return to Rome roused new anxieties. He was working on a complicated plan for baptism of his son by proxy, as a device to avoid detection in Rome as long as possible. Since the procedure was irregular, it was necessary to resort to irregular, even shady, methods. To Margaret he said guardedly: "I must warn you that Ser Giovanni [the landlord] told me that while he was in Rome he could arrange for a *procura* [similar to a power-of-attorney] to baptise the baby by a person of my choice . . . . Use caution—don't tell him what I have written because he might get to know our situation too clearly."

Next day Margaret replied, "The only thing I said to Ser Giovanni was that it would be nice to have a friend as godfather. I am not in much of a position to give advice about this baptism, which I don't understand well. But the godfather I should like for the boy is my friend the Pole. He knows of the baby's existence, and is a devout Catholic, a distinguished man who could be of help to the baby in the future. I should like to have a friend in case something befell us. Keep the Pole in mind if you don't have a trustworthy friend you would like as godfather. You must remember that your nephew knows about this matter through Catalani. But I don't know your relatives, nor if it is possible for you to trust one of them. As for the Pole, as I don't know where he is now, I can't get a certificate from him. We should have to leave the space for the godfather blank; but I am sure he would take it, and we can say we are waiting for his consent. I am sorry I can't explain better by letter; in Italian it is too difficult for me. The dear baby seemed to look for you after your departure the other night. Before morning he was awake, wanting his milk, crying a great deal, and seemed to be seeking something he couldn't find. At last I got up and lifted him, talking to him constantly, and finally he was consoled."

To Mickiewicz, who was truly the godfather, Angelo's reaction was positive: "I too would like the Pole, as he is a famous person—but how to find him, time being so short? Otherwise I don't know what to do . . . things look difficult."

Then, to pile anxiety on anxiety, Angelo reported hurriedly from Rome on October 11, "For two days we have had earthquakes—one at 8:30 Sunday night and the other at 7:30 Monday morning." But the quakes subsided without damage, and the pair returned to the urgent matter of baptism.

"You *must* find a godfather," Margaret wrote. "Giovanni says that without a legal proxy the baptism would not be legal; and if we don't do it while we are here the authorities will make great difficulties after our departure and would probably write to Rome. It is too late to try to get a proxy from the Pole . . . . I am very sorry, but you will have to speak to some friend of yours about it."

While Angelo began the search for a godfather, he also began a search for an apartment for Margaret. It had to be small, inexpensive, and available for a very short term, as Margaret refused to commit herself to a long rental without her child beside her. She was afraid, too, that Giuditta might reveal her secret, and she would be forced to leave Rome suddenly. She had found a wet nurse to her liking—Chiara, a handsome, strong young woman with a healthy baby. Chiara had agreed to take Angelino and treat him as if he were her own.

With the wet nurse problem settled, another arose. Smallpox in near epidemic proportions broke out in Rieti and surrounding villages, and frantically Margaret begged the local doctor to come at once to inoculate Angelino. The doctor promised; but, both indolent and overworked, he failed to fulfill his promise. Day after day passed, and the doctor did not appear. Angrily Margaret wrote Angelo: "He is like the other people of Rieti—the worst I ever saw!" And again: "Dr. Mogliani is detestable, untrustworthy like the others. I can't tell you how much I am suffering, because I don't want to leave Rieti without having vaccinated the baby, with everyone around dying of smallpox." Finally the doctor came, offering the excuse that he had no vaccine, and was waiting for its arrival. Immediately Margaret wrote Angelo, imploring him to seek vaccine in Rome.

Meanwhile Angelo had spoken to his nephew Pietro, a jovial young man in the financial guards of the Vatican, about the baptism, " . . . not finding anyone else in whom to confide part of my affairs, and our secret. So now the only thing left to do is to find the formula for the *procura*." And he added, "My dear I urge you not to worry and get depressed; let us hope God will watch over our loved one and guard him from all mishaps."

Then for several letters, as if in an effort to distract Margaret from the tenseness of the Rieti scene, he described in detail riots in the Jewish ghetto—riots which were found to have been deliberately provoked by agents paid by the ultrareactionary party.

Plans were made for Angelo to come to Rieti, bringing the vaccine if possible, on November 4, a Saturday. But Angelo wrote that " . . . to leave in the morning will be impossible, because uncle doesn't take the day off from his office; but I hope to leave with the mail coach in the evening."

Margaret's reaction was tart: "I am very sorry that your uncle is the only Italian who does not observe holidays, just to annoy us. It will be very cold on the 4th for you to come during the night, and I suppose it will rain . . . . Now the days are nice, and I should like to stay another week with our child. He is more interesting every day. But I also need to be with you for a while, and return to the world from which I have been absent five months now. I don't want to settle permanently in Rome, for I would be too unhappy thinking about the baby . . . . How sorry I am not to hear that Milan is rising against Radetsky at this important time. I am afraid they will trust in this damnably wicked Carlo Alberto too long and that Italy will be lost, whereas it was still possible for her to be happy."

From Angelo at last came the so welcome news that he had found a supply of vaccine, and was rushing it to Rieti at once. More: "I also obtained this morning the formula for the *procura* from a lawyer friend of mine. I thought we must get my nephew to fill it out, but on reading it I see that it says the person in question must insert an individual of his choice. However, I think anyone can present the *procura* in nephew's stead —so I'll leave the name space blank and we'll fill it in when I am with you."

In the intensity of her relief, Margaret replied with a confession: "I love you much more than during the first days, because I see from experience how good and pure of heart you are. When we see each other again I will tell you all my reasons for being worried, and you won't be surprised . . . . I don't dare go out with the baby any more. I thought I was safe in taking him to the Bishop's garden; but a child died of smallpox there last week, and it was just an accident that Angelino didn't catch it. So now I am a prisoner here . . . . Giovanni is trying to *corrupt Chiara,* and she is very angry and wants very much to go home. But she won't leave before my departure. This I can tell you only: she is very afraid her husband will find out. (She told Giovanni that if he spoke to her again she would tell me.) He retorted that he had done so much for us and that we haven't given him anything. Be sure to get something valuable for him. They are all the same; only the sisters dissemble their attitude a little better. I am so glad you found a godfather in your family; for every reason it is better so."

The following day Margaret exulted: "The vaccine arrived. The vaccination has been done. I thank you so much, as does our dear baby with a thousand smiles."

She was totally exhausted. She had caught cold and was full of aches and moods. On the first of November she wrote her last note, confining it to little more than, "Addio, my love; I hope to embrace you soon."

Angelo, having dared to ask his uncle for the holiday off, arrived precisely on schedule, bearing with him the *procura.* It was a curious document. He himself had been named proxy to baptise his own child with his nephew as the authorizing agent as godfather. With this document, and an official bribe, the true names of the parents could be left blank, and the child nevertheless be given the Ossoli name. Tacitly it was understood by the priest that the actual father was Angelo, and that he did not wish to reveal the name of the mother—a typical Italian circumlocution, bred of bureaucracy and historical necessity. But Angelo was prepared to go beyond tacit acknowledgment of his child and accept legal responsibility.

The *procura* read: "With the present mandate, I the undersigned, of my own free will, elect, constitute, and delegate as my real, legitimate and undisputed proxy and agent, Signor Gio Angelo Marchese Ossoli, who is delegated on my behalf and in my name and stead to bring to the baptismal font the infant born of Signora ————, married to Signor ————, who are absent from Rome. My agent shall then give the infant those names which his parents find pleasing, and to that end shall carry out all the rites, customs, ceremonies and solemn proceedings which are prescribed and ordered by our Holy Mother Church and by the Council of Trent. Conferring on this agent, constituted for the above-mentioned reasons, all the fullest and most extensive powers, and naming him *alter ego* not only in this but in all other matters in good faith, by mandate: Pietro Ossoli, Marchese." It was signed by two witnesses and dated the fourth of November.

On the sixth of November, the two-month-old Angelo Eugenio Filippo Ossoli was baptized and was given a baptismal certificate.* Also prepared was another extraordinary document, on parchment, stating in Latin that as his father's son he was heir to all the rights and privileges of the Ossoli name, including the title of marchese.

This document, signed by the priest and embellished with the Ossoli crest, was the father's thoughtful effort to protect his son against any disadvantages that might in the uncertain future be incurred by illegitimacy.

---

* The records in Rieti were destroyed by an American air raid in 1943, during World War II. The military objective was the ancient Roman bridge over the little river. It was blown up.

26

With tears and sighs Margaret forced herself to part with her darling, but an unexpected obstacle arose. Describing the episode in a long letter to her mother, the first she had attempted in months, she spoke as if the misadventure had occurred to her alone. But Ossoli was at her side, and *I* should be read as *We*. "As to my life," she wrote, "I think that it is not the will of Heaven it should terminate very soon. I have had another strange escape.

"I had taken passage in the diligence to come to Rome; two rivers were to be passed—the Turano and the Tiber—but passed by good bridges, and a road excellent when not broken unexpectedly by torrents from the mountains. The diligence sets out between three and four in the morning, long before light. The director sent me word that the Marchioness Crispoldi had taken for herself and family a coach extraordinary, which should start two hours later, and that I could have a place in that, if I liked; so I accepted. The weather had been beautiful, but, on the eve of the day fixed for my departure, the wind rose, and the rain fell in torrents. I observed that the river which passed my window was much swollen, and rushed with great violence. In the night, I heard its voice still stronger, and felt glad I had not to set out in the dark. I rose with twilight, and was expecting my carriage, and wondering at its delay, when I heard that the great diligence, several miles below, had been seized by a torrent; the horses were up to their necks in water, before anyone dreamed of the danger. The postilion called on all the saints, and threw himself into the water. The door of the diligence could not be opened, and the passengers forced themselves, one after another, into the cold water—dark, too. Had I been there I had fared ill; a pair of strong men were ill after it, though all escaped with life.

"For several days, there was no going to Rome; but, at last, we set forth in two great diligences, with all the horses of the route. For many miles, the mountains and ravines were covered with snow; I seemed to have returned to my own country and climate. Few miles passed, before the conductor injured his leg under the wheel, and I had the pain of seeing him suffer all the way, while 'Blood of Jesus,' 'Souls of Purgatory,' was the mildest beginning of an answer to the jeers of the postilions upon his paleness. We stopped at a miserable *osteria* [inn], in whose cellar we found a magnificent remain of Cyclopean architecture—as indeed in Italy one is paid at every step, for discomfort or danger, by some precious subject of thought. We proceeded very slowly, and reached just at night a solitary little inn, which marks the site of the ancient home of the Sabine virgins, snatched away to become the mothers of Rome. We were there saluted with the news that the Tiber, also, had overflowed its banks, and it was very doubtful if we could pass. But what else to do? There were no accommodations in the house for thirty people, or even for three, and to sleep in the carriages, in that wet air of the marshes, was a more certain danger than to attempt the passage. So we set forth; the moon, almost at the full, smiling sadly on the ancient grandeurs, then half draped in mist, then drawing over her face a thin white veil. As we approached the Tiber, the towers and domes of Rome could be seen, like a cloud lying low on the horizon. The road and the meadows, alike under water, lay between us and it, one sheet of silver. The horses entered; they behaved nobly; we proceeded, every moment uncertain if the water would not become deep; but the scene was beautiful, and I enjoyed it highly. I have never yet felt afraid when really in the presence of danger, though sometimes in its apprehension.

"At last we entered the gate; the diligence stopping to be examined, I walked to the gate of Villa Ludovisi, and saw its rich shrubberies of myrtle, and its statues so pale and eloquent in the moonlight."

Thus began the second Roman phase of Margaret's great Italian adventure.

"I am situated for the first time entirely to my mind," she explained to her mother, remembering the errors of her Corso lodgings. "I have but one room, but large; and everything about the bed so gracefully and adroitly disposed that it makes a beautiful parlor, and of course I pay much less. I have the sun all day, and an excellent chimney. It is very high and has pure air, and the most beautiful view all around imaginable. Add, that I am with the dearest, delightful old couple one can imagine, quick, prompt, and kind, sensible and contented. Having no children, they like to regard me and the Prussian sculptor, my neighbor, as such; yet are too delicate and too busy ever to intrude.

"In the attic dwells a priest, who insists on making my fire when Antonia is away. To be sure, he pays himself for his trouble by asking a great many questions. The stories below are occupied by a frightful Russian princess with moustaches, and a footman who ties her bonnet for her; and a fat English lady, with a fine carriage, who gives all her money to the Church, and has made for the house a terrace of flowers that would delight you. Antonia has her flowers in a humble balcony, her birds, an immense black cat—always addressed by both husband and wife as *Amoretto* (little love)!

" . . . You cannot conceive of the enchantment of this place. So much I suffered here last January and February, I thought myself a little weaned; but returning, my heart swelled even to tears with the cry of the poet: 'O, Rome, *my* country, city of the soul!' Those have not lived who have not seen Rome.

"Warned, however, by the last winter, I dared not rent my lodgings for the year. I hope I am acclimated. I have been through what is called the grape-cure, much more charming, certainly, than the water-cure. At present I am very well; but, alas! because I have gone to bed early, and done very little. I do not know if I can maintain any labor." She was of course, merely being playful—for the "grape-cure" was only plenty of wine. Then she grew serious again.

"You, loved mother, keep me informed, as you have, of important facts, *especially* the *worst.* The thought of you, the knowledge of your angelic nature, is always one of my greatest supports. Happy are those who have such a mother!

"Of other circumstances which complicate my position I cannot write. Were you here, I would confide in you fully, and have more than once in the silence of the night recited to you those most strange and romantic chapters in the story of my sad life. At one time when I thought I might die, I empowered a person . . . to communicate them to you on his return to the United States. But now I think we shall meet again, and I am sure you will always love your daughter, and will know gladly that in all events she has tried to aid, and never striven to injure, her fellows."

Fortified by the grape-cure, and again enchanted by Rome, Margaret was ready to enter vigorously into revolutionary activities once more—with Angelo of course close by. It was astonishing how political events seemed to seek her even more than she sought them. Even the position of her room was a perfect vantage point for an acute observer.

"The house looks out on the Piazza Barberini, and I see both that palace and the Pope's," she told her mother. "The scene today has been one of terrible interest. The poor, weak Pope has fallen more and more under the domination of the Cardinals, till at last all truth was hidden from his eyes."

She then went on to describe for her no doubt totally bewildered mother one of the few important and dramatic episodes of those months which for some reason she did not personally cover. It was the assassination of the pope's minister Pellegrino Rossi (that Rossi who had served Louis Philippe as ambassador from France), as on November fifteenth he attempted to enter the chamber of deputies. It was an assassination with shattering consequences for all sides, an act of violence which aroused both violent fears and violent hopes.

Rossi had summoned the regular papal troops of the line to protect him because he did not trust the *Guardia Civica.* The troops were deployed along his route and around the exterior of the chamber. The crowd was dense, and, as Margaret said, "howled and hissed." As Rossi descended from his carriage with his official party, the crowd surged against the protecting soldiers, pushing toward Rossi. They managed somehow to reach him, and as he turned he was stabbed in the throat. Scores of persons simultaneously had drawn daggers, so that it was impossible to identify the assassin. Bleeding profusely, Rossi fell back into the arms of a cardinal and died. The assassin probably was Luigi Brunetti, a son of Ciceruacchio who was as hotblooded as his father. (Many months later, two other young men were condemned by a papal court for the murder; one was killed in prison and the other was beheaded.)

The dagger thrust was greeted by an almost total silence, and the troops watched coolly without taking any action. Almost unanimous were the soldiers and the people in their reaction: in the evening they walked the streets arm-in-arm, singing and crying out, "Happy the hand which rids the world of a tyrant!"

"Had Rossi lived to enter the Chamber," said Margaret, "he would have seen the most terrible and imposing mark of denunciation known in the history of nations—the whole house, without a single exception, seated on the benches of opposition. The news of his death was received by the deputies with the same cold silence as by the people. For me, I never thought to have heard of a violent death with satisfaction, but this act affected me as one of terrible justice."

Then Margaret went on with events as viewed from her window, providing one of the most graphic eyewitness accounts recorded in either English or Italian: "Today, all the troops and the people united and went to the Quirinal to demand a change of measures. They found the Swiss Guard drawn out, and the Pope dared not show himself. They attempted to force the door of his palace, to enter his presence, and the guard fired. I saw a man borne by, wounded. The drum beat to call out the National Guard. The carriage of Prince Barberini has returned with its frightened inmates and liveried retinue, and they have suddenly barred up the courtyard gate. Antonia, seeing it, observes, 'Thank heaven, we are poor, we have nothing to fear!' This is the echo of a sentiment which will soon be universal in Europe . . . .

"All is quieted now in Rome. Late at night the Pope had to yield, but not till the door of his palace was half burnt, and his confessor killed. This man, Parma,* provoked his fate by firing on the people from a window. It seems the Pope never gave the order to fire; his Guard [Swiss] acted from a sudden impulse of their own. The new ministry chosen are little inclined to accept. It is almost impossible for anyone to act, unless the Pope is stripped of his temporal power, and the hour for that is not yet quite ripe; though they talk more and more of proclaiming the Republic, and even of calling my friend Mazzini . . . .

"Never feel any apprehensions for my safety from such causes. There are those who will protect me, if necessary, and besides, I am on the conquering side. These events have, to me, the deepest interest. These days are what I always longed for—were I only free from private care!"

A week later she described the situation in a letter to Marcus Spring: "Mazzini has stood alone in Italy, on a sunny height, far above the stature of other men. He has fought a great fight against folly, compromise, and treason—steadfast in his convictions, and of almost miraculous energy to sustain them. He

* Monsignor Palma, not Parma. The use of this name indicates that Margaret's sources were verbal, not written—else she would not have misspelled the name. He was also reported as the pope's Latin Secretary.

has foes; and at this moment, while he leads the insurrection in the Valtellina, the Roman people murmur his name, and long to call him here.

"How often rings in my ear the consolatory words . . . 'Though the million suffer shipwreck, yet noble hearts survive!'

"I grieve to say, the good-natured Pio has shown himself utterly derelict, alike without resolution to abide by the good or the ill. He is now abandoned and despised by both parties. The people do not trust his word, for they know he shrinks from the danger, and shuts the door to pray quietly in his closet, whilst he knows the Cardinals are misusing his name to violate his pledges. The Cardinals, chased from Rome, talk of electing an anti-Pope; because, when there was danger, he has always yielded to the people, and they say he has overstepped his prerogative, and broken his papal oath . . . . Who would have believed, a year ago, that the people would assail his palace? I was on Monte Cavallo yesterday, and saw the broken windows, the burnt doors, the walls marked by shot, just beneath the loggia on which we have seen him giving the benediction."

Then abruptly she shifted from the grand events about her to her inner life: "Of me you wish to know; but there is little I can tell you at this distance. I have had happy hours, learned much, suffered much, and outward things have not gone fortunately with me. I have had glorious hopes, but they are overclouded now, and the future looks darker than ever, indeed, quite impossible to my steps. I have no hope, unless that God will show me some way I do not know of now; but I do not wish to trouble you with more of this."

Meanwhile the carabinieri and the civic guard, Angelo among them, had taken over the task of guarding the pope's Quirinale palace, so close to Margaret's lodging. Within were the *Guardia Nobile,* with Angelo's three brothers. Though restraints on movement were not severely imposed, the pope considered himself a prisoner, and took measures to escape from his "confinement." On the evening of November 24, Pius IX disguised himself as a simple priest, and wearing large spectacles, passed through the great gateway of the palace in the carriage of the Bavarian envoy to the papal court. Accompanied by the Bavarian minister and his wife, he drove without hinderance along the Appian Way into the territory of the Bourbon king of Naples, and took refuge in the vast, grim fortress of Gaeta. When the news became known, it created a worldwide sensation. Mazzini's comment was concise: "Pius IX has fled: the flight is an abdication." Margaret, resuming on December 2 her dispatches to the *Tribune*, told Americans both the story of Rossi's murder and the pope's abandonment of Rome. Angrily she expressed her own opinion: "The only dignified course for the Pope to pursue was to resign his temporal power. He could no longer hold it on his own terms; but to it he clung . . . . I cannot forgive him some of the circumstances of his flight. To fly to Naples to throw himself in the arms of the bombarding monarch, blessing him, and thanking his soldiery for preserving that part of Italy from anarchy; . . . to choose a commission for governing in his absence, composed of men of princely blood, but as to character, so null that everybody laughed and said he chose those who could best be spared if they were killed (but they all ran away directly) . . . . These acts have not had the effect the foes of freedom hoped. Rome remained quite cool and composed . . . . In a few days all began to say: 'Well, who would have thought it? The Pope, the Cardinals, the princes, are gone, and Rome is perfectly tranquil, and one does not miss anything, except that there are not so many rich carriages and liveries.' The Pope may regret too late that he ever gave the people a chance to make this reflection . . . .

"*Don Pirlone,* the *Punch* of Rome, has just come in. This number represents the fortress of Gaeta. Outside hangs a cage containing a parrot (*pappagallo*), the plump body of the bird surmounted by a noble large head with benign face and Papal head-dress. He sits on the perch now with folded wings, but the cage door, in likeness of a portico, shows there is convenience to come forth for the purposes of benediction, when wanted. Outside, the king of Naples, dressed as Harlequin, plays the organ for instruction of the bird (unhappy penitent, doomed to penance), and, grinning with sharp teeth, observes: 'He speaks in my way now.' In the background a young republican holds ready the match for a barrel of gunpowder, but looks at his watch, waiting the moment to ignite it."

In the United States Margaret's *Tribune* articles had not gone unnoticed by the hierarchy of the Church, and her dispatches about the flight of the pope from Rome seemed outrageous to clerical eyes. Bishop John Hughes of New York, who was active in politics and had vigorously protested the use of the Protestant Bible in the public schools, complained privately and publicly about the matter. While deploring the tone of Margaret's letters, and endeavoring to halt them, he organized mass meetings in support of Pius IX and attacking the Italian Republicans. Greeley, however, gave no ground, and Margaret's dispatches continued to appear exactly as she wrote them.

For a moment Margaret paused to look forward: "Italy is being educated for the future, her leaders are learning that the time is past for trust in princes and precedents . . . . Of all this great drama I have much to write, but elsewhere, in a more full form, and where I can duly sketch the portraits of actors little known in America. The materials are over-rich. I have bought my right in them by much sympathetic suffering."

She closed with a practical suggestion to the American public: "Pray send here a good Ambassador—one that has experience of foreign life, that he may act with good judgment . . . . And send a man capable of prizing the luxury of living in, or knowing, Rome; the office of Ambassador is one that should not be thrown away on a person who cannot prize or use it. Another century, and I might ask to be made Ambassador myself . . . but woman's day has not come yet . . . . *

"A happy New Year to my country! May she be worthy of the privileges she possesses, while others are lavishing their blood to win them."

* The first woman ambassador to Italy, Mrs. Clare Booth Luce, arrived from the United States in 1953.

27

Margaret's private life now was no less intense than her political, and again was gilded with a measure of happiness. She wrote to William Story at about this time: "I have thus far passed this past month of fine weather most delightfully in revisiting my haunts of the autumn before. Then, too, I was uncommonly well and strong; it was the golden period of my Roman life . . . . To you I may tell that I always go with Ossoli, the most congenial companion I ever had for jaunts of this kind. We go out in the morning, carrying the roast chestnuts from Rome; the bread and wine are found at some lonely little *osteria;* and so we dine. And reach Rome again just in time to see it, from a little distance, gilded by the sunset.

"The moon having been so clear, and the air so warm, we have visited on successive evenings all the places we fancied: Monte Cavallo [the Pope's Palazzo Quirinale], now so lonely and abandoned—no lights but the moon and stars; Trinità dei Monti, Santa Maria Maggiore, and the Forum. So now, if the rain must come, or I be driven from Rome, I have all the images fair and fresh in my mind."

She was, obviously, still haunted by fears that her secret might be discovered, else she would not have used the phrase, "or I be driven from Rome"—driven like a Biblical sinner, and perhaps even stoned. For all her relaxation and joy in Ossoli's presence, the Puritan fathers of New England must have haunted her dreams with their broad-brimmed hats and large buckles.

As she was burning with the need for confession, and the confessionals were closed to her, she wrote to Caroline Sturgis Tappan, revealing the existence of her baby but demanding that Caroline keep the secret. It was a risky test of friendship, and after the letter was posted, she must have suffered qualms. Caroline, after all, had been the last to break the news of her marriage to William Tappan. How would she now, so respectably married, react to so wild a confidence of so serious a moral lapse? This Margaret must have wondered.

Margaret was granted, fortunately, a brief reprieve from all her problems—a week with her baby. It was a kind of interlude between bombardments. She could not endure the thought of Angelino alone at Christmas. And no matter how glowing the letters about his well-being, she no longer trusted fully any of the Rietini. The only solution was to go and see for herself. She left early on the morning of December 21, and the drafty diligence was hardly out of sight before Angelo was writing to her.

"Today in Rome is excessively cold," he dashed off in a note, " . . . the sky is leaden with snow, so I fear that on the road you will have had a great deal to suffer from the cold and snow. So let me know immediately how you fared and how is our dear one and remember to give him many kisses from me." The next day he wrote almost exactly the same words, except that he added, "I fear you might harm your health if you don't have a good fire and a warm room."

On the same day Margaret was replying to Angelo's letters, not yet received. "I made the trip well, arriving here at four-thirty. I find our dear one little changed—much less than I expected. What surprises me is that he appears quite fat. He seems to be very well, but he is not much bigger than when I left. At the same time he is very sweet, and gets on much better than with me. He sleeps so well at night, cries very rarely, and then not hard. He has pleasure in this family, seeing everyone going back and forth. They all play with him and seem to love him.

"The house is terrible. Wind enters from all sides, but he doesn't seem cold, and I hope he will be sturdier for having been so exposed during the coming months. He had a dreadful pox [probably chickenpox]. His head and body were covered with spots, and it is only thanks to God that he recovered so well. Dr. Mogliani never came to visit him; his family says I am avaricious. I suppose they thought it wasn't worth while to save our child. His face is not blemished . . . . When I held him, he leaned his dear head a long time on my shoulder. At night I very much enjoyed sleeping with him. The days are not so good—it is so cold . . . . "

What it cost Margaret emotionally to admit to Angelo that the baby throve without her can only be surmised. But it was part of the pattern of Margaret's psychic honesty that in this matter, as in so many other unflattering things, she must tell the truth. Only about her affair with Angelo did she dissemble, tell half-truths, and invent explanations. Perhaps a part of her honesty about Angelino was derived from her relief at finding him well and strong after what seemed a serious illness—a relief intensified by the distressing news, just received in Rome, that her brother Eugene's newborn baby was dead.

Angelo, in his answer to Margaret, expressed satisfaction that his son was progressing so nicely. But he sounded lonely, and remarked, "I will expect letters from you often, so as to console myself at least in this way. Meanwhile I wish you a merry Christmas and give many kisses to our dear love. p.s. Let me know what they think in Rieti of the Government's activities."

On the same day Margaret was already making plans for her return. She was freezing in the dank stone house, which was so poorly insulated at the windows and doors. "Tell Antonia to have a good fire ready for me," she asked. "Don't meet me outside the city gate [the Porta Salaria] if you are on guard duty

—it would be too difficult for you. But come after dinner, because I will have a thousand things to tell you about our dear baby."

Two days after Christmas she wrote: "I am coming on Friday. I am sorry to leave our dear one, but if I wanted to I couldn't stay in this house any longer. I have a bad cold, and my head aches . . . . [Angelino] with every passing day becomes more interesting. He has great fun with his rattle. He has no hair yet . . . . He passed a nice Christmas Eve; he seemed all excited by the bells, and wouldn't sleep nor let the others sleep."

Thus spoke the haughty transcendentalist intellectual about a bald-headed baby, his rattle, and Christmas Eve bells.

Once she had written: "Very early I knew that the only object in life was to grow." Now through the growth of her child she was achieving the growth previously denied her.

28

On New Year's Day Margaret opened a fresh notebook to the first page and wrote "Italy, 1849." It was to be a strictly political journal, avoiding personal entries—additional raw material for her *History of Italian Liberation*. She began:

"This year cannot fail to be rich in events most important for Italy, Europe, and the world. Rome has at last become the focus of the Italian revolution, and I am here. I shall in this book make brief notes of the events of the day, to be filled out as a journal at my leisure. The Pope is still about at Gaeta, and in his absence the temporal power of the papacy has received the last blow. The Costituente Romana was proclaimed on Friday, 29th Nov., 1848. It will be followed by the Costituente Italiana, which ought in the natural order of things to constitute Italy one and one republic. There may be many breakers yet before that shore is reached, but it must finally be attained, since no other can yield safety for the ship's crew. May the difficulties yet to be overcome lead to union and teach them the soberness of wisdom necessary to reconstruct.

"I believe, now that I have seen so much of Italy, that the

power of the priests must be utterly overthrown before anything solid can be done for this people. But everything tends to destroy their authority; only as it has long been founded on habit and not on illusion, an appeal to reason will not suffice. A hundred discharges of artillery announced the *Costituente*. The Piazza del Popolo was illuminated with lights all around (except on the Pincian) and a great fire on the Piazza which sent up its beautiful tribute of sparks to the deepest black blue sky, the most thoughtful fair sky I ever saw in Italy from which hung the crescent moon. The orchestra was on the platform of the obelisk. The lights of the musicians were reflected in the fountain. A fair scene! The people were very quiet and showed little feeling about the great step that had been taken. Also in the Corso were few lights except those of the casinos.

"2nd Jan. . . . Evening on the Campidoglio . . . The troops and a detachment of Civica assembled in the Piazza del Popolo and with artillery, arms and torches marched in the Campidoglio with a new tri-color banner, a gift from Venice. This was placed in the hands of Marcus Aurelius [the ancient bronze equestrian statue of the emperor], those of all the Rioni [wards] and casinos ranged around, the bands sounded, a discourse was made which none could hear but which had its effect none the less. The moon looked down, the bengal lights and torches shone on the palaces of Michelangelo and the piazza full of glittering lights.

"January 5 . . . There are many wagers pending, some to a considerable amount, that the Pope will return to Rome this evening and be present at the celebration of Epiphany tomorrow. I hope not. Read *Ricordi di giovani d'Italia* by Mazzini, a word of fire, a thought pure, solid, illustrious as diamond. Man of Italy. Thy bride is unworthy of thee, yet if any could redeem and educate her, it is now. Tomorrow celebration of the King's Magi coming to adore the infant of Bethlehem. What mockery!

"6th . . . Instead of the Pope comes from him an excommunication against those engaged in the movements of the 15th and 16th of November and in the changes to which they led and are leading *in somma,* against the major part of Romans in this city or in the provinces. I have not yet seen the document, but it is said to be worded in all the most foolish phrases of ancient superstition. The people received it with jeers, tore it at once from the walls, and yesterday (Saturday) evening carried it in procession through the Corso round a candle's end, the only light in the procession. They ran along giggling and mumbling in imitation of priestly chants, detachments occasionally digressing to throw copies into some privy. Such is the finale of St. Peterdom."

Three days passed before Margaret was able to secure a copy of the document, and then only in manuscript, so thorough was the destruction of the printed copies by the people. "Have now finally seen the mandate of the Pope. It is not a formal excommunication but an advise that all who took part in that 'detestable' act of the constitutional assembly will be excommunicated. It is the silliest document possible, an astonishment in this age." To support her judgment, she translated the entire manifesto and sent it to the *Tribune,* with the hopeful comment, "It is probably the last document of the kind the world will ever see."

The pope's words certainly were less than temperate, though he began with a salutation, "To Our most beloved subjects." Writing from the "pacific abode [the fortress at Gaeta] to which it has pleased Divine Providence to conduct Us," Pius stated that he was waiting for testimonies of remorse. "But We have seen nothing except a sterile invitation to return to Our capital, unaccompanied by a word of condemnation for those crimes or the least guaranty for Our security against the frauds and violences of that same company of furious men which still tyrannizes with a barbarous despotism over Rome and the States of the Church." Instead of remorse, a " . . . New and more monstrous act of undisguised felony and of actual rebellion" was committed—the calling of the "so-called General National Assembly." Thereupon he prohibited everyone, "of whatever class or condition," from taking part in these meetings, and restated the excommunication formula to be incurred by anyone "guilty of whatsoever attempt against the temporal sovereignty of the Supreme Pontiff."

As the constituent assembly was the first ever elected by secret ballot in Italy on the basis of direct and universal suffrage for all citizens over the age of twenty-one, the implications of the papal threat were enormous. The members of the assembly ignored it, and its tone made much more difficult any reconciliation between the new popular government and the pope as a temporal ruler. The recalcitrance of Pius IX in refusing to receive envoys from the Assembly and the staunchness of the people meant that the pope could be restored to his throne only by the intervention of foreign bayonets. Secretly Pius already had appealed to his Bourbon host, King Ferdinando, and to the heads of state of France, Spain, Austria, and astonishingly to the President of the United States, urging each "to bring his weight to bear in this calamitous time for the preservation of the temporal power of the Holy See."

Margaret probably knew nothing of these secret appeals, but her political sensitivity was very much in operation. As a prophetess of almost unbelievable perception, as early as January 26 she noted in her journal, "The Romans go on as if nothing were pending. Yet it seems very probable that the French will soon be at Civita Vecchia [the port of Rome] and with hostile intentions. Monstrous are the treacheries of our time."

All the while items only partially political were creeping into the diary, such as her pleasure at seeing marionettes enacting a farce as "anti-ecclesiastical as the *Tartuffe* of Molière. The audience laughingly extolled the ejaculations of the hypocrite 'Pazienza.'" Then, with the Republican takeover, the halls of the palaces on the Campidoglio were opened to the public: "For the first time I saw the original Lupa [She-Wolf] with the twins [Romulus and Remus], and the boy taking the thorn from his foot [a famous sculpture from antiquity]. Lupa affected me much." Lupa was suckling the twins.

In February she prepared new letters for the *Tribune,* elaborating the material she had recorded in only a line or two. Invariably the language became more involved, losing some of its color and directness. For herself she wrote as she thought; for her audience she tried to clothe her sentences with some of the ponderous style of the times. Happily she never succeeded in writing like a pompous Victorian. Even in a dispatch she could be very concise: "The revolution, like all genuine ones, has been instinctive, its results unexpected and surprising to the greater part of those who achieved them."

The opening of the constituent assembly was scheduled for the early days of February, and, Margaret wrote in the *Tribune,* " . . . gave occasion for a fine procession. All the troops in Rome defiled from the Campidoglio; among them many bear the marks of suffering from the Lombard War. The banners of Sicily, Venice and Bologna waved proudly; that of Naples was veiled with crepe. I was in a balcony in the Piazza di Venezia; the Palazzo di Venezia, that sternest feudal pile so long the headquarters of Austrian machinations, seemed to frown as the bands in passing struck up the *Marseillaise.* The nephew of Napoleon and Garibaldi, the hero of Montevideo, walked together as deputies. The deputies, a grave band, mostly advocates or other professional men, walked without other badge of distinction than the tri-colored scarf."

This was Margaret's first glimpse of Garibaldi. He was wearing a long red tunic and a black broad-brimmed felt hat trimmed with an ostrich feather—the two bizarre elements which soon came to mark all the uniforms of the Garibaldini. He was a powerful man of middle height, with light chestnut hair flowing to his shoulders, blond moustache and beard, and an expression of such sublime serenity that more than once he was compared to the paintings of Christ the Savior. That Margaret did not describe him until much later was no doubt due to her suspicions of him, as indicated in her journal. She entered: "Arm in arm with foolish Bonaparte walked Garibaldi. Why?"; and also because she continued to think of him as some sort of wild bandit chief, as indeed did most of the upper classes. She may have heard, too, that Mazzini was disappointed in him for having offered his sword to King Carlo Alberto, so that he and Mazzini had quarreled.

But whether Garibaldi walked arm in arm with a Napoleonic prince (Carlo Luciano Bonaparte, prince of Canino and Musignano, one of the Republican officials), or took off his hat at a procession of the Virgin (as he always did), he remained what he was: a vigorous Republican and a professed atheist. He had been on the way to aid still-besieged Venice with the remnants of his band, when the asassination of Rossi changed his plans and drew him toward the center of the stage. Elected to the assembly, he had come to Rome not as warrior but as legislator, leaving his legion temporarily in Rieti. And once in his legislator's seat in the back row, where he had to be carried because his arthritis that day was so crippling, he declared immediately, "Why are we losing time in vain formalities? The delay of even a minute is a crime. Long live the Republic!" But for all his practical impatience, the other deputies wanted to talk, and it was not until four days later, on February ninth at 2 A.M., that the decision was forged.

"Early next morning," Margaret wrote to the *Tribune*, "I rose and went forth to observe the Republic. Over the Quirinal I went, through the Forum, to the Capitol. There was nothing to be seen except the magnificent calm Emperor [Marcus Aurelius], the tamers of horses [the Dioscuri], the fountain, the trophies, the lions, as usual; among the marbles, for living figures, a few dirty, bold women, and Murillo boys in the sun just as usual. I passed into the Corso; there were men in the liberty cap—of course the lowest and vilest had been the first to assume it; all the horrible beggars persecuting as impudently as usual.

"I met some English; all their comfort was, 'It would not last a month.' 'They hoped to see all those fellows shot yet.' . . . Mr. Carlyle would be delighted with his countrymen. They are entirely ready and anxious to see a Cromwell for Italy.

" . . . I met an American. He 'had no confidence in the Republic.' Why? Because he 'had no confidence in the people.'

Why? 'Because they are not like *our* people.' Ah! Jonathan and John—excuse me, but I must say the Italian has a decided advantage over you in the power of quickly feeling generous sympathy, as well as some other things which I have not time now to particularize.

"At last (noon) the procession mounts the Campidoglio. It is all dressed with banners . . . . The deputies mount the steps, and one of them reads, in a clear, friendly voice, the following words:

" 'FUNDAMENTAL DECREE OF THE CONSTITUTIONAL ASSEMBLY OF ROME.

" 'ARTICLE I. The Papacy has fallen in fact and in right from the temporal government of the Roman State.

" 'ARTICLE II. The Roman Pontiff shall have all the necessary guarantees for independence in the exercise of his spiritual power.

" 'ARTICLE III. The form of government of the Roman State shall be a pure democracy, and will take the glorious name of the Roman Republic.

" 'ARTICLE IV. The Roman Republic shall have with the rest of Italy the relations exacted by a common nationality.'

"Between each of these expressive sentences the speaker paused; the great bell of the Capitol gave forth its solemn melodies; the cannon answered; while the crowd shouted, *Viva la Repubblica! Viva l'Italia!*"

Margaret seemed unaware that the United States consul in Rome, Nicholas Brown, marched in the procession in his official diplomatic uniform. He did so, as he informed Washington, because "I thought it my duty as an American citizen to do homage to the principle of popular sovereignty of which our glorious Republic is the living incarnation." Brown did more than march: He recommended to the State Department that the Roman Republic be recognized immediately—but his urgent letters remained unanswered.

Within a few days posters appeared on walls, urging that Giuseppe Mazzini, who had been elected to the assembly, be invested with Roman citizenship. This was done by an overwhelming vote of the assembly, and the hunted exile was called to Rome as an idol of the people. On the way Mazzini paused in Florence to try to persuade the Florentines to throw in their lot with Rome, as the grand duke had fled to keep Pius IX company at Gaeta.

Addressing Mazzini at Florence, Margaret wrote a letter to offer " . . . my tribute of affection. When I think that only two years ago you thought of coming into Italy with us in disguise, it seems very glorious that you are about to enter Republican Rome as a Roman citizen . . . . Yet, even in that first thrill of joy, I felt 'He will think his work but beginning now.' . . . For your sake I would wish at this moment to be an Italian and a man of action. But though an American, I am not even a woman of action; so the best I can do is to pray with the whole heart: Heaven bless dear Mazzini . . . . "

It is doubtful if Mazzini received this letter before he arrived in Rome on March fifth, entering by the Porta del Popolo on foot at night, to avoid pomp. Immediately Margaret heard the electric news, but inscribed in her journal only: "Mazzini is arrived in Rome. He is at the Albergo [Hotel] Cesari." Next day she noted: "The people went under his windows and he made them a simple noble address in which he said he would stay with them to the last."

To her *Tribune* readers Margaret commented: "He is not an orator, but the simple conversational tone of his address is in refreshing contrast with the boyish rhetoric and academic swell common to Italian speakers in the present unfledged state . . . . The speech of Mazzini is laden with thought—it goes straight to the mark by the shortest path, and moves without effort, from the irresistible impression of deep conviction and fidelity in the speaker. Mazzini is a man of genius . . . ."

She reported in full his first address to the assembly, which afterward became so widely quoted because of the phrases: "After the Rome which was wrought by conquest of arms, the Rome which was wrought by conquest of words, must come a third which shall work by virtue of example. After the Rome of the Emperors, after the Rome of the Popes, will come the

Rome of the People. The Rome of the People is arisen; do not salute with applause, but let us rejoice together!"

Then Margaret added an evaluation of her own: "He said, 'We will conquer'; whether Rome will, this time, is not to me certain, but such men as Mazzini conquer always—conquer in defeat."

On the third day after his arrival in Rome Mazzini sought his American friend, and found her entertaining the Marchese Ossoli in her room. This, however, she did not mention when she described the event to Marcus Spring: "Last night, I heard a ring; then somebody speak my name; the voice struck upon me at once. He looks more divine than ever, after all his new, strange sufferings. He asked after all of you. He stayed two hours, and we talked, though rapidly, of everything. He hopes to come often, but the crisis is tremendous, and all will come on him; since, if anyone can save Italy from her foes, inward and outward, it will be he. But he is very doubtful whether this be possible; the foes are too many, too strong, too subtle. Yet Heaven helps sometimes . . . . He has sent me tickets, twice, to hear him speak in the Assembly. It was a fine, commanding voice. But, when he finished, he looked very exhausted and melancholy. He looks as if the great battle he has fought had been too much for his strength, and that he was only sustained by the fire of his soul.

"All this I write to you, because you said, when I was suffering at leaving Mazzini—'You will meet him in Heaven.' This I believe will be, despite my faults."

For the avalanche of events had made the thought of death lie heavily upon them all.

29

By springtime tourists had almost disappeared from the streets of Rome. Even as early as *Carnevale* the pinch was felt. This year Margaret attended in good weather and was filled with delight, but admitted to her readers: "The Republican Carnival has not been as splendid as the Papal, the absence of dukes and princes being felt in the way of coaches and rich dresses; there are also fewer foreigners than usual, many having feared to assist at this most peaceful of revolutions. But if less splendid, it was not less gay; the costumes were many and fanciful—flowers, smiles, and fun abundant." She went on to describe the *Moccoletti,* the game in which each person tried to blow out someone else's candle, but her thoughts were much too much with politics to launch into a travelog.

As if to counteract the tourist trend, William and Emelyn Story returned to Rome, and helped by Margaret, set up housekeeping—a residence that was to last, with only a few interludes, for more than four and one-half decades. Margaret wrote to her mother that they were " . . . more interesting and agreeable to me than any of the other Americans." And as the Roman crisis grew, they became her closest friends.

Their association began with such pleasant interludes as breakfasting together as guests of sculptor Thomas Crawford and his wife at the Villa Negroni, with its orange trees along sheltered alleys and lines of cypresses planted by Michelangelo. The Crawfords had leased the floor above the owner, Prince Massimo. For fifteen years they had been in Rome, Thomas carving marbles for the Capitol building in Washington, including the pediment and the statue to top the dome. He had built a dozen studios among the ruins of the Baths of Diocletian, where he kept a small army of stonecutters hacking away, for he had become both famous and fashionable. He had just finished a model for his statue of George Washington, which Margaret described fairly and dispassionately in the *Tribune,* without being overly impressed—yet they remained friends.

The Storys and Margaret went together, this time including Ossoli, to the Teatro Argentina to hear Vincenzo Bellini's opera *Beatrice di Tenda*—the story of the middle-aged widow of a fifteenth-century condottiere who was married by the young Milanese Duke Filippo Maria Visconti for her fortune, conjugally spurned, then executed for alleged adultery with a page. It was all very sad and beautiful.

When Margaret was lonely or depressed, Emelyn stayed with her, talking woman talk, which included the subject of Ossoli. It was William who rose to her defense when she was attacked, unfairly as he thought, by James Russell Lowell in a long, meandering poem called *A Fable for Critics.* It included a spiteful tirade on one "Miranda"—a thinly disguised Margaret Fuller.

In her essay "American Literature" published (1846) in the collection *Papers on Literature and Art,* Margaret had stated with candor her opinion of Lowell as a poet. He was, she said, "absolutely wanting in the true spirit and tone of poesy . . . his great facility at versification has enabled him to fill the ear with a copious stream of pleasant sound. But his verse is stereotyped; his thought sounds no depth, and posterity will not remember him."

Lowell retaliated with many verses—copious but hardly a pleasant stream of sound. Typical was the following:

> She may enter on duty today, if she chooses
> And remain Tiring-woman for life to the Muses.
> Miranda meanwhile has succeeded in driving
> Up into a corner, in spite of their striving
> A small flock of terrified victims, and there
> With an I-turn-the-crank-of-the-Universe air
> And a tone which, at least to my fancy, appears
> Not so much to be entering as boxing your ears,
> Is unfolding a tale (of herself, I surmise,
> For't is dotted as thick as a peacock's with I's).

Though the poem had been published the preceding autumn, a copy did not reach Story, and Rome, till March. William wrote immediately to his old friend Lowell, taking him to task. "The *Fable for Critics* is very witty and, as the English say, 'amazingly clever.' There is but one thing I regretted, and that was that you drove your arrow so sharply through Miranda. The joke of 'Tiring-woman to the Muses' is too happy; but because fate has really been unkind to her, and because she depends on her pen for her bread-and-water (and that is nearly all she has to eat), and because she is her own worst enemy, and because through her disappointment and disease, which (things) embitter everyone, she has struggled most stoutfully and manfully, I could have wished you had let her pass scot-free."

After a long while Lowell acknowledged Story's letter. "It will seem a very old affair for me to speak of the *Fable for Critics* . . . . Set down the parts about Miss Fuller as errors of the press. You speak of her as poor. I did not know that she was so, but thought the departure of her Uncle Abraham to his namesake's bosom had made her independent. I only knew that she was malicious, and it was not what she had written of me, but what I had heard of her saying, which seemed to demand the intervention of the satiric Nemesis. You may be sure I have felt more sorry about it than anyone . . . . Nevertheless I imagine the general verdict was 'Served her right.' "

Margaret's reaction was summed up in a letter to Caroline: "I sent you a sad cry from my lacerated affections. Now I have learned more fortitude. I feel very calm but sternly towards fate. This last plot against me has been too cruel and cunningly wrought. I shall never acquiesce. I submit because a useless resistance is degrading, but I demand an explanation. I see that it is probable that I shall receive none while I live here . . . . I shall never again be perfectly, religiously generous. I understand why others are not. I am worse than I was. But enough of this—it makes my head ache . . . . Meanwhile I live day by day, though not on manna."

The Storys were well aware of Margaret's chronic crisis—absence of money—and helped in little ways when they could. As her economic position declined, fate seemed to enjoy playing fiendish little tricks. Dolefully Margaret wrote to her brother Richard about one of his bank drafts, "Now it seems someone, intercepting that letter, has forged my signature and taken the money." This for her was a true disaster. Her misfortune in not becoming an heiress also remained constant. The wealthy "Aunt" Mary Rotch had died in December, leaving a fortune of $150,000 to be divided between one friend and her lawyer. "It seems dreadful," Margaret protested to her mother, "that a person who understood so well the wants of others should have neglected this great occasion of making many happy." Mary Rotch had totally ignored Margaret's cogent advice to avoid the evil example of Uncle Abraham.

Family problems, too, were somewhat disturbing—the exceptionally long silences between letters; Richard's abrupt marriage without any warning; Ellen's tearful separation from her erratic poet-husband.

But as if by consolation, the correspondence with Costanza Arconati Visconti was resumed. The marchesa wrote that she had been very ill, and had supposed that Margaret had not returned to Rome, but Margaret had been always in her thoughts.

And also she had been profoundly discouraged by political developments: "The Italians are unworthy of liberty, incapable of using it, and are more disunited between themselves than ever."

To this Margaret replied in terms even more intimate: "I am so delighted to get your letter that I must answer on the instant. I try with all my force to march straight onwards—to answer the claims of the day, to act out my feeling as seems right at the time and not heed the consequences—but in my affections I am tender and weak. Where I have really loved, a barrier, a break, causes me great suffering. I read in your letter that I am still dear to you as you to me . . . . I was afraid you might change, or become indifferent; now I hope not. True, I have written, shall write, about the affairs of Italy what you will much dislike, if ever you see it. I have done, may do, many things that would be very unpleasing to you. Yet there *is* a congeniality, I dare to say, pure and strong and good at the bottom of the heart, far, far deeper than these differences, that would always on a real meeting keep us friends. For me, I could never have but one feeling toward you.

"Now, for the first time, I enjoy a full communion with the spirit of Rome. Last winter, I had here many friends; now all are dispersed, and sometimes I long to exchange thoughts with a friendly circle; but generally I am better content to live thus . . . . The sun shines always, when last winter it never shone. I feel strong; I can go everywhere on foot. I pass whole days abroad; sometimes I take a book, but seldom read it—why should I, when every stone talks?"

She seemed once more on the verge of telling Costanza Arconati about her liaison with Ossoli, and it was odd that she did not. But she was waiting for a favorable set of circumstances, as she explained in a long letter to Caroline, her only confidant. Caroline had kept the secret, though uneasily, as was affirmed by Caroline's letter just received. Margaret, in relief, replied on the following day (March 16). Now she felt free to unburden herself in greater detail.

"I intend to write all that relates to the birth of Angelino in a little book, which I shall, I hope, show you sometime. I have begun it and then stopped; it seemed to me he would die. If he lives, I shall finish it, before the details are at all faded in my mind. Rieti is a place where I should have liked to have him born, and where I should like to have him now, but that the people are so wicked, the most ferocious and mercenary population of Italy. I did not know this, when I went there, and expected to be solitary and quiet among poor people. But they looked on the Marchioness as an ignorant *Inglese,* and they fancy all *Inglesi* have wealth untold. Me they were bent on plundering in every way. They are so still. They made me suffer terribly in the first days and disturb me greatly still in visits to my darling.

"To add to my trouble, the legion Garibaldi is now stationed there, in which so many desperadoes are enlisted. The Neapolitan troops 6 miles off are far worse, and in case of conflict I should fear for the nurse of Angelino, the loveliest young woman there. I cannot take her from her family, I cannot change him to another place without immense difficulty in every way. That I could not nurse him was owing to the wickedness of these people, who threw me into a fever the first days. I shall tell you about it sometime. There is something very singular and fateful in the way all has wrought to give me more and more sorrow and difficulty. Now I live from day to day watching the signs of the times: when I asked you for the money I meant to use it to stay with him in Rieti, but now I do not know whether I can stay there or not. If it proves impossible, I shall at all risks, remove him. I may say every day is to me one of mental doubt and conflict: how it will end, I do not know. I try to hold myself ready every way, body and mind, for any necessity.

"You say no secret can be kept in the civilized world and I suppose not long, but it is very important to me to keep this, for the present, if possible, and by and by to have the mode of disclosure at my option. For this I have made the cruellest sacrifices: it will, indeed, be just like the rest, if they are made to no effect.

"After I wrote you I went to Rieti. The weather was mild when I set out, but the fatality that has attended me throughout, the night changed to a cold unknown in Italy and remained so all the time I stayed. There was, as is common in Italy, no fireplace except in the kitchen. I suffered much in my room with its brick floor, and windows through which came the cold wind freely. My darling did not suffer, because he was a little swaddled child like this * and robed in wool beside, but I did very much. When I first took him in my arms he made no sound but leaned his head against my bosom, and stayed so, he seemed to say how could you abandon me. What I felt you will know only when you have your own. A little girl who lived in the house told me all the day of my departure he would not be comforted, always refusing the breast and looking at the door; he has been a strangely precocious infant; I think it was through sympathy with me, and that in that regard it may be a happiness for him to be with these more plebeian, instinctive, joyous natures. I saw he was more serene, that he was not sensitive as when with me, and slept a great deal more. You speak of my being happy, all the solid happiness I have known has been at times when he went to sleep in my arms. You say when Ellen's beautiful life had been so wasted, it hardly seemed worth while to begin another. I had all those feelings too. I do not look forward to his career and his manly life: It is now I want to be with him, before prescience ends and bafflings begin. If I had a little money I should go with him into strict retirement for a year or two and live for him alone. This I cannot do: all life that has been or could be natural to me is invariably denied. God knows why, I suppose.

"I receive with profound gratitude your thought of taking him, if any thing should happen to us. Should I live, I don't know whether I should wish him to be an Italian or American citizen; it depends on the course events take here politically, but should we die, the person to whom he would naturally fall is a sister of his father, a person of great elegance and sweetness but entirely limited in mind. I should not like that. I shall think about it. Before he was born I did a great deal, having the idea I

* Margaret here pasted on the letter an engraving of the Christ child heavily swaddled. It remains attached.

might die and all my spirit remain incarnated in him, but now I think I shall live and carry him round myself, as I ride on my ass into Egypt.

"You talk about your mangers, Carrie, but that was only for a little, presently came kings with gold cups and all sorts of things. Joseph pawned them; with part of the money he bought this nice donkey for the journey; and they lived on the rest till Joseph could work at his trade. We have no donkey and it costs a great deal to travel in diligences and steamers, and being a nobleman is a poor trade in a ruined despotism just turning into a Republic . . . .

"Speaking of the Republic, you say do I not wish Italy had a great man. Mazzini is a great man; in mind a great poetic states-man, in heart a lover, in action decisive and full of resources as Caesar. Dearly I love Mazzini, who also loves me. He came in just as I had finished this first letter to you. His soft radiant look makes melancholy music in my soul . . . . *

"Ah well! what is the use of writing, dear Caroline. A thousand volumes would not suffice for what I have to say . . . ." Then she gave instructions to burn her letters—instructions not carried out.

In her diary next day she returned to business: "It appears that the Roman ambassadors have not been received in Paris, that the French government will not be friendly to the Italian republic." And for the eighteenth: "Charles Albert has declared war [against the Austrians]. Ten days after, he was defeated at Novara, abdicated in favor of his son Victor Emanuel II, and fled into Spain. Victor Emanuel sues for peace and takes up with the most shameful terms of armistice . . . . Now follows the infamy of France sending her troops here to restore the Pope. The consummation of her downward course, do what she will, she can sink no lower." It was to be the last entry but one, six weeks later.

Hurriedly she turned her attention to another dispatch for

* Margaret sent two letters to Caroline at the same time; the first is now lost. In the *Memoirs*, Emerson deleted the paragraph about Mazzini from this letter to Caroline and attached it to one addressed to him.

the *Tribune*—hurriedly because she was longing to be off to Rieti again, and the letter to Caroline had only accentuated her need to see her baby. Most of her article dealt dispassionately with American artists in Italy, as if all were calm and no disasters were in the offing. She reported only briefly on the impending deceit of France, explaining the perilous state in which Italy had been left by the Austrian victory over the Piedmontese army of King Carlo Alberto. She nevertheless was able to take satisfaction from the collapse of Gioberti, who had been made prime minister by King Carlo Alberto in response to liberal pressure. The Marchesa Arconati would have been most pained at her denunciation.

"The 'illustrious Gioberti' has fallen—fallen forever from his high scaffold of words. His demerits were too unmistakable for rhetoric to hide . . . . Now the name of Gioberti is erased from the corners of the streets to which it was affixed a year ago."

While Margaret was preparing her dispatch, the assembly met to deal with the latest crisis, which had been forced upon the fledgling republic from the north. The deputies decided that extraordinary measures were needed to meet an extraordinary situation. The Republic would, if necessary, fight for its life—with arms.

30

As was required for every trip, Margaret went to police headquarters to secure her travel document to Rieti. She found that despite the revolution and the stirring speeches in the assembly, the bureaucracy was still the same old bureaucracy—corrupt, lazy, and inefficient. The life of the Republic had as yet been too short to change even the printed forms of the old order, much less the personnel.

Nevertheless the familiar form was changed in various ways. It was no longer issued by the *Governa Pontifica—Direzione Generale di Polizia,* but by an office created by the deletion and insertion of words with a pen, so that it became *Direzione di Publica Sicurezza.* Equally significant was the deletion of the phrase requiring the bearer to present himself to the authorities at his destination for an identity check within a specified number of days. The document had become more of an ordinary passport and less of a device for police control.

As a passport it was surprising in certain personal aspects. Margaret gave her name merely as Margherita Ossoli, as if "Ossoli" were her maiden name. Had she been married she probably would have used "Signora Marchesa Margherita Fuller Ossoli"—including her true maiden name, for the maiden name traditionally is all-important for women's official documents in Italy. She gave Rome as her place of birth. And she gave her age as twenty-nine years, when actually she was approaching her thirty-ninth birthday. As this document was retained by Margaret among her papers, it raises doubts as to whether the exceptionally truthful Margaret ever told Angelo the truth about her age—though he, like everyone else, accepted the obvious fact that she was older.

When she reached Rieti (March 27), she found the town full of young bearded men, dressed largely in red tunics, wide-brimmed black felt hats trimmed with ostrich feathers, and armed with lances, sabers, old muskets, and any other weapons that had come to hand. They were in Margaret's eyes (as she had written Caroline before she saw them), a ragtag and bobtail collection of brigands: the hard core of Garibaldi's fabled legion. Among them was a giant Negro wearing a blue poncho and carrying a lasso—Garibaldi's bodyguard; the friar Ugo Bassi of Bologna, sent by Mazzini to be Garibaldi's chaplain; and a woman, short, dark, large-breasted and in her own way beautiful—Garibaldi's wife. She was that Anita whom he had first seen through his telescope when his ship was in a South American port, and had literally abducted from her husband (not, probably, from her fiancé, as said). She was perfect for him—as wild and adventurous and vital as he.

Despite the fact that this motley collection had come to defend the Republic, Margaret's reaction was to hide herself away at once, and avoid any possible contact with the Garibaldini. Once off the street, she dismissed them temporarily from her mind and concentrated on the object closest to her heart: Angelino. She wrote immediately to Ossoli, "I found our dear one in excellent health, and now he is very good. He sleeps alone in bed day and night. He's sleeping now, sucking his little hand. He is very fat but strangely small. His hair doesn't grow at all, and he still wears those hideous black bonnets. Just now everyone was talking so loudly that he waked, and looked at me all surprised and a little tearfully. But when he was alone with me he seemed to recognize me, and leaned over and wrinkled his forehead the way he used to during the first days. I will write more another day; now I am in such pain with my teeth I can't even think to write . . . . I hope to hear that you aren't ill after that bad night. I am always yours, M."

Angelo, who was on late guard duty, replied merely that he was too tired to go to the post office. Margaret answered: "I received the papers and your letter from the Castle * this morning. I am sorry to hear that you have been sent back into hard service so soon, and after that bad night with me, too. Write how you are in detail. I am beginning to feel better . . . .

"Yesterday the family was downstairs at supper and our dear one upstairs asleep in bed. I was sitting at his side thinking how sweet because I had washed him and dressed him and he looked like another child. Suddenly I heard, from below, table and chairs falling and the women crying terribly for help. I flew downstairs and found Pietro and Nicola trying to kill one another. I spoke to Nicola and he didn't answer, just looked at me like a wild animal. The women were holding his arms so that he couldn't get his knife, and he was pulling their hair. Pietro, who didn't have a knife, threw a big piece of wood, which missed my head by inches. All the neighbors came running immediately, and Nicola's employer seized his knife; but if our child had been downstairs, it is probable that he would have been killed . . . .

"But don't worry about our dear one for the moment. I won't leave him alone. I think that when you see him again, you'll agree that he is worth all we have to suffer for him. Chiara is as good as always; she has done her best for him . . . . I am calm and hope that we can find some reasonable solutions. If it is necessary for him, we will tell our secret; who knows if it might not be best in the end? But we must think of everything because all our future depends on our discretion at the moment."

Angelo was concerned with events larger than the quarrel of two brothers over the amount of housework done by their respective wives—the subject which had touched off their vio-

* Probably Castel Sant'Angelo.

lence. "Here we are, still in the usual uncertainty. So much gossip, especially of the betrayal by Carlo Alberto. As usual, kings are always kings. This morning people are saying that Garibaldi has entered the Realm [the Kingdom of Naples] with his troops—so you can hardly believe how agitated I am. But certainly I hope to see our dear one soon . . . I will derive a little pleasure from your letters about him.

" . . . Yesterday in the Chamber a Triumvirate was formed: Saffi, Armellini, and Mazzini. They undertook some urgent programs. Last night we were called to arms to search the afore-mentioned persons' rooms for assassins, as the clerical party wanted to kill them. The reactionary party is doing its utmost —in vain, I hope. Towards daylight, the members of the Triumvirate were accompanied to their respective residences. Everything calmed down, and we were sent home at about 6 in the morning.

"I am very sorry to hear of the things that are happening in the house, and very worried by all you tell me. I don't know if I can come on Tuesday; otherwise I will leave next Saturday evening. I should so like to come tonight, but I can't get permission right away. Please find out about everything that is going on in Rieti, and if ever the situation should be unfavorable return as quickly as you can—with Angelino if you think fit. Meanwhile plan some course of action for our dear one, so as not to leave him unprotected if the entire clerical party should rise.

"Tomorrow, the 1st of April, the Mazzini newspaper, *L'Italia del Popolo,* is being published again, so I will wait to subscribe to *Epoca* . . . . For the coming season at the Teatro Metastasio, Gustavo Modena will act for twenty nights, so you will be able to hear this sublime actor. So I take leave of you. If you think it wise, you can inform Chiara that I am very upset about the difficulties with Nicola. Hugging you . . . . "

On Sunday Angelo could not come to Rieti, as he was given extended guard duty. So they were unable to discuss the important news about the Triumvirs. Count Aurelio Saffi was well known as an old-time liberal, mild and philosophic; Carlo Armellini was an inconspicuous Roman lawyer; Mazzini was

—Mazzini. Margaret's letter giving her reaction is lost, but she must have rejoiced at the naming of Mazzini. Soon Mazzini would dominate the Triumvirate, and its policies would be his policies.

Meanwhile in Rome a provocation had occurred. "On Sunday and Monday the Holy Office [the administration for the Inquisition] was opened to the public, and it was much visited," Angelo wrote. "On Sunday in the evening, someone (the usual party, I suppose) tried to provoke a reaction. There were a few wounded, and it is rumored two dead. We hear that on Monday evening also about 800 persons tried to demonstrate with the Pope's banner, thinking to make the Republic fall. But I well believe they changed their minds, after seeing how few people would stand behind them. Notwithstanding, we are still in a state of agitation."

A bit later Angelo dashed off a note on a subject which had momentarily slipped his mind in all the excitement: "*Cara*— how I wish I could spend tomorrow with you, because I know you remember what day is April 4th. I hope that you at least will enjoy the day with our dear one. As for me, far away as usual, I hope he will never suffer a fate like mine. Give our dear angel a kiss for me, recalling that today is the 3rd of April." (April 4 was the anniversary of that Easter Sunday when they met.)

Margaret's attention for the moment was not on demonstrations in Rome but on the fact that April 4 had arrived. "*Mio caro*—How strange it is that we can't be together on this day," she wrote. "We must pray to be much happier another year. Yesterday I bought small birds for our dinner and I very much hoped to see you. I didn't eat because you didn't arrive. But today I am not sorry you didn't come, because it is raining hard; and Angelino, who was so happy before, so captivating that I kept wishing you could see him, feels out of sorts today. He was in pain all night with his teeth, and today, poor little thing, he is tormented. Let us hope he will be well when you are able to come.

"I think God sent me to protect him during these terrible

days. Nicola was crazy for more than 40 hours, with Chiara desperate, crying continually. Last night Nicola slept and today he is sensible again.

"Garibaldi has not passed the border. More Neapolitan troops have arrived in Aquila, and more Roman troops are arriving here from Terni to reinforce Garibaldi. Here they don't think the Neapolitan troops will enter, but that they are making a feint to move part of the Roman forces from Terracina—and will probably invade from there. Garibaldi has no control over the desperadoes in his band. On Sunday they killed a priest, two citizens and perhaps nine, it is being said. Two corpses were found in the river. The presence of the regular troops could prevent these excesses. I certainly don't have the courage to go out alone now. There is a small garden near here where I take Angelino on nice days. I never go in the road."

Without question Margaret accepted the stereotyped rumors that everywhere were set afloat about Garibaldi's legion. Throughout all Italy, throughout all Catholic Europe "it was said" that the Garibaldini were killing priests, raping women, garroting those who refused to give them food and drink and money. They were, "it was said," brigands and not patriots. And the knowledge of their approach aroused fear in all except a very few.

The legion, which in Rieti had increased in numbers from a bare five hundred to about one thousand men, was in fact governed by the strictest discipline. Garibaldi was merciless in ordering the pillory for looting or execution for rape, and the behavior of his men was actually superior to the usual semiliterate troops of the period. His greatest problem lay in his lack of money, for no government thus far saw fit to support him, and it was necessary for his men to live off the land. It was in the official requisitioning of supplies, for which Garibaldi could not pay or could pay very little, that the reputation of the Garibaldini suffered. It was true, too, that they enjoyed relieving fat monks of the larders stored in the monasteries, and offered insults or violence when opposed.

The composition of the legion differed basically from the

normal regiments of the regular armies. It was made up chiefly of workmen (artisans and tradesmen), leavened by professional men and many students (some as young as fourteen). Peasants were very few. Surprising numbers of the aristocracy had enrolled, such as the rich young Bolognese Angelo Masina, who brought with him forty-two lancers, paid from his own purse. The high level of culture in the legion was attested by a Dutch artist who told of his amazement at hearing one of Garibaldi's ordinary sentries singing a stanza of Tasso's *Gerusalemme Liberata.* Little difference existed between officers and men, and promotion was made on the spot for an act of bravery. To offset these positive aspects, Garibaldi in one of his dreamier moments had admitted a number of convicts, on the assumption that to fight for the unity of Italy would purify the worst of men. Some were purified, but by no means all—as Garibaldi eventually had to admit. One thing they all were: volunteers ready to fight for a cause in which they believed, under a leader they adored.

Normally Margaret, as an accurate journalist and historian, would have informed herself of these facts—but the presence of her baby totally changed her reactions. She believed her child menaced, and was eager for his father to come to his protection. Angelo, as a soldier himself, was much less agitated. In reply to Margaret's somewhat hysterical letter he said merely that he had arranged to leave on the mail coach. "I asked uncle for permission to be absent tomorrow—Friday—until time to go on guard duty. He was very angry." In spite of his uncle's anger Angelo arrived as promised and remained a week.

Evidently they concluded that the Garibaldini were not so threatening as believed, for Angelino was left in Rieti. Five days after Angelo's departure, Margaret hired a light carriage and set off for Rome. Their optimism was put to the test while she was resting at an *osteria,* a little wayside inn. It was Emelyn Story, not Margaret, who wrote an account of the incident.

"While there, she was startled by the *padrone,* who with great alarm rushed into the room and said, 'We are lost! Here is the

Legion of Garibaldi! These men always pillage, and if we do not give all up to them without pay, they will kill us.' Margaret looked out upon the road, and saw that it was true that the legion was coming thither with all speed. For a moment, she said, she felt uncomfortable; for such was the exaggerated account of the conduct of the men that she thought it quite possible that they would take her horses, and so leave her without the means of proceeding on her journey. On they came, and she determined to offer them a lunch at her own expense, having faith that gentleness and courtesy was the best protection from injury.

"Accordingly, as soon as they arrived and rushed boisterously into the *osteria,* she rose and said to the *padrone,* 'Give these good men wine and bread on my account, for after their ride they must need refreshment.' Immediately the noise and confusion subsided; with respectful bows to her they seated themselves and partook of the lunch, giving her an account of their journey. When she was ready to go, and her *vettura* was at the door, they waited upon her, took down the steps, and assisted her with much gentleness and respectfulness of manner. And she drove off, wondering how men with such natures could have the reputation they had."

She was returning to a Rome where she would speedily learn of their other qualities—for Rome at last would cry aloud for Garibaldi, the one man who now could save it.

3 1

After no more than three weeks' absence Margaret re-entered a Rome vastly changed. It was a circle within a circle of enemies—a Catholic noose gradually being drawn tight about the center of the Catholic world, and the people already were beginning to feel the effects of strangulation. Not since 1527, when combined German Protestant and Spanish Catholic armies had sacked Rome with a ferocity equaling that of the Goths and Vandals, had the city been faced with so ghastly a prospect. The people shivered and withdrew within the walls.

To the south were the armies of the Bourbon king of Naples, already across the frontier. To the north and east were the armies of the Austrian emperor, reoccupying bit by bit all the territories they had lost, and moving slowly but inexorably toward Rome. To the west, at sea, were ships bearing soldiers of the king of Spain, steaming at full speed to the aid of the pope. Only the position of the young French Republic remained equivocal among the Catholic powers.

On the day Margaret reached Rome, the French publicly made known their intention. The French assembly, responsive to the maneuverings of its President Louis Napoleon, voted credits for a military expedition to Italy. The French expeditionary force, it was explained, was not intended for an attack on the Roman Republic—but merely as a stabilizing element. Secretly Louis Napoleon—who as a young man had been a liberal, a Carbonaro, and actually had fought against tyranny in the Papal States—now had other intentions. The first was to counterbalance Austria and reestablish French military power in the Italian peninsula; the second was to promote himself from "prince" president to emperor. To accomplish the first objective he needed money and bayonets. To accomplish the second, he needed the pope to consecrate his rule as ordained by the divine right of kings.

"The struggle is now fairly, thoroughly commenced between the principle of democracy and the old powers," Margaret reported to the *Tribune*. Then she indulged in a little prophecy: "That struggle may last fifty years, and the earth be watered with the blood and tears of more than one generation, but the result is sure. All Europe . . . is to be under republican government in the next century."

At the moment in Rome the next century seemed less like a century and more like a millenium. Money was tight. Ossoli had experienced irritating difficulties with exchange and dispatch of funds to Margaret while she was in Rieti; and on her return cash was almost not to be had. The Republic was printing new money, but gold went into hiding, and the financial problems of the government became increasingly grave. As for Margaret, even the receipt of one hundred dollars from her childhood friend and mentor Eliza Farrar was little help, because she was forced to lose so heavily in the exchange.

Early in April the triumvirate had published a statement of its basic program: "No war of classes, no hostility to existing wealth, no wanton or unjust violation of the rights of property; but a constant disposition to ameliorate the material condition of the classes least favored by fortune." It was clear that no radical changes were intended in the structure of Italian society, for the economic bases of the aristocracy and the Church were to be left intact. And the preservation of wealth of course meant the preservation of power, however temporarily modified—as Machiavelli could have informed Mazzini.

In its general reforms, despite the pressure of time and lack of dependable personnel, the Republic was moving with surprising efficiency. Already it had forbidden star-chamber courts and annulled the jurisdiction of bishops over schools and universities. It had removed all press censorship, and both republican and clerical pamphlets were widely circulated. Its only economic blow to the Church had been the nationalization of ecclesiastical benefits—that is, the seizure of ecclesiastical estates. They were vast in extent, and immense in value. This measure was intended as a step toward agrarian reform, as the Church properties were to be apportioned among the poverty-stricken, land-hungry peasants. And, as evidence of freedom of religious belief, the High Tribunal of the Holy Office (the Inquisition) had been abolished, and its rooms converted into apartments for the poor—as Ossoli had reported sketchily to Margaret.

To the Triumvirs religious freedom included freedom of Protestants and priests, so the Republic vigorously opposed any persecution of clerics. (The papal government had forbidden any Protestant church within the walls of Rome.) Though many cardinals and other high prelates had fled to Gaeta, others did not flee, restraining themselves from overt hostility to the Republic.

Margaret reported the situation thus: "The people of Rome took the confessionals out of the churches, and made mock confessions in the piazzas, the scope of which was, 'I have sinned, Father so and so.' 'Well, my son, how much will you *pay* the Church for absolution?' Afterward the people thought of burning the confessionals, or using them for barricades; but at the request of the Triumvirate they desisted, and even put them back into the churches. But it was from no reaction of feeling that they stopped short, only from respect for the Government."

Pius, in another severe Allocution, launched a new propaganda initiative against the Republic. "Who does not know," he proclaimed, "that the city of Rome, the principal seat of the Church, has now become, alas, a den of wild beasts, overflowing with men of every nation, apostates, or heretics, of leaders of communism and socialism and animated by the most terrible hatred against Catholic truth, strive to teach and disseminate pestiferous errors of every description."

So effective were the pope's words that the London *Times* correspondent, who happened *not* to be in Rome, filed reports on the terror in the republican city, describing luridly how priests "who had the courage to appear in public" had been "butchered in open day and their flesh, cut up in morsels, thrown into the Tiber." The *Times'* man was followed by other absentee journalists throughout Europe, and the clerical parties everywhere accused the Roman Republicans of equaling the "reds" of the Paris barricades.

But the New York *Tribune's* woman was on the spot, ready and willing to give eyewitness accounts: "Both in France and England the grossest falsehoods have been circulated with unwearied diligence about the state of things in Italy. An amusing specimen of what is still done in this line I find just now in a foreign journal, where it says there are red flags on all the houses of Rome, meaning to imply that the Romans are athirst for blood. Now, the fact is that these flags are put up at the entrance of those streets where there is no barricade, as a signal to coachmen and horsemen that they can pass freely. There is one on the house where I am, in which is no person but myself, who thirst for peace, and the *Padrone,* who thirsts for money."

Soon Margaret's indignation at the distortions in the *Times* led her to attack it openly in the *Tribune:* "I am surprised to see the air of perfect good faith with which articles from the London *Times,* upon the revolutionary movements, are copied into our papers. There exists not in Europe a paper more violently opposed to the cause of freedom than the *Times,* and neither its leaders nor its foreign correspondents are to be depended upon."

The actual situation was being reported dispassionately to Washington by the able new United States chargé d'affaires,

Lewis Cass, Jr., who had arrived in Rome during Margaret's absence in Rieti. The first chargé, appointed in response to American public opinion aroused by Margaret's *Tribune* articles, had died immediately on reaching Rome, and a hiatus of six months had ensued. Lewis Cass, Jr., had served as a major in the Mexican War, and was the son of that Lewis Cass who had been American minister to France and eventually was to become Secretary of State. Lewis, Jr., had spent his formative years in France, and in many respects fulfilled the sophisticated qualifications laid down by Margaret in her appeal for a "good" ambassador. He was well educated, a linguist, cautious, and shrewd.

Cass was under instructions to withhold recognition from either the papal or the republican government until the situation stablilized. As a result he was distrusted by both the Romans and the Americans in Rome. Margaret wrote in the *Tribune* about " . . . the irritation and surprise occasioned here by the position of Mr. Cass, the Envoy. It is most unfortunate that we should have an envoy here for the first time, just to offend and disappoint the Romans . . . . Now it seems to me that the only dignified ground for our government, the only legitimate ground for any republican government, is to recognize for any nation the government chosen by itself."

Cass's actual choice for recognition gradually became apparent in his careful analytic messages, of which Margaret of course was not aware. In his official communication of April 21 to Secretary of State John M. Clayton he stated: "With every allowance for misrepresentation, arising from ignorance or the reaction of popular sentiment, the power wielded by the Cardinal college must unquestionably have been immense. Being in complete possession of the courts of justice, if they deserve the name, and of the confessional, this body were enabled to convert all and every influence to their own personal and class aggrandisement, as they are accused of having done. In illustration of this system I will quote the law of '*fiducia*' which is a matter of record, and familiar to every Roman. By this law a dying man can give his property in trust to the priest attending his last moments, the secret words which the priest declares were uttered by him being considered his valid testament. Of course such a law alone gives the priesthood the power of disinheriting any family and succeeding to any heritage.

"The belief prevails in the United States that the party which insisted on reform and which showed its discontent of the Pope's government is merely an ultra-democratic faction in the unfavorable sense of those words. But such is far from being the case. I have learned to my surprise that there is a large party of moderate, educated, and comparatively wealthy men in the Assembly, who care nothing whatever for a republic—who abhor communism, who desire more than all things protection of property, and who express the conviction that no right or freedom or happiness is possible under the sway of the Cardinals whom they have always regarded as the real government."

In the end Cass's overcaution, combined with the slowness of communications, proved the abnegation of the policy he gradually sought to promote. For time, like all else, was running against the Republic, and whatever was to be done for it, had to be done at once.

Three days after Cass's missive to Clayton, the first French ship arrived at Civita Vecchia, the port of Rome forty miles northwest of the city. The French forces, under the command of General Nicolas Charles Victor Oudinot, second duke of Reggio, were about ten thousand strong. Though no military opposition was offered, the townspeople were alarmed and hostile. General Oudinot, with a great flourish, issued a conciliatory proclamation: "The government of the French Republic, animated by liberal and friendly motives, declares that it will respect the wishes of the majority of the Roman nation—it comes as their friend, with the view of maintaining their legitimate influence, and will not suffer to be imposed upon them a form of government they do not desire." Such were the French words, but the words remained to be tested by deeds.

On April 25 Emelyn Story noted in her diary that Margaret brought news "that all Rome was in a state of excitement, the news that the French had landed at Civita Vecchia having been

The great Italian patriot Giuseppe Mazzini, as he appeared when Margaret became his intimate friend. Mazzini, a lifelong Republican and founder of the revolutionary organization "Young Italy," assumed the dominant role in the Triumvirate formed after the proclamation of the Roman Republic in 1849. (*An engraving after the painting by Ashurst, Museo Centrale del Risorgimento, Rome*)

The Roman popular leader Angelo Brunetti, nicknamed "Ciceruacchio" or "Big-Boy" for his girth, was wildly cheered when he announced in the Piazza del Popolo the grant of a provisional constitution by Pope Pius IX. (*Museo di Roma*)

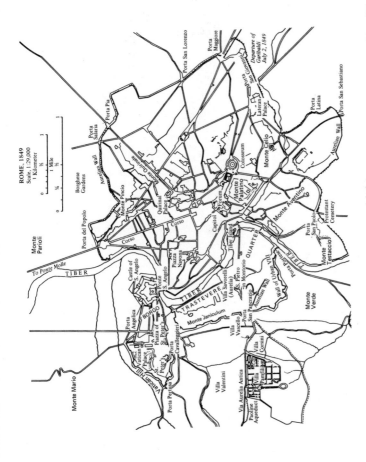

Rome in 1849, as contained within the ancient walls. The French attack on the city, to restore Pius IX to his temporal throne, centered around the Janiculum Hill—at the left of the map. (Adapted from *Garibaldi's Defence of the Roman Republic*, by G. M. Trevelyan; *Longmans, Green & Co., London*)

Giuseppe Garibaldi in his flamboyant red cape and plumed hat, as he appeared during the siege of Rome. Though not commander-in-chief of the Roman forces, his brilliant defense of the city established his reputation as the great military genius of the Italian Risorgimento and captured the imagination of the world. (*Museo Centrale del Risorgimento, Rome*)

The elegant Villa Savorelli on the Janiculum Hill served as Garibaldi's headquarters during the siege, and was demolished by the French artillery. Today, restored, it is called the Villa Aurelia, and is a part of the American Academy in Rome. (*Museo Centrale del Risorgimento, Rome*)

The beautiful and wealthy Principessa Cristina Trivulzio Belgioioso was known throughout Europe as "the revolutionary princess," and was greatly admired by Margaret. She was political activist, intellectual, and writer; and during the siege of Rome served as directress of hospitals, with Margaret as her assistant. (*Private collection of the Marchesa Maura 'dal Pozzo, Belgirate*)

The battle at the Porta San Pancrazio, as seen from the roof of the Villa Savorelli. This is one section of the first panoramic photograph ever made of a battlefield (June 1849). The main gateway is at the left, and the Villa Vascello defense point is just outside the walls in the center. (*Museo Centrale del Risorgimento, Rome*)

received. We went with her to the Piazza del Popolo to hear the addresses made to the people, and there we met, standing on a bench, the Princess Belgioioso." William Story, in his diary, added a few more details: "Sterbini [Pietro Sterbini, a minister whom Margaret knew and considered 'untalented'] arose in a carriage and said that the *generosissimi Romani* [the most generous Romans] must be quiet, that the French had been deceived into a supposition that there was anarchy here, and that when they learned the facts they would embrace the Romans as brothers. I met the Princess Belgioioso, grown much older and negligently dressed. We walked along together up beyond the Pantheon, and I then left her. She was very cordial and agreeable . . . ."

On the twenty-sixth, Oudinot's aide arrived in Rome and conferred with Mazzini. He declared that the French sought to block Austrian or Neapolitan (Bourbon) intervention, and to promote an accord between the Roman people and the pope. "And if the people do not want the Pope restored, what then?" Mazzini said.

The answer was coldly polite: "He will be restored, just the same."

Mazzini went to the assembly with this message, and asked if the deputies willed that the gates of Rome be opened to the French, or if they preferred to call on the people to defend themselves. After a brief tumult the Triumvirs directed by unanimous vote to assume the responsibility "to save the Republic and to repulse force with force."

While this news was being spread by posters, ink not dry, on the walls of Rome, not only Margaret but her friends became frenetically active. "To Porta Cavalleggieri and Porta Angelica to see the barricades, or rather earth-mounds, ramparts, stockades, which the Romans are building in the event of the French," William Story entered in his diary. " . . . I understand from Vincenzo Bassanelli that the *Guardia* are nearly unanimous in desiring the return of the Pope and the abolition of the Triumvirate and Republic, and that they will not fight." Next day he records the opposite: "Went early with Margaret

Fuller to Piazza Santi Apostoli to see the *Guardia Civica* meet and be harangued. Sterbini asked them if at the cost of their blood they were ready to defend the city; to which they screamed 'Si!' and held up their hats on their bayonets, making the piazza ring with huzzas. But the enthusiasm did not seem of the right stuff—it was rather a *festa* demonstration." And among the *Guardia* that day was the Sergeant Giovanni Angelo Ossoli.

By now Margaret had become too busy to make daily entries in her journal. On a page confusedly noted "It is the 25th April 28th" she made her final comment: "The anniversary of the Pope's encyclic letter. The tragedy so begun is tending to a close. Rome is barricaded, and the foe daily, hourly, expected. Will the Romans fight? Outwardly they express great order. The Chamber of Deputies has warmly and unanimously voted to persist. At the review of the Civic Guard yesterday they gave great promise, yet somehow I doubt them all. From my window I see now where they are bringing boards. I suppose to make a support for cannon, and it seems to be such play for men and boys alike."

In a dispatch from French headquarters the London *Times'* correspondent neatly summed up the situation for doubting Europe and confused America. The "degenerate remnant of the Roman people," he said, was arming itself to do battle, and "believe they are heroes."

On the afternoon of April 27 Garibaldi and his bronzed, dust-covered legion, with their wide hats, ostrich feathers, lances, blue and red tunics, marched into Rome. And the degenerate common people gazed at the bearded, statuesque leader on his splendid white horse and shouted, "He has come, he has come!"

32

Early on the hot, still morning of April 30 Margaret received by messenger this note in English: "Dear Miss Fuller, You are named Regolatrice of the Hospital of the Fate Bene Fratelli. Go there at twelve if the alarm bell does not ring before. When you arrive there, you will receive all the women coming for the wounded and give them your directions so that you are sure to have a certain number of them, night and day. May God help us. Christine Trivulzio of Belgioioso."

As yet not a shot had been fired, but the note told Margaret the one thing she most dreaded to know: Angelo soon would be in danger.

With the Hospital of the Fate Bene Fratelli she was very familiar. It was situated on the Tiber island, shaped like a ship. Since antiquity the island had been associated with healing the ill. Once a temple to Aesculapius had stood there, and the two original Roman bridges remained intact. In the Middle Ages monks had built the hospital. Now it was all too conveniently close to what might prove the front lines if the French attacked. And that they would attack, Margaret did not for a moment doubt. This was to be a part of her own destiny, along with the larger whole.

Already the French army was advancing in close ranks toward Rome. General Oudinot, after leaving guards to protect his communications with the sea, mustered more than six thousand infantry and all his batteries of field guns. His siege guns and scaling ladders remained behind, as he did not believe they would be needed. His scouts ranged only shortly in advance of the main body of troops. The troops felt no anxiety and were bothered chiefly by the heat. In their briefing, General Oudinot had repeated the information received from clerical agents in Rome: "We shall not meet as enemies either the citizens or the soldiers of Rome. Both consider us as liberators." Then, giving vent to nationalistic sentiments not sustained by historical experience, added contemptuously, "The Italians never fight." General Oudinot, a victim of a persistent myth, could have read with profit one of Margaret's maxims: "We must leave off despising if we would begin to learn."

For all the French optimism, it was apparent that they were not welcome. Villages, farmsteads, and roads were empty of people. And at intervals on houses and roadside walls was written in large letters in the French language: "FRANCE RESPECTS FOREIGN NATIONALITIES; HER MIGHT WILL NEVER BE EMPLOYED AGAINST THE LIBERTY OF ANY PEOPLE." This was the text of Article Five of the new French constitution. As an experiment in psychological warfare by humanitarians against a professional army, it proved a total failure. If the French soldiers could read, it had no effect on them whatever. Their officers, of course, were antidemocratic. But the irony of the words increased the outrage of the defenders, and strengthened their will to fight.

Pathetically inadequate were the arms and men of whom the people of Rome could sing. To confront a disciplined, well-equipped enemy, the Romans had at their disposal a hodgepodge force of some fourteen hundred miscellaneous volunteers; three hundred university students; one thousand volunteers in the national guard (formerly civic guard), who had never seen action; twenty-five hundred papal regular troops of the line, who had come over to the Republic merely because they had been jealous of the favors lavished on the Swiss regiments by the pope; a brigade of refugee Lombard *Bersaglieri* (sharpshooters with feathered hats), whose sympathies lay with the Piedmont king; and twelve hundred Garibaldini. Thus while the Roman forces equaled or outnumbered the French, they were anything but a heterogeneous army. For armament they could boast of the fine equipment provided the former troops of the papal army, but the rest were sketchily equipped with inferior or outdated pieces, or indeed, whatever could be snatched to hand. The Republic had ordered, in its first days, ten thousand new muskets from French manufacturers—muskets that never arrived, as with appropriate foresight they had been diverted by General Oudinot.

Equally disadvantageous, the command structure of the Roman forces had been hastily improvised. The capable General Giuseppe Avezzana, an admirer of Garibaldi, had been named minister of war. Avezzana had spent many years in New York as an exile, and had imbibed American democratic ways. But for all Avezzana's respect for Garibaldi, Colonel Pietro Roselli shortly was to receive the supreme command. Roselli was a conventional gentleman-soldier, definitely not a Republican, by whose appointment and promotion to general the Triumvirs hoped to give respectability to their army in the eyes of the aristocratic governments of Europe. To have appointed Garibaldi commander-in-chief was almost as unthinkable to the Triumvirs as it would have been to either the Austrian or French generals. His South American training in guerrilla warfare was outside the scope of positional warfare as understood in Europe. He was further disqualified as (in the European word) a proletarian. And the wild appearance of his "legion" also augered heavily against him. Proper soldiers, like the French, wore white gloves.

Finally, for the defense of the city there remained the walls, for so many centuries the last line to be held against the barbarian invaders. Once upon a time the might of ancient Rome had made the old Republican walls superfluous, and not until the regime of the Emperor Aurelian, toward the end of the third century A.D. had an anxious Rome been constrained to build a new wall around its own periphery. These walls were constructed of the justly famous Roman brick, to great thickness, with walkways and inner chambers for catapults and other engines of war. They could not, however, under any circumstances, withstand the artillery of the nineteenth century. But from the Vatican to below the Tiber island, the right bank, and most especially the Janiculum hill, had been enclosed in its entirety by Pope Urban VIII at about midpoint in the seventeenth century. These walls had incorporated the most advanced skills of the Italian military engineers of the time, and still offered a formidable barrier to any besieging army. Their great defect was that the terrain at key points outside the walls was as high or higher than the terrain within the walls.

It was a measure of the importance of the Janiculum hill that Garibaldi was posted there by the astute Avezzana; and, as the cards fell, the *Guardia Nazionale* on the walls above the Vatican gardens, including, in the second battalion, Sergeant Ossoli. This was the side from which the French army approached, expecting to enter directly into the Vatican. During the night before their arrival, placards appeared upon the walls of Rome calling on the papal party to rise.

Margaret now temporarily ceased to write, and concentrated all her energies—as she always had longed to do—on action. Thus it was left to her friends to record the day-to-day account of the siege of Rome, which might otherwise have been found in her journal. Both Emelyn and William Story described the same events. It was Emelyn who better gave the setting for April 30 and the arrival of the French.

"All the streets have been deserted, and as we walked this morning through the Babuino we were forcibly struck by the pause and hush of everything, the lull of the city as before the storm presently to fall upon it. It was as if the hour had come, and one could only pray for safe deliverance. We met on our way the terrified H., who urged us to remove to Casa Diez, whither he proposed to summon all Americans and place them under the protection of our flag. While we were walking home we heard the first cannon and went quickly to move the children to Casa Diez, whence we have been seeing the whole battle. All day long the greatest interest and excitement continue. The house was filled with Americans, and as Frank Heath's rooms, which we have taken possession of, commanded the finest view, they all flocked thither. Margaret Fuller, who had been at the Hospital, came to tell us about the wounded, of whom there were already seventy. At five o'clock, as the firing seemed to have abated, we went to the Pincio, whence we could see that the French had moved their position and, having been repulsed at Porta Cavallaggieri, were now before the Vatican gardens. The streets were kept lighted all night and all things prepared for a night attack. Rumors of all sorts were flying about and many persons greatly alarmed. We remained at Casa Diez, as our own house was cut off from the rest of the city by a barricade which would be disagreeable in case of attack. We kept looking at the watch-fires of the enemy as they blazed in the distance, and we got little sleep."

In spite of all her distractions and fears, Margaret later forced herself to prepare an article for the *Tribune:* "War near at hand seems to me even more dreadful than I had fancied it . . . . I have, for the first time, seen what wounded men suffer. The night of the 30th of April I passed in the hospital, and saw the terrible agonies of those dying or who needed amputation, felt their mental pains and longing for the loved ones . . . . The impudent falsehoods of the French general's dispatches are incredible. The French were never decoyed on in any way. They were received with every possible mark of hostility. They were defeated in open field, the Garibaldi legion rushing out to meet them; and though they suffered much from the walls, they sustained themselves nowhere. The vanity that strives to cover over these facts is unworthy of men. The only excuse for the imprudent conduct of the expedition is that they were deceived, not by the Romans, but by the priests of Gaeta, leading them to expect action in their favor within the walls. These priests themselves were deluded by their hopes and old habits of mind." Lewis Cass, at almost the same time, was reporting in diplomatic language almost the same subject matter to Washington.

The details of the French defeat were quickly known to every inhabitant of Rome. The invading troops had advanced along the outlying roads lined with cypress, umbrella pine, and marble statuary, and at eleven o'clock had reached the walls near the ancient Vatican gate, the Porta Pertusa. It was said later that Oudinot had marked this as his objective on a map which did not show that the gate had been walled up for centuries—though many found it difficult to believe that he should have been so ill informed. Within a hundred yards of the gate two cannons fired, and some of the French actually thought the shots were the traditional Roman cannon marking midday. The rapidly succeeding bursts of grapeshot quickly convinced them otherwise, and their own artillery swung into action. On the walls, not far from Ossoli's sector, the first Roman fell, crushed by a cannonball—a young volunteer from the University, a student of philosophy and mathematics. Now it was clear to the French that the people of Rome intended, as the assembly had declared, to resist force with force. Momentarily the French soldiers were overcome with irresolution and confusion.

Garibaldi, recognizing that tactically the defense must be carried on outside the walls because of the height of the terrain and the presence of enemy artillery, had stationed his men at the large and beautiful Villa Corsini. The villa lay not far from the Porta San Pancrazio, flanking the ancient Roman Via Aurelia, and was about a mile from the point of the initial engagement. Watching through his glass, Garibaldi made the decision to attack. To draw first fire, he sent his student volunteers rushing down the slope. With bayonets and slogans they flung themselves on the French infantry, who were bewildered by the shouting and the frenzy of such an assault by amateurs, "clawing with their hands." But the advantage swayed back and forth, until Garibaldi led out his reserves in a sharp assault, which forced the French into a hurried retreat. Garibaldi, though wounded in the stomach, maintained throughout the superlative calm that helped to make him famous—and revealed nothing of his pain. General Oudinot stopped his flight at about four hours' march from Rome, and there regrouped his forces. He was indignant at his reception, and seemed to feel that he had been betrayed. He had abandoned 500 dead and wounded, lost 365 prisoners, but in his official communiqué he claimed that the "affair of 30 April" was "one of the most brilliant in which French troops have taken part since our great wars." Urgently he requested secret instructions from Paris.

"Contrary to all expectations, the Romans have made a brave and gallant resistance," Cass reported to Washington. "These actions have infused a spirit into the population, the effect of which it is impossible to predict."

And William Story hurriedly scribbled in his diary: "May 1st. the French have retreated, and though we have been spying from the windows nothing can be seen. The Romans are all elated and surprised even at themselves . . . . The report is that a large force of Neapolitans is marching on Rome and is now at Velletri or Albano. This seems most unfortunate . . . ."

It was more than unfortunate, as coming weeks would reveal. The people of Rome were indignant at this treachery from the south. The Triumvirs became additionally alarmed, under the apprehension that the Bourbon troops might unite with the French in a coordinated military action against the city. Garibaldi, even more than the Triumvirs, who lacked military experience, was aware of the dangers of conducting a defense on two fronts. He therefore urged that, as the French force was the smaller and was disorganized, he be permitted to pursue the French and thrust them into the sea.

To this proposal, the Triumvirs, and in particular Mazzini, conscious of the Bourbon presence so near Rome, and the Austrian armies not far away, replied that "the Republic is not at war with France, merely in a state of defense." With this posture Mazzini hoped that public opinion in France would rally to the support of the Roman Republic. Alas, he was either misinformed about the true situation in France, or misconceived Louis Napoleon's intentions.

To Garibaldi, not to act decisively against the French implied fatal disaster, and was the source of a bitter private quarrel with Mazzini—the first of many more to come. It was said, too, that Garibaldi stood no chance of defeating so well-equipped a professional army as Oudinot's, just as the Roman Republic stood no chance of resisting the full might of so great a power as France. Such arguments were to Garibaldi meaningless rationalizations. He saw only that defeat was defeat, and victory was victory—and with victory the Republic could buy time, just as time was being bought by driving the French away from the walls of Rome. Of the Bourbon army, for all its multitudes, he had no fear. He would take care of it in his own way.

It is to be wondered that Margaret did not seek an interview with Garibaldi at this point, but she lacked the experience to judge the revolutionary significance of his mode of warfare. Through lack of contact her remarkable intuition momentarily failed to grasp the largeness of the role looming for Garibaldi. Certainly she was aware of the intoxicating effect his presence had on the people, and the combination of Mazzini and Garibaldi in Rome together literally inspired the population to actions that would normally have seemed totally beyond them. Reading between the lines of her letters and dispatches, it is clear that she herself doubted while others believed—it did not seem to her that the Republic could survive. Yet she was devoting herself and her Ossoli without reservation to a cause that to her was both just and noble.

Somberly she observed in the *Tribune*, "Should guns and bayonets replace the Pope on the throne, he will find its foundations, once deep as modern civilization, now so undermined that it falls with the least awkward movement." And as a reminder, " . . . Two of the balls that struck St. Peter's have been sent to Pius IX by his children."

33

An odd and dreamlike lull in the siege now ensued. The whole of the month of May was devoted to a *pas de deux* between Oudinot and Mazzini, assisted by a few secondary figures, while the armed *corps de ballet* watched and waited expectantly and Garibaldi practiced prodigious leaps in the wings offstage. "To every proposal on the part of the Romans, General Oudinot has briefly returned for answer, that he would talk of terms when he was in the city of Rome, not before," wrote Cass to Washington. "And to this the Romans now retort that he will only enter the city of Rome as a prisoner." But in fact no offensive action was taken against Oudinot, because Mazzini preferred pantomime.

The May ballet began *adagio,* as is indicated by the entries in William Story's diary. "May 2nd—We went to carry our money [raised by the Americans, and reported by Margaret as $250] to the Princess Belgioioso, directress of all the hospitals, whom we found sitting surrounded with men and women, giving her various orders with calmness and clearness and showing the greatest practicality and good sense in all her arrangements.

She has laid down strict rules and reduced the establishment to order and discipline; for three days and two nights she has been without sleep and still is strong. Then we went to Spillman's to get her an ice-cream to cool her parched throat, and while we were there came screaming and hooting a crowd which dragged along two Cardinals' carriages magnificently painted and gilt. These with pick-axes and clubs they tore entirely to pieces and set fire to, crying out, 'This is the blood of the poor!'—'*É il sangue dei poveri!*' Going along, we met Garibaldi's party, which had met a French detachment and taken 30 prisoners. Returning to the hospital we carried our ice to the Princess, and she partook of it, giving part to her little child, into whose stifling room I went to give it to her. Then we went over the wards—but how horrible is this reverse side of war! . . . I wish Pio Nono could have been there to see the result of his irresolution and vacillation, or rather of his weak and cruel inconsistency . . . .

"May 3rd—At the Vatican gardens, where we went to see Ossoli and saw the whole plan of battle, the men talked with great spirit, told me all the particulars and said the Romans were a little timid at first, but grew hotter and fiercer as the battle continued, and at last were full of courage and confidence, even to heroism."

Emelyn Story's diary enlarges some of the details. They "walked along the wall and saw the posts of the Guard who had fought so well, and the ground held by the French. As we looked from the wall this third day after the battle we saw the monks under the black flag looking for the unburied dead who had fallen in the ditches or among the hedges. The French had retreated without an effort to bury their dead, and in one instance a living wounded man was found on this third day with the bodies of two dead soldiers lying across him." As for Margaret, she was denied "a chance to say anything of a private nature" to Ossoli, because one of his relatives was present.

The following day Emelyn Story made an entry with the exciting news that Garibaldi had slipped away from Rome—on

Mazzini's orders—with a puny band of 2,300 men to meet King Bomba's well-heeled army of 10,000 camped in the Alban hills overlooking Rome. Perhaps Story spoke of this when he went to Mazzini to request an armed guard to protect the Americans in Rome. Mazzini lodged in an ordinary room in the Palazzo Quirinale—one, as he said, "small enough to feel at home in." Flowers were delivered to him every morning from an unknown admirer. For recreation he played the guitar and sang.

Noted Story: "May 5th—Called on Mazzini the Triumvir, whom I found haggard and worn in appearance, with rather an agreeable face, dim black eyes, full forehead, straight black hair, and grizzled beard. He speaks English and wished that America could give the republic its sympathy and adhesion. His practicality, I cannot but think, has been veneered over his mind by his English life."

Shortly thereafter came news that Garibaldi, by a series of tricks, rapid attacks and withdrawals, and a surprise night march, had defeated a major segment of King Bomba's vastly superior army and forced it to halt its advance toward Rome. Garibaldi was prepared to continue his guerrilla harassment, but Mazzini, fearing a new approach of the French coordinated with King Bomba, recalled the battle-worn legion to Rome. Nevertheless Garibaldi had given a convincing demonstration of how he would deal with Oudinot.

On the very day of Garibaldi's victory over Bomba, Louis Napoleon, twisting his fierce handlebar moustaches in fury, made public a letter to Oudinot in which he stated: "Our soldiers have been received as enemies; our military honor is involved; I will not tolerate that it should become in any way impaired. Reinforcements will not be lacking."

These words were clear evidence that Mazzini's policy of conciliation had already failed; nevertheless Mazzini continued to hope that the French might be approached in good faith, because a small French republican opposition to Louis Napoleon had surfaced. As evidence of the Roman Republic's lack of hostility toward the French Republic, the Triumvirs had ordered their French prisoners to be feted, taken on sight-seeing tours of Rome, and returned to their units with large quantities of good cigars.

Louis Napoleon was not interested in cigars; he was interested only in playing for time, until the clerical party could consolidate its power in France, and until sufficient reinforcements could reach General Oudinot. Thus he chose the device of negotiation, to raise false hopes among the Romans and lull their vigilance. For his agent he chose Ferdinand de Lesseps, a sincere, youngish consul-general already dreaming of a great engineering achievement—the Suez Canal. De Lesseps, who arrived in Rome the middle of May, approached his task in a spirit of compromise. He was impressed by Mazzini and the other Triumvirs, and with General Oudinot's agreement arranged for a twenty-day truce between the French and the Roman forces.

It was at about this time that Lewis Cass, Jr., called on Margaret to make her acquaintance. He urged her to join the rest of the Americans at the Casa Diez in the Via Gregoriana, for it was much less exposed to danger than the Piazza Barberini. They felt an immediate rapport, as was indicated by Margaret's subsequent remarks about him, and by the letters that passed between them. He offered to keep Margaret informed, as a journalist, about the progress of the impending negotiations, and thereafter did so. Thus Margaret was able not only to report procedures step by step, but to give the text of documents that passed between the Triumvirs and the French envoy. Unlike Mazzini, she was harshly skeptical, and called the de Lesseps negotiations the "Second Act of the French farce."

"Now appears in Rome M. Ferdinand Lesseps, Envoy Etc. of the French Government. He declares himself clothed with full powers to treat with Rome. He cannot conceal his surprise at all he sees there, at the ability with which preparations have been made for the defense, at the patriotic enthusiasm which pervades the population. Nevertheless, in beginning his game of treaty-making, he is not ashamed to insist on the French occupying the city. Again and again repulsed, he again and again returns to this point."

The Triumvirs replied to de Lesseps with a long, wordy, and involved moral justification of the Republic's position. While de Lesseps continued to spin fine spider webs, Oudinot continued to regroup and reinforce. As Margaret quoted de Lesseps "Friendship and violence are incompatible. Thus it would be inconsistent on our part to begin by firing our cannon upon you, since we are your natural protectors."

While the duel with words was proceeding, Garibaldi again demonstrated his capacities, in spite of serious hindrances imposed on him by the Triumvirs. He was ordered to attack again the forces of King Bomba, and was assigned nearly eleven thousand men. The high command was not given to him but to Pietro Roselli, however, and he was left with only the central unit of the army. Thereupon occurred the bewildering spectacle of a commander-in-chief attempting to dissuade his subordinate from winning victories with too great rapidity and ease. For Garibaldi continued to operate as a guerrilla, personally carrying out his own thorough reconnaissance with the advance guard (sometimes disguised as a peasant), hitting the enemy troops again and again where they were weakest, and driving them ahead. Thus Roselli was left to arrive, sullenly, after the fighting was over, and his own carefully conventional battle plans had been completely disarrayed.

In spite of lack of support, so badly did Garibaldi demoralize the Bourbon forces that he was able to drive them back across the Neapolitan frontier—and would have penetrated deep into King Bomba's territory had not Roselli vetoed his proposal. He was permitted nevertheless to continue harassment with his legion for a short time, while the bulk of the Republican army was recalled to Rome. Now the Austrians had crushed the Bolognese and were advancing rapidly, and Mazzini feared their threat more than the threat of Oudinot.

No one believed that the French would permit the Austrians to capture Rome, but also no one believed that France would go to war with Austria. The French meanwhile had advised King Bomba that they did not want his assistance, thus leaving him free to crush his revolting subjects in Sicily. Pius was dismayed, for he much preferred the Bourbon king to Louis Napoleon as big brother. Shortly thereafter the Spanish expeditionary force of four thousand men disembarked at Gaeta and marched to the border town of Terracina on the sea, equally unwelcome to the French.

It was an odd contretemps among friends—the pope, it seemed, was too greatly beloved by them all.

34

As Margaret was so well informed of these events, she felt keenly the strain of what seemed to her an approaching apocalypse. Now she caught hardly more than a glimpse of Angelo from time to time, and they were forced to resort once more to a hectic correspondence. When she returned exhausted from the hospital, notes were often waiting.

"*Mia Cara*—It would have been such a relief to have seen you. It was a terrible cruelty to have come three times, and not found you when I passed by Casa Diez. The porter told me you had been out since midday. I thought certainly I would find you at home. It is very difficult for us to get leave now, and we don't know anything. I would so have liked to see you. I was much consoled by the few lines you wrote, and much pleased to hear that Angelino is well. I beg you not to overtire yourself, and to take care of your health so that you can take good care of Angelino—so that if I die he will at least have you . . . ."

She was suffering anxiety not only for Angelo, but for herself. She wrote to her brother Richard that "amid the apparatus of war and fresh from the sight of blood, it seemed as if some accident might prevent my ever again seeing my kindred." So acute was her fear of not surviving the siege that she made the drastic decision to reveal at least part of her secret to Emelyn Story— though extracting a vow from Emelyn to tell no one, not even William, her husband. She resolved to say that she and Angelo had been married in December of the year they had met, and the marriage had been kept secret to avoid penalties imposed by his brothers and also to secure whatever patrimony might be impending from his father. Accordingly she did so.

"I well remember how exhausted and weary she was," Emelyn wrote later; "how pale and agitated she returned to us after her day's and night's watching; how eagerly she asked for news of Ossoli . . . .

"After one such day, she called me to her bedside and said that I must consent, for her sake, to keep the secret she was about to confide. Then she told me of her marriage; where her child was, and where he was born; and gave me certain papers and parchment documents which I was to keep; and in the event of her and her husband's death, I was to take the boy to her mother in America, and confide him to her care and that of her friend Mrs. Caroline Sturgis Tappan . . . . At the time when she took me into her confidence she was so full of anxiety and dread of some shock, from which she might not recover, that it was absolutely necessary to make it known to some friend . . . .

"The papers thus given me, I had perfect liberty to read; but after she had told me her story, I desired no confirmation of this fact, beyond what her words had given. One or two of the papers she opened, and we together read them. One was written on parchment, in Latin, and was a certificate given by the priest who married them, saying that Angelo Eugene Ossoli was the legal heir of whatever title and fortune should come to his father . . . . There was also a book, in which Margaret had written the history of her acquaintance and marriage with Ossoli, and of the birth of her child. In giving that to me, she said, 'If I do not survive to tell this myself to my family, this book will be to them invaluable. If I live, it will be of no use, for my word will be all that they will ask.' I took the papers and locked them up. Never feeling any desire to look into them, I never did; and as she gave them to me, I returned them to her when I left Rome for Switzerland. After this, she often spoke to me of the necessity there had been, and still existed, for her keeping her marriage a secret . . . .

"Ossoli's post was one of considerable danger, he being in one of the most exposed places; and, as Margaret saw his wounded and dying comrades, she felt that another shot might take him from her or bring him to her care in the hospital. Eagerly she watched the carts as they came up with their suffering loads, dreading that her worst fears might be confirmed. No argument of ours could persuade Ossoli to leave his post to take food or rest. Sometimes we went to him, and carried a concealed basket of provisions, but he shared it with so many of his fellows that his own portion must have been almost nothing. Haggard, worn, and pale, he walked over the Vatican grounds with us, pointing out, now here, now there, where some poor fellow's blood sprinkled the wall. Margaret was with us, and for a few moments they could have an anxious talk about their child.

"To get to the child, or to send to him, was quite impossible, and for days they were in complete ignorance about him. At length a letter came, and in it the nurse declared that unless they should immediately send her, in advance-payment, a certain sum of money, she would altogether abandon Angelino. It seemed at first impossible to forward the money, the road was so insecure and the bearer of any parcel was so likely to be seized by one party or the other, and to be treated as a spy. But finally, after much consideration, the sum was sent to the address of a physician who had been charged with the care of the child."

To Ossoli Margaret sent this message: "How hard it was for me, love, to miss you yesterday . . . . God keep you! I have received the letter from Rieti; our Nino is perfectly well, thanks for this . . . . In event of the death of both of us, I have left a paper with a certificate in regard to Angelino, and some lines praying the Storys to take care of him. If by any accident *I* die, you can revoke this paper if you will, from me, as being your consort. I have wished Nino to go to America, but you will do as seems best to you. We ought to have planned this better . . . . If you live and I die, be always most devoted to Nino. If you ever love another, think first of him, I pray, pray, love."

By the third week in May, the Storys decided that they and their two children had experienced enough of the siege. On the twenty-first, Angelo, fearing to miss them, appeared. Emelyn noted in her diary, "Ossoli came in the evening, one of the last sad days in Rome."

Margaret next morning wrote brother Richard that she had been with the Storys. "Very kind friends they have been in this strait. They are going away, so soon as they can find horses— going into Germany. I remain alone in the house, under our flag, almost the only American [in Rome]. But Mr. Cass, the Envoy, has offered to do anything for me, and I feel at liberty to call on him if I please." Within two days the Storys were gone, passing without difficulty through the French lines under a white flag—and Margaret was truly alone.

To disperse the loneliness of her few unoccupied hours, she chose to sit for a miniature portrait, by the garrulous, conventional painter Thomas Hicks, whose studio was in the bohemian Via Margutta. He too was almost alone; the remaining artists, Thomas Crawford and Frederick Mason, had been fighting at the Porta San Pancrazio. Now Margaret was less interested in the portrait than in the comfort of speaking English. But the insensitive Hicks painted her unsympathetically, emphasizing the fatigue that steadily eroded her face.

On the last day of May Garibaldi reentered Rome with his tired and tattered legion, to the shouts and generous admiration of the people. He had returned on official orders, hoping to rest before fighting the Austrians. And indeed from the de Lesseps negotiations it appeared that all was well between the Republic and the French.

Early in the morning of Friday, June 1, Margaret received an urgent note from Cass: "Dear Madame, I am in this moment informed by Canino [the prince of Canino, Carlo Luciano Bonaparte, vice president of the assembly] that an arrangement, under which France engages to regard the Republic as a friendly power, to retire from the immediate vicinity of the city, and to occupy the Roman territory only so long as is necessary to defend it against foreign invasion, has been signed and a copy sent to Paris for final ratification."

The note was premature in the hopes it raised. Margaret's terse report to the *Tribune* described the denouement: "Oudinot protested that the Plenipotentiary had 'exceeded his powers'—that he should not obey—that the armistice was at an end, and he should attack Rome on Monday. It was then Friday. He proposed to leave these two days for the few foreigners that remained to get out of town. M. Lesseps went off to Paris to get *his* treaty ratified. Of course we could not hear from him for eight or ten days. Meanwhile the honorable chief, alike in all his conduct, attacked on Sunday instead of Monday."

All had been carefully planned. The charming ballet was over.

35

"The attack began before sunrise, and lasted all day," wrote Margaret in an agitated, confused, and incomplete *Tribune* dispatch (as she herself pointed out), reflecting the desperation of the Roman response.

"I saw it from my window, which, though distant, commands the gate of San Pancrazio . . . . If they could take it, the whole town would be cannonaded, and the barricades useless; but it is the same with the Pincian gate. Small parties made feints in two other directions, but they were at once repelled. The French fought with great bravery, and this time it is said with beautiful skill and order, sheltering themselves in their advance by movable barricades. The Italians fought like lions, and no inch of ground was gained by the assailants. The loss of the French is said to be very great; it could not be otherwise. Six or seven hundred Italians are dead or wounded. Among them are many officers, those of Garibaldi especially, who are much exposed by their daring bravery, and whose red tunic makes them the natural mark of the enemy."

A few days after the attack, in a note to Emelyn Story, she

added more details: "The musket-fire was almost unintermitted; the roll of the cannon, especially from St. Angelo, almost majestic . . . . I saw the smoke of every discharge, the flash of bayonets; with a glass could see the men."

Very quickly Margaret learned the full truth. When Mazzini saw General Oudinot's so-unanticipated and so-menacing letter, at once he sought Garibaldi's advice. Garibaldi had taken to his bed, suffering from a severe bout of arthritis and the month-old festering stomach wound. Garibaldi replied with his usual directness: "Mazzini—You ask me to choose what I want. I tell you that I can exist for the good of the Republic only in one of two ways—a dictator with unlimited powers or a simple soldier. Choose! Always yours, Garibaldi." This response was typical of Garibaldi's vice-virtue of oversimplification, which often was both wrong and right. His appointment would rouse the wrath of the Catholic powers as no other possible act of the Republic. On the other hand, a series of victories might rouse the people of Italy as the people of Rome had been roused, and the reimposition of the old order would be made immensely more difficult.

The Triumvirs quibbled. They asked again for his military judgment of the situation, and his response was to say that General Avezzana should be given Roselli's job as commander-in-chief. In not taking this advice, the Triumvirs committed an error which proved fatal. They hedged again, and asked Garibaldi if he would resume command of the Porta San Pancrazio section of the walls. He declined, saying he was ill, but that if necessary he would serve as an ordinary soldier. So he stayed in bed, intending to remain until the expiration of the truce.

General Oudinot, while the talks were in progress, had proceeded systematically to reinforce his army with seasoned troops from the Algerian wars, to a total of 35,000 men, plus 75 heavy siege guns. He imported engineering specialists in siege warfare, including the famous General Jean Baptiste Vaillant, reputedly a genius. He shifted his position remote from Rome to an easy striking distance. Certainly all this was known to the Triumvirs. De Lessep's armistice had given Oudinot all the time that he needed, and he intended to fulfill his orders from Paris: "to enter Rome as soon as possible." He planned to do so by the Porta San Pancrazio, seize the Janiculum hill, and dominate the city.

To defend Rome against the French, the Republic was able to muster an army of nineteen thousand, of which only twelve thousand were trained soldiers. The cannon, in number about one hundred, were mostly of small calibre, and half were old and rusty, unusable after a shot or two, though five new cannon had been cast in local forges. Munitions were short, but workshops were feverishly producing more. The Republic for its military genius had Garibaldi, but Roselli—alas for the Republic—remained in supreme command.

Before any attack on the Porta San Pancrazio could be successful, the villas that dominated its approaches must be captured—as Garibaldi on April 30 had so clearly foreseen. The villas, abutting the Via Aurelia Antica with high stone walls, had been garrisoned with a skeletal four hundred volunteers, and neither entrenched nor strengthened in any other way. General Roselli on Saturday had toured the posts, tranquilly assuring the defenders that the French would not attack before Monday morning, as General Oudinot had promised. And that the promise would be kept, the defenders did not doubt, for it was well known that Oudinot was " a strict Catholic and a very religious man."

The immediate result of General Roselli's behavior, conceivable only as the grossest stupidity or outright sabotage, was that the French forces swarmed up the outer slopes at three o'clock on Sunday morning—with all the defenders asleep except the sentries. The surprise was complete. By the time the dawn light had turned from gray to pink, the key villas, Pamphili, Corsini, and Vascello, were in French hands, and the Porta San Pancrazio itself was under fire. Only the Villa Vascello, closest to the gate, had been recaptured when Garibaldi and his men arrived on the scene. Two desperately valuable hours had been wasted. Immediately Garibaldi, naturally reassuming command, determined that all the villas must be taken if the Republicans were successfully to hold the walls.

Rome meanwhile had become frenzied with indignation, anger, and excitement. The people poured into the streets to the clanging of bells, thumping drums, and wild shouts of "*Roma o Morte!*" (Rome or Death). Thus began the day of blood and heroism that was to create the legends necessary for the eventual rise of a new state in Italy, free of foreign invaders and overt papal temporal sovereignty. Mazzini's morning proclamation was in the same tone: "Romans—To the crime of assailing a friendly Republic with Republican troops, General Oudinot has added the infamy of treachery. He has violated his written promise, now in our hands, that he would not begin the attack before Monday. Romans, arise! To the walls, to the gates, to the barricades! Let us show that not even treachery can vanquish Rome . . . ."

The situation outside the Porta San Pancrazio was such that flank attacks on the villas were not practical, and there remained only the possibility of suicidal charges up narrow lanes lined by trees and box hedges. The French sharpshooters were so situated as to be well protected, and the villas themselves contained many troops with concentrated firepower. Such frontal attacks by the Italians therefore could have been successful only if masses of men were available for the assault, and further masses available for support in case a breakthrough was achieved—for the French reserves were both relatively inexhaustible and immediately available. Garibaldi had only his legion, belatedly the handful of Lombard *Bersaglieri* under the command of Luciano Manara, and finally, a small body of the ex-papal troops. For covering fire, he had only one battery on the walls. As General Roselli declined to send reinforcements, the outcome was almost inevitable. The single incalculable factor was the will of the Italians to fight.

For the Italians, the battle was impromptu from the beginning—thanks to Roselli's manifold negligence. For the French it was a carefully planned and executed slaughter. All the while a band on the walls played the *Marseillaise* to shame the French; but the French were not shamed. The Villa Corsini, on its commanding height with its narrow entranceway, crumbling from the fire of the Roman battery on the wall, was three times seized by the Republicans and three times relinquished. On its steps the handsome young Bolognese Angelo Masina, who had brought his lancers to Garibaldi, was killed, and his body lay putrefying for a month. Here too perished other young men, to be classified by later Italians as among the immortals: Enrico Dandolo, Francesco Daverio, Goffredo Mameli so gravely wounded in one leg that he died of gangrene. The Italians charged with bayonets in groups as small as twenty men into a fire so intense that it meant almost certain death. Yet they went willingly again and again to attack the incredulous French. Only the small Casa Giacometti and the broken and battered Vascello stayed firmly in Italian hands. The resistance had proved that Rome could be taken only by cannonade.

By the end of the day, when the exhausted Italians ceased to charge among the corpses, the extent of the Roman disaster was evident. Garibaldi, said the conventional generals, had proved that he did not know how to maneuver masses of men. But perhaps he had a deeper wisdom. True, the battle had been lost; but the legend had been won. *Roma o Morte!* held a meaning baptized with blood. Rome, and only Rome, henceforth, could be the Capital of Italy.

Mazzini's evening message to the people in these bitter hours sounded a note of exaltation: " . . . Romans! This is a day of heroes, a page of history. Yesterday we said to you, be great; today we say to you, you are great. Continue so."

Margaret's life now centered totally about the hospital on the Tiber island, and the wards set up in the Palazzo Quirinale. Almost unbearably magnified was her terror that the stretchers and carts bringing in the wounded might include that one she most dreaded to see. But of this she confided nothing to anyone, not even to the Principessa Belgioioso, to whom she had become a chief assistant.

Lewis Cass wrote later: "The weather was intensely hot, her

health was feeble and delicate, the dead and dying were around her in every form of pain and horror, but she never shrank from the duty she had assumed. Her heart and soul were in the cause for which these men had fought, and all was done that woman could do to comfort them in their suffering. I have seen the eyes of the dying, as she moved among them, extended upon opposite beds, meet in commendation of her unwearied kindness . . . nothing of tenderness and attention was wanting to soothe their last moments. And I have heard many of those who recovered speak, with all the passionateness and fervor of Italian natures, of her whose sympathy and compassion throughout their long illness fulfilled all the offices of love . . . . "

Repeated with an even greater intensity were the earlier scenes described by Emelyn Story: "I have walked through the wards with Margaret, and seen how comforting was her presence to the poor suffering men . . . . They raised themselves up on their elbows to get the last glimpse of her as she was going away. Some of the sturdy fellows of Garibaldi's legion were there, and to them she listened as they spoke with delight of their chief, of his courage and skill—for he seemed to have won the hearts of his men in a remarkable manner."

To Emelyn, Margaret wrote (June 6): "The cannonade on one side [of Rome] has continued day and night (being full moon), till this morning . . . the French throw rockets into the town; one burst in the courtyard of the hospital just as I arrived there yesterday, agitating the poor sufferers very much."

Out of the distant and unreal past came a letter from Dear Waldo, who seemed so pallid as to be himself unreal. She had lost almost all interest in attempting to communicate with him. Nevertheless she replied at once, describing her hospital experiences, which to him must have seemed unintelligible: "I received your letter amid the round of cannonade and musketry . . . . Since the 30th April, I go almost daily to the hospitals, and though I have suffered—for I had no idea, before, how terrible gunshot wounds and wound-fever are—yet I have taken pleasure, and great pleasure, in being with the men. There is scarcely one who is not moved by a noble spirit . . . . When they begin to get better, I carry them books and flowers. They read, and we talk.

"The palace of the Pope, on the Quirinal, is now used for convalescents. In those beautiful gardens I walk with them—one in his sling, another on his crutch. The gardener plays off all his water-works for the defenders of the country, and gathers flowers for me, their friend.

"A day or two since, we sat in the Pope's little pavilion, where he used to give private audience. The sun was going gloriously down over Monte Mario, where gleamed the white tents of the French light-horse among the trees. The cannonade was heard at intervals. Two bright-eyed boys sat at our feet and gathered up eagerly every word said by the heroes of the day. It was a beautiful hour, stolen from the midst of ruin and sorrow . . . .

"Should I never return—and sometimes I despair of doing so, it seems so far off, so difficult, I am caught in such a net of ties here—if ever you know of my life here, I think you will only wonder at the constancy with which I have sustained myself; the degree of profit to which I have put the time, at least in the way of observation. Meanwhile, love me all you can. Let me feel that, amid the fearful agitations of the world, there are pure hands with healthful, even pulse, stretched out toward me, if I claim their grasp.

"I feel profoundly for Mazzini. At moments I am tempted to say, 'Cursed with every granted prayer'—so cunning is the demon. He is become the inspiring soul of his people. He saw Rome, to which all his hopes through life tended, for the first time as a Roman citizen, and to become in a few days its ruler. He has animated Rome, he sustains her to a glorious effort, which if it fails this time, will not in the coming age. His country will be free. Yet to me it would be so dreadful to cause all this bloodshed, to dig the graves of such martyrs . . . .

"I know not, dear friend, whether I ever shall get home across that great ocean, but here in Rome I shall no longer wish to live. O Rome, *my* country! could I imagine that the triumph of what I held dear was to heap such desolation on thy head!"

By now Mazzini was almost inaccessible. The previous

day (June 9) he had written to Margaret: "Dear Friend, will you be *woman* and forgive? I well deserve to be forgiven. Could you spend a whole day near me you would wonder not at my being *silent* with those I love, but at my *living*. From seven o'clock in the morning yesterday to seven o'clock in the evening I have been continually writing, writing even while I speak with people, writing *à la vapeur* [under pressure]. At seven o'clock I was called to the Trinità dei Pellegrini [hospital] to the bedside of a friend, Mameli, a young poet and soldier of promise, whom I had to decide to bear the amputation of the leg, and whom I found so ill that even *that* could not be done; I left him at nine o'clock: went for the first time to eat something, came back to the palace, then to begin again till one o'clock after midnight. Everything, from the detail of a soldier arrested at St. Angelo to the defense, from a quarrel between two officers to a dissenting between two generals comes down to me. I scarcely even write a few words to my mother. Should the thing last long, there is no human strength or will that can resist it. Keep this note for you: it is for you only. I do not like people to know that I am working more than another man. I have been very often *thinking* of you; the only thing I could do. Keep faithful and trustful; pray for Rome and Italy; it is centered here."

On the basis of the events before his eyes, Chargé Cass came to an important decision with respect to the Republic. Carefully he prepared the ground in his diplomatic reports to Washington. "The work of the defences is pushed with unremitting labor. The roads leading from the gates are planted with iron spears, rendering the movements of cavalry impossible. The adjacent houses are pierced for musketry, and the gates are raked by pieces of cannon planted on the neighboring bastions. The gates themselves are mined, should all other obstacles be overcome. Every house in the streets through which the enemy must pass, after having forced the outworks, is provided with oil and stones, the former of which is directed to be kept boiling hot, to be cast from the windows . . . . The hardships of the siege are beginning to be felt by all classes. Yesterday and the day before the market supplies failed, having been intercepted by the French cavalry . . . . A still greater calamity is the threatened scarcity of water. The aqueducts leading from the Sabine hills, by which the principal reservoirs are fed, have been sundered by General Oudinot . . . . The actual object of the intervention is shaking the edifice of the Catholic religion to its very foundations, crushing that faith in thousands of hearts. Almost the entire state of Rome has declared the downfall of the temporal power of the Pontiff . . . . This can hardly be called the voice of a mere faction. The consequence, naturally, is that many are now asking themselves whether he who represents a religion of peace has a right to reassert temporal power by force of arms . . . . The confidence arising from the successful resistance thus repeatedly opposed to the entrance of the French into the Capital, the unanimity and enthusiasm, which increases every hour in favor of the Republican cause, combine to render permanent establishment of the existing government highly probable. Probable, I mean, on the supposition that it is the design of those Powers, who have intervened on the Roman question, to regard in the slightest degree the sentiments of the Roman people."

The chief blot on the regime, sporadic assassinations, Cass also reported. A rumor swept Rome that in the dungeons of the Inquisition a pit had been discovered crammed with human bones. Immediately several priests, called "retrogrades," were senselessly murdered for revenge. Killed, too, were three peasants believed (without evidence) to be spies. But the real substance of Cass's document was a cautious request for authority to recognize the Republican government in the name of the United States. But his caution was to prove as self-defeating as Consul Brown's enthusiastic endorsement of the Republic.

In the midst of all this chaos Margaret received the news from home that her sister Ellen, now tearfully separated from husband Ellery for some months, had borne another child—a boy. Margaret replied, referring only obliquely to the fact that she too was the mother of a baby boy. It was a letter filled with foreboding for the end of the Republic, and for her own: "As was

Eve, at first, I suppose every mother is delighted by the birth of a man-child. There is hope that he will conquer more ill, and effect more good, than is expected from girls. This prejudice in favor of man does not seem to be destroyed by his shortcomings for ages. Still, each mother hopes to find in hers an Emanuel. I should like very much to see your children, but hardly realize I ever shall. The journey home seems so long, so difficult, so expensive. I should really like to lie down here, and sleep my way into another sphere of existence, if I could take with me one or two that love me and need me, and was sure of a good haven for them on the other side.

"The world seems to go so strangely wrong! The bad side triumphs; the blood and tears of the generous flow in vain. I assist at many saddest scenes, and suffer for those whom I knew not before. Those whom I knew and loved—who, if they had triumphed, would have opened for me an easier, broader, higher-mounting road—are every day more and more involved in earthly ruin. Eternity is with us, but there is much darkness and bitterness in this portion of it. A baleful star rose on my birth, and its hostility, I fear, will never be disarmed while I walk below."

36

Late in the sultry afternoon of June 12 General Oudinot sent an ultimatum to the authorities in Rome. Though the message was shrouded with the velvet niceties of diplomatic jargon, its meaning was curt: *Open the gates or I will batter them down.* The various authorities replied with closely reasoned letters, *No.* All the documents were quoted by Margaret in their entirety in her dispatch to the *Tribune.* Momentarily her indignation overcame her fears.

She was again writing history while it was being made. "After receiving these answers to his letter and proclamation, Oudinot turned all the force of his cannonade to make a breach, and began what no one, even in these days, has believed possible: the bombardment of Rome. Yes! the French, who pretend to be the advance guard of civilization, are bombarding Rome. They dare to take the risk of destroying the richest bequests made to man by the great Past . . . . When the bombs began to come, one of the Trasteverini, those noble images of the old Roman race, redeemed her claim to that descent by seizing a bomb and extinguishing the match. She received a medal and a reward in money. A soldier did the same thing at Palazzo Spada, where is the statue of Pompey, at whose base great Caesar fell. He was promoted. Immediately the people were seized with emulation; armed with pans of wet clay, they ran wherever the bombs fell, to extinguish them. Women collect the balls from the hostile cannon, and carry them to ours."

". . . *Ours*." By now Margaret's identification was complete. It could hardly be otherwise. Three days later, in a citation addressed not to the nobleman Signor Marchese Ossoli but to Citizen Ossoli, Angelo was promoted from Sergeant to Captain. His competence and bravery under fire had been remarked. His post remained one of the most dangerous on the walls.

Before the beginning of the new offensive, Garibaldi had utilized the time to strengthen the defenses of the Janiculum against "Cardinal Oudinot's Gallic-friars," as he called them. He had chosen for headquarters the two-hundred-year-old Villa Savorelli,* which stood high above the Porta San Pancrazio and was a perfect observation post. From the villa's roof he daily surveyed the French lines with his glass, calmly ignoring both the sharpshooters, who paid him special attention, and the cannoneers, who were gradually blasting the elegant structure to pieces.

The legion had lost so many of its officers that Garibaldi was constrained to name the aristocrat Luciano Manara as his chief of staff. Manara had called him "a devil, a panther" and had viewed him with great suspicion, but after fighting with him against King Bomba, had replaced suspicion with admiration and devotion. The defense of the all important Villa Vascello outside the gate Garibaldi placed in the hands of the Genovese Giacomo Medici, who there began his rise to fame as one of Garibaldi's toughest young generals.

Steadily the French applied pressure, daily inching their

* Today called the Villa Aurelia, a property of the American Academy in Rome. From the roof in June 1849 was made the first full 360° panoramic photograph of a battleground—a historic document then intended merely for a lithograph copy.

trenches closer to the walls and bringing up more and more heavy siege guns at shorter range. To these activities the Republicans replied with repeated bayonet forays outside the walls and surprisingly accurate shooting with their rickety old cannon. "The extreme heat of these days was far more fatal to the Romans than to their assailants," Margaret explained in the *Tribune;* "for as fast as the French troops sickened, their place was taken by fresh arrivals . . . . Ours also not only sustained the exhausting service, by day, but were harassed at night by attacks, feigned or real. These commonly began about eleven or twelve o'clock at night, just when all who meant to rest were fairly asleep. I can imagine the harassing effect upon the troops, from what I feel in my sheltered pavilion, in consequence of not knowing a night's sleep for a month."

Just at this moment, when morale was under such strain and nerves were so lacerated, clerical elements began the rumor that the Republicans had mined St. Peter's. Immediately Margaret asked Mazzini for information about the matter. He replied (June 20): "It is written that none will trust me, you too! Can you believe for a single moment such nonsense as that of St. Peter being mined, whilst *I* am here? Have I proved a vandal? Is there a Frenchwoman here who has been molested? . . . My soul is full of grief and bitterness, and still I have never for a moment yielded to reactionary feelings . . . . No one has *seen* the mines: no one will see them, I repeat, whilst I am here."

Of this rumor Margaret reported nothing, but continued her description of the main developments of the siege. "The bombardment became constantly more serious. The house where I live was filled as early as the 20th with persons obliged to fly from the Piazza di Gesù, where the fiery rain fell thickest. The night of the 21st-22nd, we were all alarmed at about two o'clock by a tremendous cannonade. It was the moment when the breach was finally made by which the French entered . . . . That was the fatal hour for the city. Every day afterward, though obstinately resisted, the enemy gained, till at last, their cannon being well placed, the city was entirely commanded from the Janiculum and all thought of further resistance was idle."

Nevertheless, resistance continued—although an acid disagreement had erupted between Garibaldi on the one hand and Mazzini and General Roselli on the other. Reinforcements were not supplied, despite Garibaldi's urgent requests, and the situation rapidly deteriorated—to the point where Garibaldi flatly refused to obey Roselli's orders. The quarrel became common knowledge, but Margaret, now loyal to both Mazzini and Garibaldi, declined to mention it.

"After the 22nd of June," she went on in her dispatch, "the slaughter of the Romans became every day more fearful. Their defenses were knocked down by the heavy cannon of the French, and, entirely exposed in their valorous onsets, great numbers perished on the spot. Those who were brought into the hospitals were generally grievously wounded, very commonly subjects for amputation. My heart bled daily more and more at these sights, and I could not feel much for myself, though now the balls and bombs began to fall round me also. The night of the 28th the effect was truly fearful, as they whizzed and burst near me . . . . However, that night passed; the next, we had reason to expect a still more fiery salute toward the Pincian [Hill], as here alone remained three or four pieces of cannon which could be used."

Here, on the Pincian, was Ossoli, shifted to help stem the French tide in that sector. Here Margaret had visited him. "I saw blood that streamed on the wall where Ossoli was," she wrote afterward. "I have a piece of a bomb that burst close to him." No longer could she endure the tension. Once more she decided to reveal portions of her secret. The chosen confidant was Lewis Cass, Jr.

"On the 29th of June, after midnight," Cass later revealed, "the bombardment from the French camp was very heavy, shells and grenades falling in every part of the city. In the afternoon of the 30th, I received a brief note from Miss Fuller, requesting me to call at her residence. I did so without delay, and found her lying upon a sofa, pale and trembling, evidently much exhausted. She informed me that she had sent for me to place in my hands a packet of important papers, which she wished me to keep for the present, and in the event of her death to transmit it to her friends in the United States. She then said that she was married to the Marquis Ossoli, who was in command of a battery on the Pincian hill. That being the highest and most exposed position in Rome, and directly in the line of the bombs from the French camp, it was not to be expected, she said, that he could escape the dangers of another night such as the last, and that therefore it was her intention to remain with him and share his fate. At the Ave Maria, she added, he would come for her, when they would proceed together to his post . . . . After a few words more I took my departure, the hour she named having nearly arrived. At the porter's lodge I met the Marquis Ossoli and a few minutes afterwards I saw them walking towards the Pincian hill."

Margaret's emotions that night, as she waited with Ossoli for a resumption of the bombardment, can only have fitted with the sweep of the bright-starred sky above the umbrella pines, and the shadowed rooftops of Rome with the massive and mysterious forms of its towers and domes. Cream white in the darkness were marble statues, like wraiths of antiquity returned; mingled among them were the few remaining guns. She must have been welcomed by Ossoli's men, and shared their tension all the night through, with thankful disbelief at dawn's light that the cannonade had not been renewed. The night was gone. And both she and Ossoli were alive.

But the Roman Republic was dead. A last incredible defense by Garibaldi and his legion along the line of the ancient Roman walls—the Aurelian—had succumbed to the vast superiority of the French. Manara was killed, and with ammunition exhausted, Garibaldi himself fought hand to hand with his sword. On the morning of July 1 Garibaldi, covered with dirt and blood, went to the assembly to say that the French cannon now could destroy the city totally, and that resistance in the streets would be futile. He proposed a withdrawal to the hills and continued resistance. Mazzini supported him. "Wherever we are, there will Rome be," Garibaldi said, and called for volunteers.

He met them in St. Peter's piazza, ringed by the great columns. The people came by the thousands. The whole vast space was packed. Wearing black feathers on his hat, and riding a white horse, he worked his way slowly to the Egyptian obelisk and there held up his hand to stop the echoing deep-throated continuous cheers. In a sonorous voice he cried: "Fortune, who betrays us today, will smile on us tomorrow. I am going out from Rome. Let those who wish to continue the war against the stranger, come with me. I offer neither pay, nor quarters, nor provisions; I offer hunger, thirst, forced marches, battles and death. Let him who loves his country in his heart and not with his lips only, follow me."

And the crowd responded not with cheers but sobs.

Margaret described the departure. "Toward the evening . . . I went into the Corso with some friends; it was filled with citizens and military. The carriage was stopped by the crowd near the Doria palace. The lancers of Garibaldi galloped along in full career . . . . all are light, athletic, resolute figures, many of the forms of the finest manly beauty of the south . . . . We followed them to the Piazza of St. John Lateran. Never have I seen a sight so beautiful, so romantic, and so sad. Whoever knows Rome knows the peculiar solemn grandeur of that Piazza, scene of the first triumph of Rienzi, and whence may be seen the magnificence of the 'mother of all churches'—the baptistry with its porphyry columns, the Santa Scala with its glittering mosaics of the early ages, the obelisk standing fairest of any of those most imposing monuments of Rome, the view through the gates of the Campagna, on that side so richly strewn with ruins. The sun was setting, the crescent moon rising. The flower of the Italian youth were marshalling in that solemn place . . . . They had all put on the beautiful dress of the Garibaldi Legion—the tunic of bright red cloth, the Greek cap or else round hat with plume. Their long hair was blown back from resolute faces; all looked full of courage."

They would need that courage. The assembly had voted capitulation, and the four thousand volunteers had chosen instead to march to the aid of Venice, which under Manin still held out against the Austrians—the last bastion of freedom in

Italy. Among the volunteers were the friar Ugo Bassi and Ciceruacchio with his young son, destined all three to be captured and shot by the Austrians.

But if it was a thrilling exodus, it was also pathetic. "I saw the wounded, all that could go," Margaret said, "laden upon their baggage carts; some were already pale and fainting, still they wished to go. I saw many youths, born to rich inheritance, carrying in a handkerchief all their worldly goods. The women were ready; their eyes too were resolved if sad. The wife of Garibaldi followed him on horseback. [She was pregnant and ill.] He himself was distinguished by the white tunic; his look was entirely that of a hero of the Middle Ages—his face still young, for the excitements of his life, though so many, have all been youthful, and there is no fatigue upon his brow or cheek. One sees in him a man engaged in the career for which he is adapted by nature. He went upon the parapet, and looked upon the road with a spyglass, and, no obstruction being in sight, he turned his face for a moment back upon Rome, then led the way through the gate. Hard was the heart, stony and seared the eye that had no tear for the moment."

Another legend was being born. Garibaldi, with his little band, was to forge a symbolic victory from defeat by the paradox of new defeat. Few were the volunteers who survived the trek, which was to become one of the great sagas of history. Surrounded by three hostile armies, Garibaldi nevertheless outmaneuvered, outmarched, and outfoxed all of them. Finally, with no more than a handful of followers, he reached the Adriatic coast and seized thirteen fishing boats, seeking to sail to Venice. By moonlight the Austrian fleet intercepted the tiny craft; but with his hand on the tiller, his boat and two others slipped away. Driven ashore in the reedy marshes of the delta of the river Po, he reached safety only to have his wife Anita die in his arms. Thenceforth, aided by an underground which not once betrayed him, he again crossed the whole of Italy and fled by sea. Eventually he sought safety in the United States, where for a time he became a candlemaker on Staten Island.

The escape of Mazzini was altogether different. Though he

approved of Garibaldi's expedition, he did not follow, because he was not a man who could follow anyone. On the day after the capitulation, as yet making no effort to hide, he wrote a note to Margaret: "Dear Friend, it is all over . . . . I don't know what I shall do: I cannot think of it. Meanwhile let me work for others. Angelo Brunetti [Ciceruacchio; Mazzini did not know that Ciceruacchio had gone with Garibaldi] and his son Lorenzo, twelve years old, but having fought bravely out of the walls, are afraid of the priests and of their agents. I have been obliged to promise to them to get, if possible, a passport for them, and I ask you to do that. I could write to Mr. Cass for that, but I prefer to avail myself of *your* help. You must have friends among the influential Americans. Could they get the passports with different names, of course, or better, to be filled in with Italian names but as subjects of the U.S. so as to have protection assured . . . . Could they add a third, it might perhaps be of some use to me hereafter."

Margaret moved at once in behalf of Mazzini's modest request for himself, and for the other Republicans. She obtained passports for Sterbini, Avezzana, and for Mazzini under the name of George Moore with a letter of introduction to the American consul at Genoa. They were not represented as American citizens, but as under American protection.

It was at this time that one of the ironic "Pasquinades" appeared on the famous "talking" statue of Pasquino. The statue itself was a fragment of a Greek marble which had survived the millenia in the Roman streets. For centuries the repressed Romans, by attaching placards to it at night, had used it as a means of expressing the barbs too dangerous to repeat elsewhere. Now Pasquino had a dialogue with his straight man Marforio, another talking statue, who proposed to flee from Rome.

Pasquino replied: *"Ma figlio bello, dove passi? Per terra, c'e sono li Francesi. Per mare, c'e sono li Tedeschi. Per aria, c'e sono li preti."* ("But my dear son, where can you go? By land, there are the French. By sea, there are the Germans. By air, there are the priests.")

But Pasquino had not thought of the American passports. Again Mazzini wrote to Margaret. "I have made my mind up, dear friend, and I shall go, that is endeavor to go. I must go to Switzerland. How to reach it is the problem. By land I have to cross Tuscany, Piedmont, etc. and the Austrians are there and the Piedmontese Government not unlike the Austrians. By sea. I have Civita Vecchia, a town *en état de siège,* and where they can, if they choose, arrest me; then Marseille, worse than any other place: I am known there. Once beyond Marseille and traveling cautiously, I have nothing to fear. Do you know of any American or English family traveling toward Switzerland or going to travel? Joining them under a little disguise and with my American passport, the thing would be made easier . . . ."

With Margaret he had a secret rendezvous before his departure. Margaret described the meeting in answer to a letter from William Henry Channing: "I did not see Mazzini the last two weeks of the Republic. When the French entered, he walked about the streets to see how the people bore themselves, and then went to the house of a friend. In the upper chamber of a poor house, with his life-long friends—the Modenas—I found him . . . . Mazzini had suffered millions more than I could. He had borne his fearful responsibility; he had let his dearest friends perish; he had passed all these nights without sleep. In two short months he had grown old. All the vital juices seemed exhausted. His eyes were all blood-shot; his skin orange; flesh he had none. His hair was mixed with white, his hand painful to the touch. But he had never flinched, never quailed; had protested in the last hour against surrender. Sweet and calm, but full of a more fiery purpose than ever, in him I revered the hero and owned myself not of that mould."

No traveling Americans materialized, and Mazzini was forced to choose the most dangerous route; by sea to Marseille. But the American passport carried him safely through to Geneva, and afterward to London. In effect his life was finished, because his great role in the unification of Italy was finished. Soon that work would pass into other hands.

Margaret and Mazzini, unlike Garibaldi, were not spared the

bitterness of watching the French army occupy Rome. It was the fourth of July, Garibaldi's birthday, and American Independence Day. "Yes—July 4th, the day so joyously celebrated in our land is that of the entrance of the French into Rome!" Margaret exclaimed to her readers in the *Tribune*. "I did not appear in the street, as I would not give any countenance to such a wrong; but an English lady, my friend, told me they seemed to look expectingly for the strong party of friends they had always pretended to have within the walls. The French officers looked up to the windows for ladies, and she being the only one they saw, saluted her. She made no reply. They then passed into the Corso. Many were assembled, the softer Romans being unable to control a curiosity the Milanese would have disclaimed, but preserving an icy silence. In an evil hour, a foolish priest dared to break it by the cry of *Viva Pio Nono!* The populace, roused to fury, rushed on him with their knives. He was much wounded; one or two others were killed in the rush. The people howled then, and hissed at the French, who, advancing their bayonets and clearing the way before them, fortified themselves in the piazzas."

At the assembly, the deputies to a man sat immobile in their seats, as the ancient Roman senators had sat when Rome was first sacked by the Gauls. Now the deputies were driven out not by clubs and spears but by bayonets.

And as Citizen Captain Giovanni Angelo Ossoli looked down from Margaret's window on the French troops who had restored the power of the pope, he sat with his head in his hands, sobbing.

Margaret sought release from hers and Ossoli's sense of tragic oppression by busying herself with her letter to the *Tribune*. She would complete her coverage of the defense and fall of Rome just as honestly and vividly as she had begun, though the days and even the hours which remained to her in Rome were certainly numbered. "Yesterday I went over the scene of conflict. It was fearful even to *see* the Quattro Venti [Villa Corsini] and Vascello, where the French and Romans had been several days so near one another, all shattered to pieces, with fragments of rich stucco and painting still sticking to rafters between the great holes made by the cannonade, and think that men had stayed and fought in them when only a mass of ruins. The French, indeed, were entirely sheltered the last days; to my unpractised eyes the extent and thoroughness of their works seemed miraculous . . . . I was struck more than ever by the heroic valor of *our* people—let me so call them now as ever, for go where I may, a large part of my heart will ever remain in Italy . . . .

"A *contadino* [peasant] showed me where thirty-seven brave are buried beneath a heap of wall that fell upon them in the shock of one cannonade. A marble nymph, with broken arm, looked sadly that way from her sun-dried fountain; some roses were blooming still, some red oleanders, amid the ruin. The sun was casting its last light on the mountains, on the tranquil, sad Capagna, that sees one more leaf turned in the book of woe. This was in the Vascello.* I then entered the French ground, all mapped and hollowed like a honeycomb. A pair of skeleton legs protruded from a bank of one barricade. Lower, a dog had scratched away its light covering of earth from the body of a man, and discovered it lying face upward all dressed. The dog stood gazing on it with an air of stupid amazement . . . ."

She had described this scene with a firm purpose: "O men and women of America, spared these frightful sights—acknowledge as the legitimate leaders and rulers those men who represent the people, who understand their wants, who are ready to die or to live for their good . . . . Friends, countrymen, lovers of virtue, lovers of freedom, lovers of truth! be on the alert. Rest not supine in your easier lives, but remember '*Mankind is one, and beats with one great heart.*' "

It was Margaret's last passionate plea that the United States of America, land of freedom and democracy, align itself always with the progressive forces of the people and not the forces of reaction throughout the world. For this dispatch to the *Tribune* was to be her last.

Slightly more than a fortnight later, Chargé d'Affaires Lewis Cass received permission from Washington to recognize the

* It remains in ruins—a national monument.

Roman Republic. Too late, too late. The representatives of the old order were trooping back to Rome, secure behind the cold steel and cold hearts which were to remain as the pope's protectors for more than twenty years—until the Franco-Prussian War of 1870.

But all the pope's horses and all the pope's men could not stop the acceleration of the freedom forces which the defense of Rome had put in motion. Garibaldi's epic escape was to have far-reaching consequences. In 1860 he would return, to lead the "Thousand" in two leaky steamboats against Francis II's forces in Sicily—and at Palermo would defeat an army of 24,000 men. Thereafter, he would march half the length of Italy, acclaimed and followed by the people, to drive the king from Naples. Then, though remaining politically a steadfast Republican, he would unite with the armies of King Vittorio Emanuele II to defeat and expel the Bourbons from Italian soil. Already Cavour had wrested most of northern Italy from the Austrians. Thus would Italy become one nation.

And in 1870 the walls of Rome again would be breached—this time by an Italian army—and the papacy, in the person of aging Pope Pius IX, relieved of its temporal power. The Church's advance reaction would be (1869) to declare the dogma of papal infallibility. So the popes would retreat into the Vatican, and there remain until the Fascist Concordat (1929) would restore many of the Church's privileges within and over the Italian State. In 1945, after World War II, an Italian Republic would come at last—almost a century after the men of Rome under Mazzini and Garibaldi died, crying "Viva la Repubblica!"

37

The hostile reception of the French forces convinced General Oudinot that he must use the iron hand without the velvet glove. The *Guardia Nazionale* was immediately disarmed, martial law declared, early curfew imposed (though in the crowded slums the people were accustomed to staying late in the streets during the summer heat). The press was stifled. And a proclamation was issued that all foreigners who had aided the Republic must quit Rome within twenty-four hours or face the consequences.

Urgently Margaret sent a note to Lewis Cass: "I beg you to come and see me and give me your counsel and, if need be, your aid to get away from Rome. From what I hear this morning, I fear we may once more be shut up here; and I shall die, to be again separated from what I hold most dear. There are as yet no horses on the way we want to go, or we should post immediately. You may feel, like me, sad in these last moments to leave this injured Rome. So many noble hearts I abandon here, whose woes I have known! I feel, if I could not aid I might soothe. But for my child I would not go till some men, now sick, know whether they shall live or die."

The situation was in fact dangerous. The death penalty had been decreed for anyone who impeded a French soldier. "Three families were carried to prison because a boy crowed like a cock at the French soldiery," Margaret recorded. "The Italians went out of the caffès if Frenchmen entered . . . . The French yesterday violated the domicile of our Consul, Mr. Brown, pretending to search for persons hidden there. Mr. Brown, banner in one hand and sword in the other, repelled the assault, and fairly drove them downstairs. Then he made them an appropriate speech, though in a mixed language of English, French, and Italian, that the crowd vehemently applauded . . . . He then donned his uniform and went to Oudinot to make his protest." (Reported in detail to Washington by Cass. General Oudinot apologized.) The next day Brown left Rome, taking with him one of the Republican leaders (Sterbini) disguised as a servant; but of this Margaret apparently knew nothing.

Her greatest indignation was reserved for the French handling of the hospitals. "The wounded have been warned to leave the Quirinal at the end of eight days," she noted, "though there are many who cannot be moved from bed to bed without causing them great anguish and peril; nor is it known that any other place has been provided as a hospital for them." Indeed no other hospital had been provided, for the French command had ordered the transfer of all patients, "except those to whom Extreme Unction had been administered," to the Termini prison. To help the wounded, "could I have sold my hair or blood from my arm, I would have done it," Margaret said. Her efforts were useless: female attendants were prohibited, and the Italian doctors were banished. The Principessa Belgioioso, who was curtly ousted, took a cue from Margaret's dispatches and wrote a letter of denunciation to a newspaper in Torino. The French, she said, "have permitted the dismissal of the chaplains, and have replaced them by fanatical monks, who threaten to leave the wounded to perish of hunger and thirst unless they incontinently confess, and unless their confession betakes of a political rather than a religious nature." For her trouble she was threatened with a bill covering all the expenses of the hospitals during her administration, on the grounds that she had usurped the proper authorities.

As Margaret hurried to pack, she dashed off a short scrawl to her brother Richard. His last letter had been in hand for two or three weeks. "Probably I shall answer it sometime," she said, "if I should ever again find myself tranquil and recreated from the painful excitements of these last days. But amid the ruined hopes of Rome, the shameful oppressions she is beginning to suffer, amid these bleeding martyrs, my brothers, I cannot fix my thoughts on anything else. I write that you may assure mother of my safety, which in the last days began to be seriously imperilled. Say that as soon as I can find means of conveyance, without an expense too enormous, I shall go again into the mountains. There I shall find some bracing air and I hope stillness for a time. Say she need feel no anxiety if she does not hear from me for some time. I may feel indisposed to write, as I do now. My heart is too full. Private hopes of mine are fallen with the hopes of Italy. I have played for a new stake and lost it. Life looks too difficult. But for the present I shall try to waive all thought of self, and renew my strength."

Margaret was now suffering from shock, and all around her seemed distorted and grotesque. Her mood became a kind of passive despair. When, later, she was reminded by Channing that she had been given a great opportunity for carrying out her principles, she replied, "Would it were so! I found myself inferior in courage and fortitude to the occasion. I knew not how to bear the havoc and anguish incident to the struggle for those principles. I rejoiced that it lay not with me to cut down the trees, to destroy the Elysian gardens for the defense of Rome. I do not know that I could have done it . . . . I forgot the great ideas, to sympathize with the poor mothers."

Many months later she wrote to her sister Ellen, "I sought solace in tending the suffering men; but when I beheld the beautiful fair young men bleeding to death, or mutilated for life, I felt the woe of all the mothers who had nursed each to that full flower, to see them thus cut down. I felt the consolation, too—for those youths died worthily. I was a Mater Dolorosa, and I remembered that the midwife who helped Angelino into the world came from the sign of the Mater Dolorosa. I thought, even if he lives, if he comes into the world at this great troubled time, terrible with perplexed duties, it may be to die thus at twenty years, one of a glorious hecatomb indeed, but still a sacrifice. It seemed then I was willing he should die."

But this willingness for Angelino to die was no more than the momentary product of physical and emotional exhaustion, a sense of individual helplessness when faced by vast events beyond personal control. And the small events were the same. A packet of letters from America brought a new blow. "The first words which met my eyes were these, in the hand of Mr. Greeley: 'Ah, Margaret, the world grows dark with us! You grieve, for Rome is fallen—I mourn, for Pickie is dead.' I have shed rivers of tears over the inexpressibly affecting letter thus begun. One would think that I might have become familiar enough with images of death and destruction; yet somehow the image of Pickie's little dancing figure, lying stiff and stark, had made me weep more than all else."

Her thoughts turned obsessively to Angelino. During the siege she said, "I often seemed to hear him calling me amid the roar of the cannon, and he seemed to be crying." As she waited for the coach and horses to carry her to her child, the cries seemed to intensify, and she became frantic at the need to go to him.

Once, when she was ten years old, she had tried her hand at prophecy. On a scrap of paper, which her father saved among his documents, she wrote: "On the 23rd of May, 1810, was born one foredoomed to sorrow and pain, and like others to have misfortunes. She had feeling which few have, which is the SOURCE of sorrow."

She could not free herself from the feeling that Angelino too was "foredoomed to sorrow and pain."

38

All the dream-cries of Angelino were not enough to prepare Margaret for the shattering reality. His nurse's milk had failed, he had suffered from an un-named illness, he appeared to be slowly starving to death.

As communications from Rome to Rieti had been completely severed, his caretakers believed that he had been abandoned— that they had been forced to accept an undesired addition to their family. They had no way of being sure that the eccentric foreign woman would ever reappear to claim her child. Their letters had not been answered. The baby, they said, would take only a little bread and wine. Margaret's first reaction was anguish; Ossoli's was fury.

Within a few days Margaret wrote to Lewis Cass, with whom she was now on the friendliest of terms: "I could find much repose of the moment . . . were it not for the state in which I find my baby. You know, my dear Mr. Cass, I flattered you with the thought you would be happy in having a child; may you never know such a pang as I felt in kissing his poor, pale little hand . . . . He is worn to a skeleton, all his sweet childish graces fled; he is so weak it seems to me he can scarcely ever re-vive to health. If he cannot, I do not wish him to live; life is hard enough for the strong. It is too much for the feeble. Only, if he dies, I hope I shall too. I was too fatigued before, and this last shipwreck of hopes would be more than I could bear."

Firmly she reiterated her own death wish in case Angelino should die. It lodged deep in her consciousness. To Caroline Sturgis Tappan she confided: "I have been on the brink of los-ing my little boy . . . . All that I have undergone seemed little to what I felt seeing him unable to smile or lift his little wasted hand. Now by incessant care I have brought him back (who knows if indeed that be a deed of love?) into this difficult world. I hope that the cruel law of my life will not at last oblige me to be separated from him . . . . But when I really saw him lin-gering as he did, for two months between life and death, I could not let him go unless I could go with him. When I saw his first smile, his poor, wan, feeble smile—and more than four weeks we watched him night and day before we saw it—new resolu-tion dawned in my heart. I resolved to live, day by day and hour by hour for his dear sake. So if he is only treasure lent, if he must go as sweet Waldo * did, as my little Pickie, as *my* children do, I shall at least have had these days and hours with him."

Exhausted from this second siege of all that she loved best, she could not resist bitterness. To a friend unknown she wrote: "I am not what I should be on this earth. I could not be. My nature has need of profound and steadfast sentiment; without this it could have no steadfast greatness, no creative power. I have been since we parted the object of great love from the noble and the humble. I have felt it towards both. Yet a kind of chartered libertine I rove. Pensively, always; in deep sadness, often. 'O God help me' is all my cry. Yet I have very little faith in the Paternal love I need; the government of the earth does seem so ruthless or so negligent.

"I am tired of seeing men err and bleed. I am tired of think-ing, tired of hoping. I take an interest in some plans, *our* social-ism, for instance—for it has become mine, too—but the

* Emerson's small son.

279

interest is shallow as the plans. They are needed, they are even good, but man will still blunder and weep, as he has done for so many thousand years.

"Coward and footsore, gladly would I creep into some green recess, apart from so much meddling and so much knowing, where I might see a few not unfriendly faces, where not more wretched would come than I could relieve. Yes! I am *weary*, and faith soars and sings no more. Nothing is left good of me, except at the bottom of the heart a melting tenderness: 'She loves much.' Thus I die daily, and well understand the dejections of other troubled spirits with whom in times past I have communed."

It seemed that in the vigil over Angelino her union with Angelo was finally and completely consummated. As their child regained his health bit by bit, they drew ever closer together. They were now two parents seared by the same emotions over the baby's fate, and therefore more than lovers. All the former reasons for maintaining secrecy had now vanished. Their fate was indeed together, and Margaret no longer resisted an open relationship. Evidently the topic of marriage was again placed on the agenda for active discussion, but no record exists that anything was yet done about it. Certainly the decision was now taken to reveal what they had made such efforts to conceal: the existence of Angelino.

For Margaret the greatest problem was how to inform her mother. "A great pang of remorse came," she told Caroline, "and I thought, if Angelino dies I will not give her the pain of knowing that I have kept this secret from her; she shall hear of this connection as if it were something new. When I found he would live, I wrote to her. It half-killed me."

This "connection" she described to her mother as marriage, when at the end of August she finally forced herself to the admission. After a few preliminaries, she plunged: "This brings me to the main object of my present letter—a piece of intelligence about myself which I had hoped I might be able to communicate in such a way as to give you *pleasure*. That I cannot

—after suffering much in silence with that hope—is like the rest of my earthly destiny.

"The first moment, it may cause you a pang to know that your eldest child might long ago have been addressed by another name than yours, and has a little son a year old.

"But, beloved mother, do not feel this long. I do assure you, that it was only great love for you that kept me silent. I have abstained a hundred times, when your sympathy, your counsel, would have been most precious, from a wish not to harass you with anxiety. Even now I would abstain, but it has become necessary, on account of the child, for us to live publicly and permanently together; and we have no hope, in the present state of Italian affairs, that we can do it at any better advantage, for several years, than now."

She then summarized Angelo's family history and personal characteristics, and went on:

"His love for me has been unswerving and most tender. I have never suffered a pain that he could relieve. His devotion, when I am ill, is to be compared only with yours. His delicacy in trifles, his sweet domestic graces remind me of Eugene. In him I have found a home, and one that interferes with no tie. Amid many ills and cares, we have had much joy together, in the sympathy with natural beauty—with our child—with all that is innocent and sweet.

"I do not know whether he will always love me so well, for I am the elder, and the difference will become in a few years, more perceptible than now. But life is so uncertain, and it is so necessary to take good things with their limitations, that I have not thought it worth while to calculate too curiously.

"However my other friends may feel, I am sure that *you* will love him very much, and that he will love you no less. Could we all live together, on a moderate income, you would find peace with us. Heaven grant that, on returning, I may gain means to effect this object. He, of course, can do nothing while we are in the United States, but perhaps I can; and now that my health is better, I shall be able to exert myself, if sure that my child is watched by those who love him, and who are good and pure . . . .

"What shall I say of my child? All might seem hyperbole, even to my dearest mother. In him I find satisfaction for the first time to the deep wants of my heart. He is a fair child, with blue eyes and light hair; very affectionate, graceful, and sportive. He was baptized in the Roman Catholic Church by the name of Angelo Eugene Philip, for his father, grandfather, and my brother. He inherits the title of Marquis.

"Write the name of my child in your Bible, ANGELO OSSOLI, *born September 5, 1848*. God grant he may live to see you, and may prove worthy of your love!"

Mrs. Fuller had gone to live with Arthur in Manchester, New Hampshire, where he had accepted a pastorate. Margaret's letter had arrived on the anniversary of Timothy Fuller's death, and Mrs. Fuller had taken four long days to think about the situation. Her reply was homey, newsy, full of warmth and love: "No words of mine could give you any idea of the effect your communication of having become wife and mother made upon me. I had thought that nothing could ever move the depths of my spirit as this did. I have had time for calm reflection, and assure you that fervent thankfulness has come out of all this tumult, that I should have suffered tortures to have known that you were to become a mother, and I so far from you . . . . You are the only one who could judge of what could make you happy. I could have given no advice had I been consulted on so momentous a subject as a husband for my beloved daughter, knowing nothing of the person thus selected. If he continues to make you happy, he will be very dear to me . . . . I can make out Angelo, Eugene, Philip, but not your husband's name. Is it Orsoli or Orsoni? As you have not received the title Marchesa,* I should like to be able to say I know the name my daughter is addressed by—so please write it in plain letters . . . . Let us hold fast our faith in the good providence of God, who has led

* Reference to the title was deleted from Emerson's version of Margaret's letter in the *Memoirs*. Had she been legally married, she would have received the right to the title.

us gently thro' all our darkest days, wiped away our tears in sorrow, and showed us the light of His countenance when we were ready to faint by the way."

Then continued miscellaneous items: Ellen was coming to visit, with the baby; poor Ellery was engrossed in painting— "when he has a hobby he is less unhappy . . . I understand and pity him from the bottom of my heart"; Eugene was well; "my poor Lloyd more deranged." And finally, the blessing: "I send my first kiss with my fervent blessing to my grandson. I hope your husband will understand a little of my English, for I am too old to speak Italian fluently enough to make him understand how dearly I shall love him if he brings you safe to me . . . . Ever your loving, tender, sympathizing mother, Margarett Fuller."

With her mother's approval of her confession, so great a burden was lifted from Margaret that she told Lewis Cass about it. He replied that he was glad. "Your mind must be much relieved. Withholding confidence when it is due brings ugly feelings." They had been in constant correspondence. He kept her informed of events in Rome, with occasional little homilies (once he jokingly asked her to find him a beautiful countess as a lady friend).

"We have not been able to find an apartment," she informed him, "so we have rooms at the rustic *locanda,* which is on the piazza, clean and airy . . . . All the dandies of Rieti in all kinds of queer uniforms are congregated below. At the barber's, the druggist's, the caffè, they sit and digest the copious slander —chief product of this, as of every *little* hive of men. The baronesses and countesses, in the extreme of Italian undress, are peeping through the blinds. At half-past seven, if the band plays, they will put on their best dresses (alas! mongrel French fashions prevail here) and parade . . . . At present the scene is varied by presence of the Spanish force, who promise to stay only three days; and I hope they will not, for they eat up everything like locusts."

The pleasing contrast of this scene with Rome was made the more apparent by Cass's recital of events. General Oudinot had ordered attendance at a *Te Deum* at St. Peter's to celebrate "the re-establishment of the Papal authority"; but no one knew when the pope would return to Rome. The city was being governed by a commission composed of three cardinals—a new triumvirate. General Oudinot was recalled to Paris in disgrace, his acts considered "too violent and antiliberal." The Principessa Belgioioso, who had been forced to flee, repeatedly inquired about Margaret's welfare. She herself was almost penniless, and had been driven from Malta to Istanbul. Commented Cass: "One might almost doubt whether this is the 19th century. Certainly these are noble times, when a woman of her age, standing for the advocacy of such principles, too, is obliged to fly from Christendom to a Pagan land for safety and tolerance." The efforts to obtain his own recall for having given passports to the three Republicans were thus far unsuccessful. And finally, a tribute to the woman who had written so negatively about him in some of her dispatches to the New York *Tribune:*

"Whenever you leave Rieti, or wherever you go, you will of course let me know. If anything whatsoever should happen to you, of whatever nature, in which I can serve you, or be of any assistance, I trust you will not do me the wrong not to apprise me without delay. I will come to you instantly . . . . You must pardon me, if necessary, for speaking so plainly, but I feel warmly. I liked you from the first time I saw you." A cheering letter, too, arrived from Adam Mickiewicz in Paris. He thought of her often and fondly.

The question of leaving Rieti was given urgency by an incident that reactivated Margaret's old anxiety for Angelo. He was actively attempting to realize whatever revenues he could from the small properties that had been left to him. The great castle of Pietraforte, once an Ossoli family stronghold, had been a feudal fief surrounded by extensive lands. The castle itself and most of the land had been lost by interfamilial rivalries and lawsuits. One day Angelo set out in the direction of the castle, which was distant. At nightfall he had not returned.

Early next morning Margaret rushed to the authorities, in panic. Already they had been informed that Angelo had strayed into the territory of King Ferdinando ("Bomba"), and was being held at Città Ducale, a garrison center—apparently on suspicion of being a Garibaldian. She dashed off a note: "*Caro* —you can imagine in what torment I passed the night, not having received a word from you. It was only this morning that I got the idea that by mistake you had entered the Realm. I went with an official to see Monsignor Bella, and he assured me that since your papers are in order you can return immediately. He will write to the Superintendent of Città Ducale . . . . I was half considering taking a carriage and coming to look for you, but was afraid it would take a long time and I would have to leave Nino far too long. But if you are exhausted and can't find a carriage or other method of travel, write and tell me what I should do."

Angelo returned safely, not so much because his papers were in order, but because he happened to be carrying a letter addressed to the Marchese Ossoli. One of the Bourbon regimental chaplains remembered the name Ossoli as connected with the *Guardia Nobile* of the pope. Thus Angelo received apologies and was freed. But the realm was periously close, and so too was Rome, for word of Angelo's Republican activities might easily filter through to the clerical authorities in Rieti. So the decision was made to move.

Early in September Angelo went reluctantly to Rome to cash one of Margaret's bills of exchange. Margaret wrote to Emelyn Story, "Feel no immediate anxiety about me. Our plans are laid till next April, and we think we have money sufficient to last till then. Meanwhile Ossoli will make an effort to have a fund of ready money from his family for renunciation of claims on a vineyard, houses, etc.; but I hardly hope he will succeed. They are angry, the brother who is administrator [Giuseppe] having been obliged to hide in a cellar and have troops quartered in his house during the rule of the Republic. Besides, ready money is very hard to raise in Rome at present. It is odd how peculiarly things have turned against us. You have read that the dispatches of Oudinot were dated from Villa Santucci. That beautiful place was the property of Ossoli's grandmother, which in the religious weakness of her last hours she gave to Monsignor Santucci, then her confessor. As he is godfather to my husband, there was reason to hope he might restore the unjust acquisition at his death. But he has had to fly and hide; his property has been ravaged by the war, and he will have little love for a godson who served on the Republican side."

Margaret's doubts were justified. Angelo was met by frigid silence; brother Giuseppe would not speak to him. Alessandro allied himself with Giuseppe, and Ottavio was too ill with asthma to care. Only sister Angela offered comfort and tried to help. Dejected, Angelo returned to Rieti.

At the end of the month, when the summer heat had passed, Angelo and Margaret and Angelino set off like three vagabonds through the grape-laden hills of Umbria. Their destination was first Perugia, then the city of Florence. True, the grand duke had returned, and Florence was occupied by the Austrians; but there at least the pope did not rule.

39

When Margaret arrived in Florence with her two males, she created a sensation among the English-speaking colony. If informing her mother of her circumstances had caused her such pain, she must have shrunk infinitely more from the public announcement. With reserve and simple dignity she concealed her quivering inward state, and pretended that nothing could be more ordinary than the sudden appearance of a maiden lady as a married lady with a small son.

The impact was described by Elizabeth Barrett Browning in a letter to a friend. Margaret had sought to meet the Brownings in London, and subsequently in Rome had been in correspondence with Mrs. Browning. By a nice ironic touch it had been Margaret's reviews that introduced the poems of both Robert Browning and Elizabeth Barrett to American readers. Robert Browning she had called "a subtle and radiant mind," but Miss Barrett had not fared so well. Though Margaret termed her the leading "female" writer, reservations were candidly expressed. "As a poet, Miss Barrett is deficient in plastic energy, and . . .

diffuse." Her writing had "many blemishes of overstrained and constrained thought and expression."

Now Miss Barrett, whose own romance had been so sensational, seized her opportunity. Rather spitefully she remarked that Miss Fuller had "taken us by surprise at Florence, retiring from the Roman world with a husband and child above a year old. Nobody had even suspected a word of this underplot, and her American friends stood in mute astonishment before this apparition of them here. The husband is a Roman marquis appearing amiable and gentlemanly, and having fought well, they say, at the siege, but with no pretensions to cope with his wife on any ground appertaining to the intellect."

The news spread with the remarkable speed always given by the impetus of scandal. "Emelyn Story wrote me," said Margaret, "that William was a little hurt, at first, that I did not tell him, even in the trying days of Rome—but left him to hear it, as he unluckily did, at the *table d'hôte* in Venice. But his second and prevailing thought was regret that he had not known it, so as to soothe and aid me, to visit Ossoli at his post, to go to the child in the country. Wholly in this spirit was the fine letter he wrote me, one of my treasures."

As the Marchesa Arconati Visconti had a house in Florence, and often returned there, it became Margaret's necessary and trying duty to confirm the rumor of which the Marchesa once had spoken: that Margaret had taken a lover. She decided on an approach which was frank and without apologies: "Reading a book called *The Last Days of the Republic in Rome,* I see that my letter giving my impressions of that period may well have seemed to you strangely partial. If we can meet as we once did and compare notes in the same spirit of candor, while making mutual allowance for our different points of view, your testimony and opinions would be invaluable to me. But will you have patience with my democracy, my revolutionary spirit? Believe me that in thought I am more radical than ever. The heart of Margaret you know—it is always the same. Mazzini is immortally dear to me . . . . You will not love me the less that I am true to him.

"Then, again, how will it affect you to know that I have
united my destiny with that of an obscure young man, younger
than myself, a person of no intellectual culture, and in whom, in
short, you will see no reason for my choosing. Yet more—that
this union is of long standing; that we have with us our child of
a year old; and that it is only lately I acquainted my family
with the fact?

"If you decide to meet with me as before, and wish to say
something about the matter to your friends, it will be true to say
that there have been pecuniary reasons for this concealment.
But *to you,* in confidence, I add, this is only half the truth. And
I cannot explain, or satisfy my dear friend further. I should wish
to meet her independent of all relations, but as we live in the
midst of 'society,' she would have to inquire for me now as Margaret Ossoli. That being done, I should like to say nothing further on the subject.

"However you may feel about all this, dear Madame Arconati, you will always be the same in my eyes. I earnestly wish
that you may not feel estranged; but if you do, I would prefer
that you act upon it. Let us meet as friends, or not at all."

Notable was the fact that Margaret had not mentioned Ossoli's title, equivalent to the Visconti title of Costanza's husband. She was content to state her case on the basis of "an obscure young man." Costanza answered: "I assure you that I see
nothing in your changed state to alter our relations. On the contrary it ought to strengthen the bond between us now that we
have in common maternal affection."

Margaret, relieved and delighted, replied at once. "My loved
friend—I read your letter with greatest content. I did not know
but there might seem something offensively strange in the circumstances I mentioned to you. Goethe [whose biography
Margaret once planned to write] says: 'There is nothing men
pardon so little as singular conduct for which no reason is
given.' . . . It gladdens my heart indeed that you do not care
for this, and that we may meet in love . . . .

"When you write by post, please direct 'Marchesa Ossoli.' I
did not explain myself on that point. The fact is, it seems to me

silly for a radical like me to be carrying a title; and yet, while Ossoli is in his native land it seems disjoining myself from him not to have it. It is a sort of thing that does not naturally belong to me—and, unsustained by fortune, is but a *souvenir* even for Ossoli. Yet it has seemed to me that for him to drop an inherited title would be, in some sort, to acquiesce in his brothers' disclaiming him, and dropping a right he may passively wish to maintain for his child. How does it seem to you? I am not very clear about it. If Ossoli dropped the title it would be a suitable moment in becoming an inhabitant of republican America."

In republican America there were certain subsurface currents of gossip which verged from smug to nasty. But not all. In a letter to Emelyn Story, Margaret commented: "Thus far, my friends have received news that must have been an unpleasant surprise to them, in a way that—*à moi*—does them great honor. None have shown littleness or displeasure at being denied my confidence while they were giving their own. Many have expressed the warmest sympathy, and only one has shown a disposition to transgress the limit I myself had marked, and to ask questions. With her, I think, that was because she was annoyed by what people said, and wished to be able to answer them. I replied to her that I had communicated already all I intended, and should not go into detail—that when unkind things were said about me, she should let them pass. Will you, dear Emelyn, do the same? I am sure your affection for me will prompt you to add that you feel confident whatever I have done has been in a good spirit, and not contrary to *my* ideas of right.

"For the rest, you will not admit for me—as I do not for myself—the rights of the social inquisition in the United States to know all the details of my affairs. If my mother is content; if Ossoli and I are content; if our child, when grown up, shall be content—that is enough. You and I know enough of the United States to be sure that many persons there will blame whatever is peculiar. The lower-minded persons everywhere are sure to think that whatever is mysterious must be bad. But I think there will remain for me a sufficient number of friends to keep my heart warm and help me earn my bread. That is all that is of any consequence."

Brother Richard was so shocked that he refused to send Margaret congratulations, or even to write at all, expressing himself as "amazed" at the "worldliness" of his sister—though later he modified his views. Arthur said guardedly, "We have not yet communicated your marriage extensively to the family." And to her sister, Margaret confided less than she had to Caroline Sturgis a year earlier: "You are anxious, my dear Ellen, to know some details of my past history. I should like to gratify you, but I hardly know how. There are some reasons, which I cannot explain further than by the remark that Ossoli is still a member of the Roman Catholic Church, why I do not go into all the matter of past history. I cannot, at least at present, tell exactly the facts; so I choose to say nothing."

Margaret's remark about Angelo's continued membership in the Roman Church indicates how seriously loomed the problem of the special dispensation to marry a Protestant. So long as Angelo was in Rome, subject to his brothers' control, it could have been their chief weapon against him. But with his espousal of the Republic he had forfeited everything, and he no longer had anything to lose by requesting a dispensation. In the Papal States a civil marriage could not be contracted. In the duchy of Tuscany it might have been. Nevertheless Angelo would have preferred to be married in the Church, and with a sufficient contribution secret arrangements could have been made with some willing friar.

The only valid clue to this mystery was contained in a letter written a year and a half later by Angelo's sister to Margaret's sister—Angela to Ellen. Angela explained, " . . . neither my husband nor I ever had the pleasure to meet [Miss Fuller]. Your sister Margaret was always in Rieti; then she moved to Florence, where I heard from my brother, Gio Angelo, that there she was married, having first in Rieti given birth to their son, Nino, who was baptized. I was surprised to learn all of this, since I had known nothing beforehand." * Surprised, but not shocked—as the baby was properly baptized and bore the father's name.

In the region around Florence small churches abounded. Perhaps Margaret left out the most essential fact—her wedding ceremony—when she wrote the following passage: "Today we have been out in the country, and found a little chapel—full of *contadine,* their lovers waiting outside the door. They looked charming in their black veils—the straw hat hanging on the arm—with shy, glancing eyes, and cheeks pinched rosy by the cold . . . . On foot we have explored a great part of the environs; and till now I had no conception of their beauty. When here before, I took only the regular drives as prescribed for all lady and gentlemen travellers. This evening we returned by a path that led to the banks of the Arno. The Duomo, with the snowy mountains, were glorious in the rosy tint and haze just before the sunset.

"What a difference it makes to come home to a child!—how it fills up all the gaps of life, just in the way that is most consoling, most refreshing! Formerly, I used to feel sad at that hour; the day had not been nobly spent, I had not done my duty to myself and others, and I felt so lonely! Now I never feel lonely."

* This is the only reference to the date and place of Margaret's marriage ever found among the Fuller papers. Apparently all references were systematically destroyed by the Fuller family because they considered the belated wedding scandalous. This letter escaped probably because it was in Italian and difficult to translate. It has never before been published in English.

40

She was not lonely—but once the hurdle of social acceptability had been leaped, there were other problems. The police, for example, viewed them with hostility, and though Angelo had been provided with a United States passport, threatened to send them away. Only the combined intercession of Horatio Greenough and Lewis Cass made possible a tentative permission; yet they remained under surveillance. In spite of these difficulties, Margaret was able to write Cass, "Here I feel better pleased than ever before. Florence seems so cheerful and busy after ruined Rome. I feel as if I could forget the disasters of the day for a while."

They took rooms in a house with windows overlooking the Piazza Santa Maria Novella, so that they could see the fourteenth-century church with Alberti's geometric marble facade, and also the campanile. Their small living room, with polished tile floor and frescoed ceiling, was sparingly furnished. Its greatest asset was a table which could be drawn near the fireplace while Margaret worked on her *History*—of which two volumes were completed. Angelo read by the brass Renaissance lamp. In the evenings he often wore the jacket of his *Guardia* uniform, with its red epaulettes, sitting quietly with a melancholy air. In the mornings, while Margaret cared for Angelino, he undertook the study of sculpture, probably under the direction of Greenough. When Americans who did not speak Italian came to call on Margaret, he usually went out to a caffè, to avoid constraining the conversation by his presence.

Their social life was modest, but not unsatisfactory. Occasionally they went to the opera, as guests. Frequently they went to vesper services together. Besides the Greenoughs and the Moziers (who had nursed Margaret when she came to Florence so ill), they came to know very well the Brownings, with whom they were particularly friendly. At first Mrs. Browning had been wary of Margaret, "she being one of the out and out *Reds* and scorners of grades of society." But when the Marchesa Arconati Visconti arrived and introduced the couple into aristocratic Italian circles, Mrs. Browning was mollified. On Margaret's part, as she said to Emelyn Story, "The society of the Brownings affords me great entertainment and pleasure, but I fancy I make but little return. I do not feel drawn out, but like to hear them, especially Browning." But Mrs. Browning, she wrote to George Curtis, "seems too gentle and faded at first sight to excite prospective feeling of any kind."

Finally there was the ever-faithful young Horace Sumner, son of Timothy Fuller's friend Charles Sumner. Horace had admired Margaret extravagantly at Brook Farm, and had come from Boston to Europe "to see cathedrals and Margaret." She described him as "a pale, erect, narrow little figure, which made my nerves tingle with old associations . . . . Imagine Brook Farm walking the streets of Florence!" Daily he knocked at the Ossoli door, bringing some little present of flowers. With Angelo he exchanged English-Italian lessons, but neither seemed to make much progress. Horace, said Margaret, "was old in his ways for one of his age." But patiently she tolerated him. Such was their little circle.

Not their social life but her husband and son were the subjects that chiefly concerned Margaret in her letters. About

Angelo she had relatively little to write; about Angelino, volumes.

To Ellen she explained something of Angelo's character: "About Ossoli I do not like to say much, as he is an exceedingly delicate person. He is not precisely reserved, but it is not natural to him to *talk* about the objects of strong affection. I am sure he would not try to describe me to his sister, but would rather she would take her own impression of me. And, as much as possible, I wish to do the same by him. I expect that to many of my friends (Mr. Emerson for one) he will be nothing, and they will not understand that I should have life in common with him. But I do not think he will care; he has not the slightest tinge of self-love. He has throughout our intercourse been used to my having many such ties; he has no wish to be anything to persons with whom he does not feel spontaneously bound, and when I am occupied he is happy in himself.

"But some of my friends and my family who will see in him the details of practical life, cannot fail to prize the purity and simple strength of his character—and should he continue to love me as he has done, to consider his companionship an inestimable blessing to me. I say *if* because all human affections are frail, and I have experienced too great revulsions in my own not to know it. Yet I feel great confidence in the permanence of his love . . . .

"Now he loves his child in the same way. I think he will make an excellent father, though he could not speculate about it, or in fact about anything . . . . The friction that I have seen mar so much of the domestic life of others does not occur with us— or at least has not."

In another letter, to a close but unknown friend, she explained, "Our relation covers only a part of my life, but I do not perceive that it interferes with anything I ought to have or be; I do not feel in any way constrained or limited or that I have made any sacrifice. Younger I might, because I should have been exposed to love some other in a way that might give him pain, but I do not now feel apprehensive of that.

"There is more danger for him, as he is younger than I; if he should I shall do all that this false state of society permits to give him what freedom he may need. I have thought a great deal about this; there are things I do not wish to put on paper. I daresay I shall tell them to you when we meet.

"You speak as if I might return to America without him. I thought of it at one time . . . but now that cannot be. He could not at present re-enter Rome without danger; he is separated from his employment and his natural friends, nor is any career open for him in Italy at present. Then I could not think of taking away the child for several months; his heart is fixed on the child as fervently as mine. Then it would not only be very strange and sad to me to be without his love and care for weeks and weeks, but I should feel very anxious about him under present circumstances."

She sent home a daguerrotype of Angelo and a lock of his dark hair, to give a tactile reality. When, two months later, they had not yet arrived, she wrote: "I know there must be a cloud of false rumors and impressions at first, but you will see when we meet that there was a sufficient reason for all I have done, and that if my life be not wholly right (as it is so difficult to keep a life true in a world full of falsities), it is not wholly wrong nor fruitless. You would have had true impressions at first if you had received the daguerrotype likeness of Ossoli. I had depended on that. It gave a view of his face different from the habitual one, but which represents him as he most is in our relation."

To Elizabeth Hoar she made a plea which in reality was a cry for tolerance from all her friends: "Never blame him for ills I may have to undergo; all that he could he has done for me, all that he had has given . . . . He has suffered enough; it has plowed furrows in his life since first we met . . . . When we look on the sweet face of our child, we think if we can keep him we shall have courage for whatever we may have to do or endure."

But it was in writing about Angelino that Margaret, more than any ordinary mother, became rhapsodic. In one of her long intimate letters to Caroline Sturgis Tappan she said: "I do not know what to write about him—he changes so much, has so many characters. He is like me in that; his father's character is simple and uniform, though not monotonous, more than are the flowers of spring, flowers of the valley. He is now in the most perfect rosy health, a very gay, impetuous, ardent, but sweet tempered child. He seems to me to have nothing in common with his first baby [hood] with its ecstatic smiles, its exquisite sensitiveness, and a distinction in gestures and attitudes that struck everybody. His temperament seems changed by taking the milk of these robust women. His form is robust . . . .

"He is now come to quite a knowing age (fifteen months). In the morning, as soon as dressed, he signs to come into our room; then draws our curtain, kisses me rather violently, pats my face, stretches himself and says *bravo*. Then expects as a reward to be tied in his chair and have his playthings. These engage him busily, but still he calls to us to sing and drum to enliven the scene. Sometimes he calls me to kiss his hand; he laughs very much at this. Enchanting is that baby laugh, all dimples and glitter, so strangely arch and innocent. Then I wash and dress him; that is his great time. He makes it [last] as long as he can, insisting to dress and wash me the while, kicking, throwing water about, full of all manner of tricks that I think girls never dream of. Then is his walk; we have beautiful walks here for him, along the Arno, by the bridges or the sunny walk at the Cascine, protected by fine trees always warm in mid-winter, the bands playing in the distance and children of all ages walking and sitting with their nurses. His walk and sleep give me about three hours in the middle of the day. Then at eight he goes to bed and we have the [evening] . . . .

"I feel so refreshed by his young life. Ossoli diffuses such a power and sweetness over every day that I cannot endure to think yet of our future. Too much have we suffered already trying to command it. I do not feel force to make any effort yet . . . . Now for two months we have been tranquil; we have resolved to repose and enjoy being together as much as we can in this brief interval—perhaps all we shall ever know of peace. It is very sad we have no money, we could be so quietly happy a while. I rejoice in all that Ossoli did, but the results in this our earthly state are disastrous, especially as my strength is now so much impaired. This much I do hope, in life or death, to be no more separated from Angelino . . . . The position of a mother separated from her only child is too frightfully unnatural . . . .

"The Christmas holidays interest me now through my child as they never did for myself. I like to go out and watch the rising generation who will be his contemporaries. On Sunday I went . . . to the Cascine. After we had taken the drive, we sat down on a stone seat in the sunny walk to see the people pass; the Grand Duke and his children; the elegant Austrian officers who will be driven out of Italy when Angelino is a man; Princess Demidoff with her hussars; Harry Lorrequer and his absurd brood; M. de Coaveilles who helped betray Rome; many lovely children; many little frisking dogs with their bells. The sun shone brightly on the Arno; a bark moved gently by. All seemed good to the baby. He laid himself back in my arms, smiling, singing to himself, dancing his feet. I hope he will retain some trace in his mind of the perpetual exhilarating picture of Italy . . . .

"Christmas day I was just up, and Nino all naked on his sofa, when came some beautiful large toys that had been sent him: a bird, a horse, a cat that could be moved to express different things. It almost made me cry to see the kind of fearful rapture with which he regarded them—legs and arms extended, fingers and toes quivering, mouth made up to a little round O, eyes dilated. For a long time he did not even wish to touch them. After he began to, he was different with all the three: loving the bird; very wild and shouting with the horse; with the cat, putting her face close to his, staring in her eyes, and then throwing her away. Afterwards I drew [for] him in a lottery, at a child's party given by Mrs. Greenough, a toy of a child asleep on the neck of a tiger. The tiger is stretching up to look at the child. This he likes best of any of his toys. It is sweet to see him when he gets used to them and plays by himself, whispering to them and seeming to contrive stories. You would laugh to know how much remorse I feel that I never gave children more toys in the course of my life. I regret all the money I ever spent on myself or in little presents for grown people, hardened sinners. I did not know what pure delight could be bestowed. I am sure that if Jesus Christ had given, it would not have been little crosses.

"There is snow all over Florence, in our most beautiful piazza. Santa Maria Novella, with its fair loggia and bridal church, is a carpet of snow, and the full moon looking down. I had forgotten how angelical all that is; how fit to die by. I have only seen snow in mountain patches for so long. Here it is the even holy shroud of a desired power. God bless all good and bad tonight, and save me from despair."

41

"It has long seemed that in the year 1850 I should stand on some important plateau in the ascent of life," Margaret told a friend, "—should be allowed to pause for a while and take more clear and commanding views than ever before. I feel however no marked and important change as yet."

In Florence the New Year began with damp, penetrating cold, and from Rome the news was bleaker than the cold. Cass, who lately had presented his official credentials to the Vatican, reported to Margaret: "Rome is in a frightful state. There is no commerce, no credit, no confidence, owing to the posture of public affairs. The French are at swords' points with the authorities. The Government is proscriptive beyond all bounds. Fines, imprisonments and banishments are inflicted every day. Scarcely a family has escaped. Even the princely families of highest rank, the heads of which never participated in the late revolution, are punished from day to day for the conduct of some of their members who have joined in that movement . . . ."

"I have twice, without any volition of my own, by circumstances been thrust between the Cardinals and the creatures whom they were hunting down, and I gave them my mind with a freedom which I expected would be followed by a cessation of diplomatic relations. For that, however, I cared very little . . . . The Cardinals are overdoing their work. A terrible reaction must come, or human nature will give the lie to the history of centuries. The priests will wake up some morning to a second and better edition of the late revolution, from which there will be no escape.

"The Government . . . is hunting out with fiendish ferocity every individual who is tainted with republicanism. They might as well undertake to exhaust the ocean by draining it."

From Angela to Angelo came more news of Rome, personal and public. She had broken entirely with brothers Giuseppe and Alessandro, and they were not on speaking terms. That "dear soul" Giuseppe, as she called him, again had failed to meet his commitments. "We will have to take him to court, as usual—he continues to act in his usual untrustworthy manner."

It was almost too painful to read her description of the pope's long-delayed return to Rome. "As you know, on the 12th of this month [April] the Holy Father made his entrance through the San Giovanni gate, announcing his arrival with 101 cannon shots and the sound of all Rome's church bells. Descending from his travelling coach, he entered the Lateran Basilica where were gathered all the most important priests, all the religious orders, and the diplomatic corps, who were waiting to welcome him. After having given the benediction to all, in the midst of a throng of cheering people, he entered his ceremonial coach. He was accompanied by the French High Command, and the *Guardia Nobile,* followed by the coaches of all the ministers, who were in full regalia. He went along the Via dello Stradone and on by the Colosseum and Trajan's Forum, passing beneath our windows. The Papal route and all the streets were decorated for the occasion. He went then to St. Peter's basilica to give thanks. For three evenings all the city, and especially the Campidoglio, was illuminated—at the latter were hung great lamps which blinded one's eyes. In many parts of the city orchestras were playing. On the following Sunday, a *Te Deum* of thanks was sung in all the churches for the Pope's safe return. On the 18th of this month, before an enormous crowd and with the salute of 300 or more cannons, the French held a parade in St. Peter's piazza before the Holy Father—who gave them his benediction."

It was abundantly evident that years must pass before Angelo could return to Rome. Had Giuseppe, in his strategic position at the papal court, been willing to help, some sort of conditional pardon might have been secured. But the probability was otherwise: Giuseppe would use his position to hound Angelo into renunciation of whatever claims might remain to the property he had inherited from their father. Angelo was almost as circumscribed as if he were already a prisoner in the loathsome dungeons of the Castel Sant'Angelo. No spot in all Italy was completely safe; there was no recourse but to emigrate.

To her mother, Margaret had carefully understated the true situation: "It will be terrible for me to leave Italy, uncertain of return. Yet when I think of you, beloved mother, of brothers and sister and many friends, I wish to come. Ossoli is perfectly willing. He leaves in Rome a sister whom he dearly loves. His aunt is dying now. He will go among strangers; but to him, as to all the young Italians, America seems the land of liberty. He hopes, too, that a new revolution will favor return after a number of years, and that then he may find really a home in Italy. All this is dark; we can judge only for the present moment. The decision will rest with me. I shall wait until the last moment, as I always do, that I may have all the reasons before me."

The reentry of Pius IX into Rome proved the ultimate reason, and Margaret began at once the arduous task of preparation. It was well that she did so, because the Austrian police showed increasing signs of restlessness at Angelo's presence.

But there were other reasons, among the most pressing of which was the real poverty of the little family. Margaret's connection with the *Tribune* had not been resumed, for reasons unannounced—but probably because rumors of her "free love" had been circulating freely in New York. With the completion of her manuscript Margaret had hoped to find at once a publisher in England, where the Roman revolution was much more meaningful than in America. She did in fact make a submission, but the *History* was declined—probably on the grounds of her interpretation of events. It would not be easy to find a publishing house sympathetic to her views, even with the proffered help of Thomas Carlyle. Also the British copyright laws recently had been changed, so that they were unfavorable to foreigners.

To Emelyn Story she wrote that it was imperative for her to go to the United States to try to make arrangements for the book. "Will I be more fortunate in person?" she said. "I do not know. I am ill-adapted to push my claims and my pretensions, but at least it will not be such slow work passing from disappointment to disappointment as here, where I wait upon the post office—wait two or three months to know the result of any proposition." Realistically she summed up her situation: "I cannot be quite independent of what is called society, as I need to earn our bread at least for the present. But I trust there will be a sufficient number of persons needing something from me to enable me to earn frugal bread. That is all I want of what is called the world."

To Emerson she had turned reluctantly for aid and advice. He replied, "I am sure it is needless that you should cross the ocean only to make a bargain for your book, whilst I am here, even if I were a far clumsier agent than I am. I can see plainly, too, the very important advantages which continued residence in Italy will give to your factors at home . . . . It is certainly an unexpected side for me to support—the advantages of your absenteeism." The truth was that he felt Ossoli had "taken her away" from him, and he rather dreaded her return, as later inadvertently he was to reveal in a letter to Carlyle.

She ignored Emerson's advice, and made a definite decision to return as soon as feasible. The major problem, as always, was money. She wrote to her brother Richard that she could not say yet when she would come home, " . . . not being sure we can get the money. The voyage, made in the cheapest way we can, must cost us about two hundred and fifty dollars, as, even if we have the length and discomforts of a voyage by a merchantman, and go without any help for care of the baby in case of being sick, we must still buy stores, and have a cow or a goat to insure him proper food. We may have in this way two months on the ocean. I have always suffered much in my head at sea. However, to go by France would be more than double the expense."

From Angelo now almost no money was forthcoming. There was no alternative but once again to ignore her pride and ask for loans, though nothing can be more humiliating for the poor than borrowing trifling sums of money from the rich. From Costanza Arconati she asked and received one hundred dollars; from a bank, with Marcus Spring as security, she asked and received three hundred dollars on a hundred-day note. She gave instructions as to how this latter sum could be collected from her family should she be lost at sea. She had raised just enough for a voyage by sailship, but not by steamer. All that remained was to choose the ship.

Suddenly she began to suffer the acute headaches which formerly had proved so debilitating. She seemed to undergo a paralysis both of will and action. Her forehead throbbed, and her myopia seemed terribly intensified. All before her was hazy and formless, as though she could grasp no firm reality. She was bled by the doctor, but found little relief. On one of these occasions a letter arrived from the Marchesa Arconati, who, writing now in Italian instead of French, commented cheerfully that a long sea voyage would restore her health and be splendid for the baby. Immediately she revived.

Through the Moziers she met Captain and Mrs. Hasty. Seth Hasty was master of the bark *Elizabeth,* a nearly new, three-masted American merchantman. Rugged and not uncultured, he was the traditional type of hardy Yankee skipper from Maine, who had lived with the sea most of his life. Margaret was greatly impressed with the captain, liked his wife Catherine, and resolved to inspect the ship, which was docked at Livorno, taking on a cargo of old paintings, almonds, olive oil, silk, 150 tons of Carrara marble, and Powers' bulky statue of John C. Calhoun—which Margaret had so admired. The *Elizabeth,* it proved, was trim, well kept, and gave every evidence of being a staunch, reliable vessel. Yet by some intuition Margaret resisted the *Elizabeth,* though she commented favorably that the ship bore the given name of Mrs. Browning.

"I am suffering as never before the horrors of indecision," she said. " . . . Now that I am on the point of deciding to come in her, people daily dissuade me, saying that I have no conception of what a voyage of sixty or seventy days will be in point of fatigue and suffering; that the insecurity, compared with packet-ships or steamers, is great; that the cabin, being on deck, will be terribly exposed in case of a gale, etc. etc. I am well aware of the proneness of volunteer counselors to frighten and excite one, and have generally disregarded them. But this time I feel a trembling solicitude on account of my child, and am doubtful, harassed, almost ill."

Preparations nevertheless went steadily forward. Carefully Margaret packed all the documents of the Republic she had so carefully saved—the printed edicts, the notes from Cass, the directives from Belgioioso, the order for Angelo's promotion, the Roman journal, and the letters from Mazzini. Someday, she knew, they would be historically invaluable. Carefully she bound together the letters she and Angelo had written one another, for no eyes except their own. The *History* she kept apart, that she might revise and perfect the style. It was an extraordinary manuscript, according to the Americans who knew about it, because it incorporated information from exceptional sources with Margaret's exceptional passion for the Republican cause. Neatly and precisely all was organized, as though love and anguish were strangers to her heart.

Angelo approached their departure as a problem in logistics. He wrote sister Angela for the papers and a diary he had left in an upper drawer of a certain desk, and for his old trunk. She replied that she was sending the papers, but that the diary and trunk had disappeared. She was having a new trunk made (at a cost which made him groan), and would pack it with all his old clothes. Then she added, "I am also sending you a Crucifix and the catechism for the little child, which you must teach him. Also other saints and amulets and the prayer book for the month of May. I wrapped all of it in a small paper parcel; and also a Rosary, which I put into a sock."

Dutifully, under the urging of Angela, Angelo wrote a farewell letter to their absent sister Matilde in Ireland. "I have been married to an American lady for some time now," he said (using an Italian phrase which implied less than a year). "We love each other very much. In addition, we have a sweet son who is our greatest consolation—especially since he makes me forget all my problems with that no-good Pepe [Giuseppe], who has tried to take advantage of me as much as he can. We are not rich but we keep each other happy in hoping for a more fortunate future . . . . "

It was spring—the time to come to Tuscany, not the time to leave. Margaret described it: "The Italian spring is as good as Paradise. Days come of glorious sunshine and gently-flowing airs that expand the heart and uplift the whole nature. The birds are twittering their first notes of love; the ground is enamelled with anemones, cowslips and crocuses; every old wall and ruin puts on its festoon and garland. And the heavens stoop daily nearer, till the earth is folded in the embrace of light, and her every pulse beats music."

But within was wintry foreboding. "I go home prepared to expect everything that is painful and difficult" she told Emelyn Story. To Costanza Arconati she wrote a last note: "I had intended if I went by way of France to take the packet-ship *Argo* from Havre . . . . I read of the wreck of the *Argo* returning from America to France. There were also notices of the wreck of the *Royal Adelaide,* a fine English steamer, and of the *John Skiddy,* one of the fine American packets. Thus it seems safety is not to be found in the wisest calculation. I shall embark more composedly in my merchant ship; praying, indeed fervently, that it may not be my lot to lose my babe at sea, either by unsolaced sickness, or amid the howling waves. Or that, if I should, it may be brief anguish, and Ossoli, he and I go together."

To that other middle-aged mother, Elizabeth Barrett Browning, she made a parting gift of a Bible for the little Robert. On its flyleaf she inscribed: "In memory of Angelo Eugene Ossoli."

To a person unknown she wrote: "You speak of my whole future. That future here on earth now seems to me short. It may be terribly trying, but it will not be so very long now . . . . My life proceeds so regularly, far more so than the fates of a Greek tragedy, that I can but accept all the pages as they turn."

42

The *Elizabeth* lay two miles offshore, looking more like a toy sailing ship for Angelino than an ocean-going vessel which could carry them all to America. It was much more graceful than the black and belching steamboat which—after the collision—had carried Margaret from Livorno to Naples. Now the *Elizabeth* rode placidly at anchor in a mild sea as brilliantly blue as the sky.

The passengers were few: Margaret and Angelo and Angelino; plus a young Italian girl named Celeste Paolini who was returning to her job in New York as a domestic servant, and had agreed to help care for Angelino; plus Horace Sumner, who refused to be detached from Margaret's magnetic field.

As they were rowed out in the ship's boat they saw the spars and rigging limned against the horizon, saw the Stars and Stripes astern undulate languidly in the breeze, heard the soft splash of waves. The ship seemed so secure, so safe, after all the horror and tragedy of the Roman revolution. It was early in the morning of May 17, 1850, and the sun was golden fresh.

Yet in the last hour before embarking Margaret had almost

backed out. During the preceding week letters had come from Marcus Spring indicating that her economic situation might be stabilized; but with the Marchesa Arconati Visconti again fearful that she would be forced with her husband into exile, it was evident that the political situation could not be stabilized for active Republicans. There was no choice but to return to America, with the hope that eventually gossip would subside. As the sailors heaved anchor, Margaret cast off her doubts. Playfully she said farewell to Italy, farewell to the umbrella pines and flowers, farewell to the glorious villas and more glorious ruins. All the passengers laughed and sang in apparent happiness.

All day the sea was calm, but next day both Margaret and Angelo were seasick. And in the evening one of Margaret's paralyzing headaches occurred. Under the tranquil surface, like the sea itself, flowed deep currents of turbulence. On the sixth day out Margaret passed her fortieth birthday. There is no record that it was celebrated, though each night the passengers played and sang in the saloon. In January Angelo had come to twenty-nine, and for a few brief months he and Margaret had been but ten years apart. Now forty sounded so much older than thirty-nine. Angelo said nothing of birthdays, and aided by Horace Sumner, went on with the study of English.

Angelino had become the toast of the ship. He had a white nanny goat to provide his milk, and he loved to cling to her fur like a miniature satyr from antiquity. The sailors—Swedish, English, and American—did tricks for him, sang to him, spoiled him. But of them all the worst was Captain Hasty. Every day in his cabin the captain played with Angelino and told him tales of gulls and fish and dolphins. On the eighth day out the captain became unwell; but not to disappoint the boy, continued to pet him.

Soon the captain became so ill that he could no longer read aloud the morning and evening selections from the Bible: so ill that he could no longer follow when his wife read. A fiery rash erupted on his skin, he coughed constantly, his throat swelled so that he could not swallow. For ten days the agony continued. At midnight on June 2 the *Elizabeth* anchored off Gibraltar, and at dawn the steward was sent for a doctor. He returned alone, but it did not matter, for Captain Hasty was dead.

All on board were denied permission to land, and the ship was held in quarantine for a week. Margaret was profoundly concerned for Angelino. She wrote to the Springs of her fears, mailing the letter to go by steamer from Gibraltar. "The last days were truly terrible," she said of Captain Hasty. "He died, we suppose (no physician has been allowed to come on board to see the body), of confluent smallpox . . . . I have seen great suffering, but nothing physical compared to this . . . . He died yesterday and was buried in deep water, the American Consul's barge towing out one from the ship which bore the body. It was Sunday and divinely calm. You cannot think how beautiful the whole thing was, the decent array and sad reverence of the sailors; the many ships with their banners flying; the stern pillar of Hercules all bathed in roseate vapor; the little white sails diving into the blue depths with that solemn spoil of the good man, when he had been so agonized and gasping . . . . "

When no new illnesses developed, the *Elizabeth* sailed on under the command of Henry Bangs, first mate. He was not a Captain Hasty, wise in the nature of the sea, but so inexperienced that he found it necessary to call on Mrs. Hasty for aid in navigation. And it was to Margaret that Mrs. Hasty turned for consolation.

On the second day out from Gibraltar, Angelino sickened. The pattern of his illness was the same as Captain Hasty's. His body was covered with pustules; his face and throat swollen shapeless; his eyes completely closed. All despaired of his life. "The father seemed resigned to this," wrote Mrs. Hasty afterward; "for he said life seemed so hard to him, he was willing baby should be spared the conflicts." But Margaret "seemed to feel she could not give him up." Throughout the long hours they applied cooling poultices, soothed and nursed him as best they could. On the ninth day of the illness, Margaret announced triumphantly to Mrs. Hasty that Nino could see again. The vaccination in Rieti perhaps had helped to save him.

Quickly he recovered, with hardly a mark on his body. All rejoiced.

The voyage continued without incident. Passage was quiet in the trade winds, but progress was so slow that the southeast wind—harbinger of danger—was hailed with joy. June had slipped away, and July had come. On the night of the last full moon, Margaret paced the deck at near midnight, and told Mrs. Hasty she did so because it was her "last moonlight night at sea—it seemed so holy."

On July 18 the *Elizabeth* was somewhere off the New Jersey coast, between Cape May and Barnegat. Mr. Bangs assured the passengers he would have them ashore in New York next day. Trunks were brought up from the hold, and Margaret selected the little frock Nino was to wear for the landing. When a supposed pilot boat was sighted, all the passengers rushed on deck in ecstasy. But the vessel slowly vanished. Night came, and all hands turned in. The southeast wind freshened; the seas became rough.

By midnight the wind had reached gale force. Mr. Bangs, under the misapprehension that the *Elizabeth* was still off New Jersey, close-reefed the sails, took an occasional sounding, and held his course.

At about four o'clock in the morning the *Elizabeth* struck. He had driven his ship into that strip of bayberry-and-poison-ivy-covered sand off Long Island called Fire Island. Here the currents were always dangerous, and the surf deadly with its undertow. The ship struck hard, and then again. The bow held in the sand while the stern swung round broadside to the waves, and the marble in the hold smashed through the bottom. Every swell washed across the deck.

In the darkness of their cabins the passengers were flung from their bunks. They could see nothing, and above the wind could barely hear the cry "Cut away!" as the main and mizzen masts went down. In the Ossoli cabin the skylight was shattered and the door wrenched ajar. Water and spray fumed above and around them. The passengers grouped together as best they could. Nino cried, and Margaret, in her white nightgown, clasped him tight to her breast. She wrapped him in whatever she could find, for the sea was cold. Angelo remained calm, as during the siege of Rome. To quiet Celeste Paolini, who screamed in hysteria, he prayed with her.

Soon after dawn, with the gale increasing, the passengers were conducted one by one from the cabin, which was breaking up, to the greater safety of the forecastle. Mrs. Hasty slipped on the slanting deck and was blown into an open hatch, but was saved by a sailor who clasped her hair. Nino was carried in a bag slung across a sailor's back. Margaret and Angelo, grasping one another, made their way through the tangled ropes and railings, drenched by the waves. Later, at Mrs. Hasty's request, a sailor returned twice for some of Mrs. Hasty's and the passengers' valuables: gold coins, necklaces, rings. Margaret remarked that her most important possession remained behind—the manuscript; but she would not ask the sailor to risk his life again for it.

The ship's boats had been swamped. As the hours passed, and on the beach no rescue efforts could be seen through the spray, Margaret gave up the one remaining life preserver to a seaman who volunteered to swim ashore for help. Another hour passed. No lifeboat had appeared. No line was received by mortar shot. At last human forms were visible. They were beach pirates, gathering salvage into wagons, interested in wrecks but not in rescues.

Now aboard ship the plan was advanced that, before the tide turned, each passenger should cling to a plank, and a sailor would swim with the plank. Mrs. Hasty volunteered, and through the pounding surf finally reached safety, gasping and near unconscious, three-quarters of a mile down the beach— invisible to those who remained behind. Then Horace Sumner leaped with a plank, but sank. Mr. Bangs urged Margaret and Angelo to try, but Margaret refused to be separated from husband and child. "Save yourselves!" shouted Mr. Bangs, and seizing a plank, abandoned ship before his passengers. Four seamen remained.

A lifeboat appeared on shore, but it was not launched. Evidently no hope was to be had from the land. A new effort was being planned by those who remained on the ship, for the steward took up Nino just as a massive wave crashed against the forecastle, and the foremast gave way. Celeste and Angelo were swept into the rigging, where Angelo clung for a moment, then disappeared. Margaret, in her white nightgown, with her hair fallen long and disheveled, had been seated at the foot of the foremast. When the wave had passed, reported a seaman who survived, she was not to be seen.

On the beach the bodies of the steward and little Nino were washed up, naked and still warm. The bodies of Margaret and her Ossoli were never found.

In Manchester, New Hampshire, Mrs. Fuller was waiting impatiently at Arthur's parsonage for the most beloved offspring to appear with her treasures. Mrs. Fuller had written instructions, which Margaret never received: "If we could know when you would arrive we would be at the Depot to conduct you to our house; but all the drivers know where my son lives—at the corner of Chestnut and Central Streets. May the great God preserve you, and conduct you in safety to your home."

All that reached home safely were a few documents and the bundle of love letters in Italian, half in Ossoli's ornate, elegant script; and half in Margaret's anguished, hurried scrawl. They were found in a small trunk buried in the dunes. The manuscript of the *History of the Roman Republic* was not among them.

At last were resolved the questions posed by Margaret in her journal as a young girl: "I remembered how, a little child, I had stopped myself on the stairs and asked, how came I here? How is it that I seem to be this Margaret Fuller? What does it mean? What shall I do about it?"

By her life the questions had been answered—and by her death, incised for posterity.

Bibliography

PRIMARY SOURCES

The Fuller manuscript collection of the Harvard University Library, Cambridge.

The Fuller manuscript collection of the Boston Public Library.

Letters from the Fuller collection of the Fruitlands Museums, Harvard, Massachusetts.

The Ossoli-della Torre family archives, Rome.

THE WORKS OF MARGARET FULLER

Eckermann's Conversations with Goethe, Boston, 1839.

Correspondence of Fräulein Günderode and Bettina von Arnim, Boston, 1842.

Summer on the Lakes, Boston, 1844.

Woman in the Nineteenth Century, New York, 1845.

Papers on Literature and Art, New York, 1856.

At Home and Abroad, edited by A. B. Fuller, Boston, 1856.

Life Without and Life Within, edited by A. B. Fuller, Boston, 1859.

Love-Letters of Margaret Fuller, 1845–1846, introduction by Julia Ward Howe, New York, 1903.

THE CHIEF BIOGRAPHIES
IN CHRONOLOGICAL ORDER

RALPH WALDO EMERSON, WILLIAM HENRY CHANNING, JAMES FREEMAN CLARKE, editors. *Memoirs of Margaret Fuller Ossoli,* 2 vols., Boston, 1852.

JULIA WARD HOWE. *Margaret Fuller (Marchesa Ossoli),* Boston, 1883.

THOMAS WENTWORTH HIGGINSON. *Margaret Fuller Ossoli,* "American Men of Letters" series, Houghton Mifflin Company, Boston, 1884.

CAROLINE W. HEALEY. *Margaret and Her Friends,* Boston, 1895.

ANDREW MACPHAIL. *Essays on Puritanism,* Boston, 1905.

KATHERINE ANTHONY. *Margaret Fuller, a Psychological Biography,* Harcourt, Brace & Howe, New York, 1920.

MARGARET BELL. *Margaret Fuller,* introduction by Mrs. Franklin D. Roosevelt, C. Boni, New York, 1930.

MASON WADE. *Margaret Fuller: Whetstone of Genius,* The Viking Press, Inc., New York, 1940.

MADELEINE B. STERN. *The Life of Margaret Fuller,* E. P. Dutton & Co., Inc., New York, 1942.

EMMA DETTI. *Margaret Fuller Ossoli e i suoi corrispondenti,* Le Monnier, Florence, 1942.

FAITH CHIPPERFIELD. *In Quest of Love—the Life and Death of Margaret Fuller,* Coward-McCann, Inc., New York, 1957.

ARTHUR W. BROWN. *Margaret Fuller,* Twayne's "United States Authors" Series, Twayne Publishers, Inc., New York, 1964.

GENERAL REFERENCES

ACTON, HAROLD. *The Last Bourbons of Naples, 1825–1861,* Methuen & Co., Ltd., London, 1961.

ANDREOTTI, GIULIO. *Lasiarda di Papa Mastai,* Casini, Rome, 1967.

ARTOM TREVES, GIULIANA. *Gli anglo-fiorentini dell'otto-cento,* Sansoni, Florence, 1953.

BEACH, SETH CURTIS. *Daughters of the Puritans—a Group of Brief Biographies,* American Unitarian Association, Boston, 1905.

BENEDETTI, ANNA. *Mazzini e Margherita Fuller,* "Nuova Anthologia," Rome, 1918.

BERKELEY, GEORGE FITZ-HARDINGE and J. *Italy in the Making —June 1846 to 1 January 1848,* The Macmillan Company, New York, 1936.

BRADFORD, GAMALIEL. *Portraits of American Women,* Houghton Mifflin Company, Boston, 1919.

BROOKS, VAN WYCK. *Life of Emerson,* E. P. Dutton & Co., Inc., New York, 1932.

——. *Flowering of New England,* E. P. Dutton & Co., Inc., New York, 1936.

——. *The Dream of Arcadia,* E. P. Dutton & Co., Inc., New York, 1958.

BROWN, JOHN L. *Un'amica di Mazzini: Margaret Fuller,* "Mondo Occidentale", No. 77, Anno VIII, Maggio 1961, United States Information Service, Rome.

BROWNING, ELIZABETH BARRETT. *Letters,* edited by F. G. Kenyon, Macmillan Company, New York, 1898.

CANBY, HENRY SEIDEL. *Thoreau,* Beacon Press, Boston, 1939.

CANDELORO, GIORGIO. *La Rivoluzione nazionale—1846–1849,* Feltrinelli, Milan, 1966.

CLARKE, JAMES FREEMAN. *Autobiography,* Houghton Mifflin Company, Boston, 1892.

COMMISSIONE ESECUTIVA PER IL MAUSOLEO OSSARIO GIANICOLENSE. *Caduti per Roma,* Rome, 1941.

EMERSON, EDWARD WALDO, and FORBES, WALDO EMERSON. *Journals of Ralph Waldo Emerson,* Houghton Mifflin Company, Boston, 1910.

EMERSON, RALPH WALDO. *The Complete Essays and Other Writings,* edited by Brooks Atkinson, Random House, Inc., New York, 1950.

FONZI, F., and GIUNTELLA, V. E., editors. *La Mostra Storica della Repubblica Romana,* Comitato Nazionale per le Onoranze a Giuseppe Mazzini, Rome, 1949.

FULLER, FREDERICK T. "Hawthorne and Margaret Fuller Ossoli," in *Literary World,* XVI, 1, Jan. 10, 1885.

FULLER, RICHARD F. *Recollections,* privately published, Boston, 1936.

GARIBALDI, GIUSEPPE. *Autobiography of Giuseppe Garibaldi,* authorized translation by A. Werner, London, 1889.

———. *The Memoirs of Garibaldi,* edited by Alexandre Dumas, translated by R. S. Garnett, D. Appleton-Century Company, Inc., New York, 1931.

GAY, H. NELSON. "Pubblica dimostrazione di simpatia per il Papa Pio IX," Biblioteca Storica, *Relazioni fra gli Stati Uniti e l'Italia negli anni 1847–71,* Torino, 1907.

GRAMSCI, A. *Il Risorgimento,* Torino, 1949.

GREELEY, HORACE. *Recollections of a Busy Life,* New York, 1868.

HIBBERT, CHRISTOPHER. *Garibaldi and His Enemies,* Longmans, Green & Co., Ltd., London, 1965.

HOWE, JULIA WARD. *Reminiscences, 1819–1899,* Houghton Mifflin Company, Boston, 1900.

JAMES, HENRY. *William Wetmore Story and His Friends,* 2 vols., Houghton Mifflin Company, Boston, 1903.

Lowell, James Russell. *Poetical Works,* Houghton Mifflin Company, Boston, 1887.

Luzio, Alessandro. "Costanza Arconati," *Profili biografici e Bozzetti storici,* Vol. II, Cogliati, Milan, 1927.

Mack Smith, Denis. *Garibaldi: A Great Life in Brief,* Alfred A. Knopf, Inc., New York, 1956.

——. *The Making of Italy, 1796–1870,* Harper Torch Books, Harper & Row, New York, 1968.

Madison, Charles A. *Critics and Crusaders,* Holt, Rinehart and Winston, Inc., New York, 1947.

Maguire, John Francis. *Rome, Its Ruler and Its Institutions,* Longmans, Green & Co., Ltd., London, 1857.

Malvezzi, Aldobrandino. *La Principessa Cristina di Belgiojoso,* Treves, Milan, 1937.

Marraro, Howard. *American Opinion on the Unification of Italy, 1846–1861,* Columbia University Press, New York, 1932.

Martin, Willard E., Jr. "A Last Letter of Margaret Fuller Ossoli," *American Literature,* V, 1, March 1933.

Martineau, Harriet. *Autobiography,* Boston, 1877.

Mazzini, Giuseppe. *Scritti editi ed inediti,* Galeati, Imola, 1906.

McKilliam, A. E. *A Chronicle of the Popes,* G. Bell & Sons, Ltd., London, 1912.

McMaster, Helen. *Margaret Fuller as a Literary Critic,* "University of Buffalo Studies," VII, 3, Dec. 1928.

Mickiewicz, L. *Adam Mickiewicz, Sa Vie et Son Oeuvre,* Paris, 1888.

Miller, Perry, editor. *Margaret Fuller—American Romantic,* Doubleday Anchor Books, Doubleday & Company, Inc., New York, 1963.

Montégut, Emile. "Marguerite Fuller," *Revue des Deux-Mondes,* XXII année, 1 avril 1852, Paris.

Morelli, Emilia. *Mazzini in Inghilterra,* Le Monnier, Florence, 1938.

NEGRO, SILVIO. *Album Romano,* Casini, Rome, 1956.

NIELSEN, FREDRIK. *The History of the Papacy in the XIX Century,* translated under the direction of Arthur James Mason, London, 1906.

NUCH, RICCARDA. *La difesa di Roma,* INCI, Milan, 1924.

PARRINGTON, VERNON LOUIS. *Main Currents in American Thought,* Vol. II, Harcourt, Brace and Company, Inc., New York, 1948.

PISANI, ARCANGELO. *Margherita Fuller,* Arpino, 1932.

PRAZ, MARIO. *Un'amica di Mazzini: Margaret Fuller Ossoli,* "Motive e Figure," Einaudi, Torino, 1945.

PREZZOLINI; GIUSEPPE. *Come gli Americani scoprirono l'Italia,* Treves, Milan, 1933.

PROCACCI, GIULIANO. *Storia degli Italiani,* Laterza, Bari, 1968.

ROSSI, JOSEPH. *The Image of America in Mazzini's Writings,* University of Wisconsin Press, Madison, 1954.

ROSTENBERG, LEONA. "Margaret Fuller's Roman Diary," *The Journal of Modern History,* XII, 2, June 1940, The University of Chicago Press, Chicago.

RUSK, RALPH L. *The Letters of Ralph Waldo Emerson,* 6 vols., Columbia University Press, New York, 1939.

———. *The Life of Ralph Waldo Emerson,* Charles Scribner's Sons, New York, 1949.

SALOMONE, A. WILLIAM. "The Nineteenth Century Discovery of Italy: An Essay in American Cultural History," *The American Historical Review,* June 1968.

SALVATORELLI, LUIGI. "Pio IX e il Risorgimento," *Il Lavoro,* 2 October 1936.

SALVEMINI, GAETANO. *Mazzini,* La Voce, Florence, 1925.

SEGNI, ANTONIO, editor. *L'Unità d'Italia—Mostra Storica,* Comitato Ordinatore della Mostra Storica, Torino, 1961.

SPELLANZON, C. *Storia del Risorgimento e dell'Unità d'Italia,* 5 vols., Milan, 1933–1950.

STOCK, LEO FRANCIS, editor. *United States Ministers to the*

Papal States, Catholic University Press, Washington, D.C., 1933.

STORY, WILLIAM W. *Roba di Roma,* Chapman & Hall, Ltd., London, 1876.

STRAUCH, CARL F. "Hatred's Swift Repulsions: Emerson, Margaret Fuller and Others," *Studies in Romanticism,* VII, 2, Boston University, Winter, 1968.

THOMAS, JOHN WESLEY, editor. *The Letters of James Freeman Clarke to Margaret Fuller,* Cram, de Gruyter & Co., Hamburg, 1957.

TREVELYAN, GEORGE MACAULAY. *Garibaldi's Defense of the Roman Republic,* Longmans, Green & Co., Ltd., London, 1912.

TREVELYAN, JANET PENROSE. *A Short History of the Italian People,* George Allen & Unwin Ltd., London, 1956.

VILLARI, PASQUALI. *Margaret Fuller,* "Scritti Vari," Zanichelli, Bologna, 1894.

WADE, MASON. *The Writings of Margaret Fuller,* The Viking Press, Inc., New York, 1941.

WARFEL, HARRY R. *Margaret Fuller and Ralph Waldo Emerson,* Publications of the Modern Language Association of America, L, 2, June 1935.

WELLISZ, LEOPOLD. *The Friendship of Margaret Fuller d'Ossoli and Adam Mickiewicz,* Polish Book Importing Co., New York, 1947.

WHITEHOUSE, H. REMSEN. *A Revolutionary Princess—Christina Belgiojoso Trivulzio,* George Allen & Unwin Ltd., London, 1906.

WILLIS, FREDERICK L. H., editor. *Alcott Memoirs,* Badger, Boston, 1915.

WYNNE, GEORGE. *Early Americans in Rome,* Daily American Printing Co., Rome, 1966.

ZABRISKIE, FRANCIS NICOLL. *Horace Greeley,* Funk & Wagnalls Company, New York, 1890.

Notes

The quotations in the text are not numbered, for ease of reading. References instead follow in sequence by chapter and page number. To aid the general reader, Latin abbreviations are not used, but references are repeated in abbreviated form by author or title or manuscript collection as listed in the bibliography.

CHAPTER 1

PAGE   2: *Memoirs* II, p. 208.
PAGE   3: *Memoirs* II, p. 208; *Abroad,* p. 218; *Abroad,* p. 218.
PAGE   4: *Abroad,* p. 218.
PAGE   5: Harvard MS; Bell, p. 191; Harvard MS.
PAGE   6: Bell, p. 57; Harvard MS; *Abroad,* p. 218; *Abroad,* p. 219.
PAGE   7: *Memoirs* I, p. 68; *Memoirs* II, p. 208—Harvard MS.

CHAPTER 2

PAGE   8: *Memoirs* I, p. 23.
PAGE 10: Chipperfield, p. 38.
PAGE 11: *Memoirs* I, p. 41; *Memoirs* I, p. 15.
PAGE 12: *Memoirs* II, p. 14; *Memoirs* II, p. 17; *Memoirs* II, p. 31.

PAGE 38: *Abroad*, p. 205; Boston Library MS; Rossi, p. 52; Chipperfield, p. 250.
PAGE 39: *Abroad*, p. 200; *Abroad*, p. 202; *Abroad*, p. 203.
PAGE 40: *Memoirs* II, p. 201; *Abroad*, p. 191; *Abroad*, p. 207; *Abroad*, p. 195.
PAGE 41: Miller, p. 160; Harvard MS.
PAGE 42: *Memoirs* II, p. 198; *Memoirs* II, p. 207.
PAGE 43: L. Mickiewicz, Vol. XI, p. 124; Welliscz, letter No. 1; Detti, p. 153; *Abroad*, p. 204.
PAGE 44: *Abroad*, p. 216.

CHAPTER 7

PAGE 46: *Memoirs* I, p. 18; Harvard MS; *Abroad*, p. 222.
PAGE 47: *Memoirs* II, p. 216; L. Mickiewicz, Vol. XI, p. 124; *Memoirs* II, p. 210.
PAGE 48: Story, *Roba*, p. 173.
PAGE 49: *Memoirs* II, p. 209; *Abroad*, p. 220.
PAGE 50: *Abroad*, p. 224; *Abroad*, p. 224; *Abroad*, p. 181; *Abroad*, p. 226.
PAGE 51: J. P. Trevelyan, pp. 335–337; *Abroad*, p. 224.

CHAPTER 8

PAGE 54: *Memoirs* II, p. 283.
PAGE 55: *Memoirs* II, p. 283.
PAGE 57: Boston Library MS.

CHAPTER 9

PAGE 58: *Memoirs* II, p. 136; Harvard MS.
PAGE 59: Chipperfield, p. 107; Harvard MS.
PAGE 60: Chipperfield, p. 147; Bell, p. 115.
PAGE 61: Strauch, p. 86; Strauch, p. 86; Chipperfield, p. 154; Miller, p. 50.
PAGE 62: Bell, p. 123; *Memoirs* I, p. 206; Rusk, *Life*, p. 253; Strauch, p. 70.
PAGE 63: *Journals*, Vol. V, p. 464; Strauch, pp. 70–71; Rusk, *Letters*, Vol. II, p. 340; Strauch, p. 71.
PAGE 64: Strauch, p. 71; *Journals*, Vol. VI, p. 87; Strauch, p. 96; Strauch, p. 97; Anthony, p. 101.

CHAPTER 10

PAGE 65: *Memoirs* II, p. 9; *Memoirs* I, p. 35.
PAGE 66: *Memoirs* I, p. 129; L. Mickiewicz, Vol. XI, p. 128.

PAGE 67: *Memoirs* II, p. 307.
PAGE 68: *Memoirs* II, p. 274.
PAGE 69: Ossoli archives, and chapel.
PAGE 70: Miller, p. 152; Chipperfield, p. 259.
PAGE 71: *Memoirs* II, p. 277; *Memoirs* II, p. 216; *Memoirs* II, p. 277.

CHAPTER 11

PAGE 72: Harvard MS; *Memoirs* II, p. 167; *Memoirs* II, p. 58.
PAGE 73: Detti, p. 164; Detti, p. 283; *Memoirs* II, p. 220.
PAGE 74: *Memoirs* II, p. 216; *Memoirs* II, p. 210; *Memoirs* II, p. 211; *Memoirs* II, p. 211; Harvard MS.
PAGE 75: *Abroad*, p. 228; *Abroad*, p. 229; *Abroad*, p. 230; *Abroad*, p. 231; *Abroad*, p. 232; *Abroad*, p. 232; *Abroad*, p. 233.
PAGE 76: *Memoirs* II, p. 217.
PAGE 77: *Abroad*, p. 239; *Memoirs* II, p. 217; *Memoirs* II, p. 213; *Abroad*, p. 237; *Memoirs* II, p. 217; *Memoirs* II, p. 231.
PAGE 78: *Abroad*, p. 241; L. Mickiewicz, Vol. XI, p. 123.
PAGE 79: *Memoirs* II, p. 220; *Memoirs* II, p. 142.

CHAPTER 12

PAGE 80: *Memoirs* II, p. 221.
PAGE 81: Harvard MS.
PAGE 82: Harvard MS.
PAGE 83: Harvard MS; Bell, p. 95; Harvard MS; Harvard MS; Harvard MS.
PAGE 84: Harvard MS.
PAGE 85: *Memoirs* II, p. 220.
PAGE 86: Brooks, *Arcadia*, p. 100; *Memoirs* II, p. 281; Harvard MS; Harvard MS.

CHAPTER 13

PAGE 87: *Memoirs* II, p. 222; *Abroad*, p. 263; *Memoirs* II, p. 221.
PAGE 88: *Abroad*, p. 267; *Memoirs* II, p. 288.
PAGE 89: *Abroad*, p. 245.
PAGE 90: *Abroad*, pp. 242–243; Story, *Roba*, p. 50.
PAGE 91: *Abroad*, p. 265; *Abroad*, p. 268.
PAGE 92: *Memoirs* II, p. 222; Wynne, p. 45; *Abroad*, pp. 246–248.
PAGE 93: *Abroad*, pp. 250 ff; *Abroad*, p. 255.

PAGE 94: *Abroad,* p. 256; *Memoirs* II, p. 223; *Memoirs* II, p. 223.

CHAPTER 14

PAGE 95: *Memoirs* II, p. 231; Boston Library MS; *Memoirs* II, p. 293.
PAGE 96: *Memoirs* II, p. 224; *Abroad,* p. 269; *Memoirs* II, p. 231.
PAGE 97: Higginson, p. 241; *Memoirs* II, p. 278; L. Mickiewicz, Vol. XI, p. 123.
PAGE 98: *Abroad,* p. 272; *Abroad,* p. 273.
PAGE 99: *Abroad,* p. 270; *Abroad,* pp. 259 ff.

CHAPTER 15

PAGE 101: *Memoirs* II, p. 225.
PAGE 102: *Abroad,* p. 280; Candeloro, p. 99; *Abroad,* pp. 280–281.
PAGE 103: *Abroad,* p. 279; *Abroad,* p. 276.
PAGE 104: N.Y. *Tribune,* 30 Nov. 1847; *Abroad,* p. 291; *Abroad,* p. 284.
PAGE 105: *Abroad,* pp. 285 ff; Candeloro, p. 114; Mazzini, Vol. XI, p. 96.
PAGE 106: J. P. Trevelyan, p. 337; Mazzini, Vol. XI, p. 96; Rossi, p. 54; Mazzini, Vol. XI, p. 96—Rossi, p. 56.
PAGE 107: Mazzini, Vol. XI, p. 96.

CHAPTER 16

PAGE 108: *Abroad,* p. 292.
PAGE 109: *Abroad,* p. 295; *Abroad,* p. 295; *Abroad,* pp. 301–302.
PAGE 110: Candeloro, p. 131; Candeloro, p. 136; *Abroad,* p. 294.
PAGE 111: Detti, p. 293; *Memoirs* II, p. 233; Detti, p. 294; Detti, p. 291.
PAGE 119: Whitehouse, p. 124.
PAGE 120: Bell, p. 259.
PAGE 121: Detti, p. 296.

CHAPTER 17

PAGE 122: *Abroad,* p. 293; *Abroad,* pp. 297 ff.
PAGE 123: Story, *Roba,* p. vi; *Abroad,* p. 297; *Abroad,* p. 296.
PAGE 124: *Abroad,* p. 300; *Abroad,* p. 300.
PAGE 125: Detti, p. 295; Detti, p. 296.

CHAPTER 18

PAGE 126: *Abroad,* p. 303; *Memoirs* II, pp. 234 ff.
PAGE 128: *Abroad,* p. 305; *Memoirs* II, p. 233; L. Mickiewicz, Vol. XVI, p. 128; L. Mickiewicz, Vol. XI, p. 127.
PAGE 130: Candeloro, p. 145; J. P. Trevelyan, p. 340; *Abroad,* p. 321.
PAGE 131: *Abroad,* pp. 306–307; *Abroad,* p. 309.
PAGE 132: Whitehouse, p. 167; *Abroad,* p. 385; *Memoirs* II, p. 235.

CHAPTER 19

PAGE 133: *Abroad,* p. 309.
PAGE 134: Detti, p. 297; Detti, p. 298.
PAGE 135: L. Mickiewicz, Vol. XI, p. 127; *Abroad,* p. 320; Candeloro, p. 14.
PAGE 136: *Abroad,* pp. 321 ff.
PAGE 138: Detti, p. 300.

CHAPTER 20

PAGE 139: *Abroad,* p. 306; *Abroad,* p. 326.
PAGE 140: Chipperfield, p. 270; Rusk, *Letters,* Vol. IV, p. 28.
PAGE 141: Rusk, *Letters,* Vol. IV, p. 61; *Memoirs* II, p. 239; Harvard MS.
PAGE 142: Chipperfield, p. 270; Harvard MS; Harvard MS.
PAGE 143: Wade, p. 230; *Memoirs* II, p. 240.
PAGE 144: *Abroad,* p. 327.

CHAPTER 21

PAGE 146: *Memoirs* II, p. 294; Detti, p. 300.
PAGE 147: Rusk, *Letters,* Vol. IV, p. 79.
PAGE 148: R. W. Emerson, *Complete Essays,* pp. 87–89–90.
PAGE 149: *Memoirs* II, p. 244; *Memoirs* II, p. 243; Harvard MS; Chipperfield, p. 176; *Memoirs* II, p. 244; *Memoirs.* II, p. 243.

CHAPTER 22

(The Fuller-Ossoli correspondence in this and succeeding chapters comes from the Harvard MS collection unless otherwise noted. As the letters are closely integrated, they are indicated only by date. The place of writing is given in the text.)
PAGE 152: 13 June 1848; 8 June 1848; 15 June 1848.
PAGE 153: 18 June 1848; 20 June 1848.
PAGE 154: Boston Library MS; 29 June 1848; 6 July 1848; 8 July 1848.

PAGE 183: Harvard MS.
PAGE 184: Harvard MS.
PAGE 185: Harvard MS; *Memoirs* II, pp. 252–253.
PAGE 186: *Memoirs* II, p. 254.
PAGE 187: Candeloro, p. 343; *Abroad,* pp. 342 ff.
PAGE 188: *Abroad,* p. 334; *Abroad,* p. 344.

CHAPTER 27

PAGE 189: *Memoirs* II, pp. 256–257.
PAGE 190: 21 Dec. 1848; 22 Dec. 1848; 22 Dec. 1848.
PAGE 191: 23 Dec. 1848; 23 Dec. 1848.
PAGE 192: 27 Dec. 1848; Harvard MS.

CHAPTER 28

PAGE 193: Harvard MS (also printed in the *Journal of Modern History*).
PAGE 195: *Abroad,* p. 350; *Abroad,* pp. 351–352.
PAGE 196: Wynne, p. 113; Harvard MS.
PAGE 197: *Abroad,* p. 349; *Abroad,* p. 357; Harvard MS, Journal entry for 5 Feb. 1849.
PAGE 198: Hibbert, p. 40; *Abroad,* pp. 358–359.
PAGE 199: Wynne, p. 11.
PAGE 200: Harvard MS; Harvard MS; *Abroad,* p. 367; *Abroad,* p. 366.
PAGE 201: *Abroad,* p. 368; *Memoirs* II, pp. 262–263.

CHAPTER 29

PAGE 202: *Abroad,* p. 346; Harvard MS.
PAGE 203: *Papers,* Vol. II, p. 132.
PAGE 204: Lowell, *Poetical Works;* James, Vol. I, p. 170; James, Vol. I, p. 180.
PAGE 205: Boston Library MS; Harvard MS; Harvard MS.
PAGE 206: Detti, p. 300; *Memoirs* II, pp. 257–258; Harvard MS.
PAGE 209: Harvard MS.
PAGE 210: *Abroad,* pp. 364–365.

CHAPTER 30

PAGE 211: document in Italian, Harvard MS.
PAGE 212: 27 March 1849.
PAGE 213: 30 March 1849.
PAGE 214: 31 March 1849.

PAGE 215: 3 April 1849; 3 April 1849; 4 April 1849.
PAGE 217: 4 April 1849; *Memoirs* II, pp. 286–287.

CHAPTER 31

PAGE 220: *Abroad,* p. 380; G. M. Trevelyan, p. 101, from Mazzini II, p. 61 (*Atti della Repubblica Romana*).
PAGE 221: *Abroad,* p. 381; Hibbert, p. 49.
PAGE 222: London *Times,* 12 May 1849; *Abroad,* p. 382; *Abroad,* p. 400.
PAGE 223: *Abroad,* pp. 385–386; Stock, p. 27.
PAGE 224: Stock, p. 26; Stock, p. 35; James, Vol. I, p. 134.
PAGE 231: James, Vol. I, p. 151; Hibbert, p. 44; Candeloro, p. 443; James, Vol. I, p. 152.
PAGE 232: Harvard MS; London *Times,* 17 May 1849; G. M. Trevelyan, p. 111.

CHAPTER 32

PAGE 233: Detti, p. 352.
PAGE 234: Hibbert, p. 55; Candeloro, p. 443; *Memoirs* I, p. 330; G. M. Trevelyan, p. 127.
PAGE 236: James, Vol. I, pp. 134 ff.
PAGE 237: *Abroad,* pp. 383–384.
PAGE 238: Hibbert, p. 57.
PAGE 239: Hibbert, p. 63; Stock, p. 36; James, Vol. I, p. 154; Mazzini, Vol. V, p. 204.
PAGE 240: *Abroad,* p. 382; *Abroad,* p. 388.

CHAPTER 33

PAGE 241: Stock, p. 37; James, Vol. I, pp. 155–156.
PAGE 242: James, Vol. I, pp. 137–138.
PAGE 243: G. M. Trevelyan, p. 147; James, Vol. I, p. 156; Candeloro, p. 447.
PAGE 244: *Abroad,* p. 391.
PAGE 245: *Abroad,* pp. 396–397.

CHAPTER 34

PAGE 247: Harvard MS, letter of Thurs. May (?), 1849; Harvard MS.
PAGE 248: *Memoirs* II, pp. 289–292; *Memoirs* II, pp. 290–303.
PAGE 249: *Memoirs* II, p. 292; Higginson, p. 264.

PAGE 250: James, Vol. I, p. 140; letter of 22 May 1849, printed in appendix to *Abroad*, p. 436; Detti, p. 319.
PAGE 251: *Abroad*, p. 397.

CHAPTER 35

PAGE 252: *Abroad*, p. 397.
PAGE 253: *Memoirs* II, p. 261; Hibbert, p. 69.
PAGE 254: Hibbert, p. 69; G. M. Trevelyan, p. 163.
PAGE 255: Hibbert, p. 79.
PAGE 256: Hibbert, p. 80; Detti, p. 343.
PAGE 257: *Memoirs* II, p. 286; *Memoirs* II, p. 262; *Memoirs* II, pp. 265–266.
PAGE 259: Harvard MS; Stock, pp. 42–43.
PAGE 260: *Abroad*, appendix, p. 439.

CHAPTER 36

PAGE 262: *Abroad*, pp. 405–406.
PAGE 263: G. M. Trevelyan, p. 205; Hibbert, p. 81.
PAGE 264: *Abroad*, p. 410; Mazzini, Vol. XI, p. 103; *Abroad*, p. 411.
PAGE 265: *Abroad*, p. 412; Harvard MS; Detti, pp. 343–344.
PAGE 266: Hibbert, p. 94.
PAGE 267: G. M. Trevelyan, p. 231; *Abroad*, p. 412.
PAGE 268: *Abroad*, p. 413; Harvard MS.
PAGE 269: Harvard MS; Story, *Roba*, p. 299.
PAGE 270: Mazzini, Vol. XI, p. 110; *Memoirs* II, p. 268.
PAGE 271: *Abroad*, p. 414; *Abroad*, p. 420.
PAGE 272: *Abroad*, p. 421.

CHAPTER 37

PAGE 274: *Memoirs* II, p. 271.
PAGE 275: *Abroad*, pp. 416–417; *Abroad*, p. 416; *Memoirs* II, p. 269; Whitehouse, p. 230.
PAGE 276: Harvard MS; *Memoirs* II, p. 269; Harvard MS.
PAGE 277: *Memoirs* II, p. 272; Boston Library MS; Bell, p. 286.

CHAPTER 38

PAGE 278: Higginson, p. 268.
PAGE 279: Boston Library MS; Boston Library MS.
PAGE 280: Harvard MS; *Memoirs* II, pp. 273 ff.
PAGE 282: Harvard MS.

PAGE 283: Detti, p. 329; Higginson, p. 267.
PAGE 284: Detti, pp. 322, 328, 330.
PAGE 285: Harvard MS, letter of 9 Aug. 1849; Boston Library MS.

CHAPTER 39

PAGE 287: *Papers,* Part II, pp. 28–31.
PAGE 288: E. B. Browning, letter to Miss Mitford; Harvard MS; Harvard MS.
PAGE 289: Detti, p. 302; Harvard MS.
PAGE 290: Harvard MS.
PAGE 291: Harvard MS; Harvard MS; Harvard MS, letter of 9 March 1851.
PAGE 292: *Memoirs* II, p. 304.

CHAPTER 40

PAGE 293: Harvard MS.
PAGE 294: Wade, p. 265; Harvard MS; Fruitlands MS; Wade, p. 262; Fruitlands MS; Harvard MS.
PAGE 295: Harvard MS; Boston Library MS.
PAGE 296: Boston Library MS; Boston Library MS; Harvard MS.

CHAPTER 41

PAGE 300: Boston Library MS; Detti, pp. 335–339.
PAGE 301: Harvard MS.
PAGE 302: Harvard MS.
PAGE 303: Harvard MS; Boston Library MS; Rusk, *Letters,* Vol. IV, p. 199; Rusk, *Letters,* Vol. IV, p. 223; Harvard MS.
PAGE 305: *Memoirs* II, p. 335.
PAGE 306: Harvard MS; Harvard MS; *Memoirs* II, p. 333; Harvard MS; Boston Library MS.
PAGE 307: Bell, p. 313; Boston Library MS.

CHAPTER 42

PAGE 310: Harvard MS; Harvard MS.
PAGE 311: Harvard MS; *Memoirs* II, p. 342.
PAGE 312: *Memoirs* II, p. 347.
PAGE 313: Harvard MS; *Memoirs* I, p. 141.

Index

Note: Page references to illustrations are in *italics*.